The Complete Diet Cookbook

650+ Healthy and Tasty Recipes Perfectly Designed to Get the Best out of the Paleo and Vegan Diet

By Eleanor Hale

Table of Contents

4

Chapter 2: Lunch Recipes ... 54

Chapter 3: Dinner Recipes 101

Chapter 4: Side Dishes 127

Chapter 5: Smoothies and Drinks 146

Chatper 6: Dessert Recipes 156

Introduction

This introduction help to clarify the many facets of this fairly complex diet.

The Pegan diet derives from Paleo and Vegan, as the name suggests, and it tries to combine the benefits of both, while trying to avoid the negative sides.

It consists of low processed dense whole foods that reduce inflammation and balance blood sugar.

It's less intuitive than Paleo diet (non-processed aliments only) and Vegan diet (vegetable-derived aliments only), but it is also less restrictive as it does not consist in the overlap of both; animal derived foods and human processed ones are allowed but usually restricted.

A Pegan diet plan is much more sustainable and much easier to stick to, health and personal satisfaction will be perfectly balanced.

A typical Pegan meal will be mostly leafy green plant based, with a massive restriction on high simple carbs and high glycemic foods, other aliments like meat and fish will be treated more as a side dish.
How much you will avoid simple carbs and high glycemic aliments depends on how much you need to control blood sugar and insulin spikes, for example if
you want or have to lose weight you will need to reduce sugary or starchy foods like some fruits and vegetables.

Common vegetable, bean and seed oils must be avoided as they are highly processed; saturated fats from unprocessed sources are allowed but not in combination with refined sugar and starches and
you also need to pay attention to junk ingredients and chemicals additives like preservatives, dyes, artificial sweeteners.

Fruit and vegetables are a must in the Pegan diet but keep in mind that the sweeter they are the harder you need to restrict them, like potatoes, squash. Healthy fats like avocado and avocado oil, extra virgin olive oil, eggs, nuts, seeds, and coconut oil can be consumed.

You need to avoid grains as much as possible with the only, very limited in quantity, exception of whole grains.

Always cook legumes like lentils thoroughly
to avoid digestion problems, also you need to exclude starchy beans from your meals. Dairy products like butter and ghee are permitted by Pegan diet's tenants but they are very processed and so they are not very good for the environment, in fact many people that choose to stick to a Pegan diet plan limit the consumption of processed aliments that are not highly sustainable

.

Chapter 1: Breakfast Recipes

Orange & Carrot Juice

Servings: 2 | Preparation: 10 min

Ingredients
- 1 pound carrots, trimmed and scrubbed
- Four oranges, peeled

Directions
1. Add all ingredients into a juicer and extract the juice according to the manufacturer's directions.
2. Place the juice into glasses and serve immediately.

Nutrition: Calories: 266; Total Fat: 0.4g; Saturated Fat: 0.1g; Protein: 5.3g; Carbs: 65.6g; Fiber: 14.4g; Sugar: 40g

Green Fruit Juice

Servings: 2 | Preparation: 10 min

Ingredients
- Two medium green apples, cored and sliced
- four large kiwis, peeled and chopped
- 1 cup seedless green grapes
- two teaspoons fresh lime juice

Directions
1. Add all ingredients into a juicer and extract the juice according to the manufacturer's directions.
2. Place the juice into glasses and serve immediately.

Nutrition: Calories: 261; Total Fat: 1.2g; Saturated Fat: 0g; Protein: 2.8g; Carbs: 66.6g; Fiber: 10.5g; Sugar: 48.4g

Apple Smoothie

Servings: 2 | Preparation: 10 min

Ingredients
- One large granny smith apple, peeled, cored, and chopped
- One large orange, peeled, seeded, and sectioned
- ½ teaspoon lemon zest, grated freshly
- ½ tablespoon fresh lemon juice
- 1½ cups chilled filtered water

Directions
1. In a blender, place all the ingredients and pulse until smooth.
2. Place the smoothie into glasses and serve immediately

Nutrition: Calories: 102; Total Fat: 0.3g; Saturated Fat: 0g; Protein: 1.2g; Carbs: 26.4g; Fiber: 5g; Sugar: 20.3g

Banana & Date Smoothie

Servings: 2 | Preparation: 5 min

Ingredients
- 3-4 Medjool dates, pitted and chopped
- two large frozen bananas, peeled and sliced
- 1½ cups unsweetened chilled almond milk

Directions
1. In a blender, place all the ingredients and pulse until smooth.
2. Place the smoothie into glasses and serve immediately

Nutrition: Calories: 135; Total Fat: 3g; Saturated Fat: 0.4g; Protein: 2g; Carbs: 28.5g; Fiber: 3.8g; Sugar: 14.4g

Fruit & Greens Smoothie

Servings: 2 | Preparation: 10 min

Ingredients
- 1 cup fresh baby spinach
- 1 cup fresh baby kale
- One frozen banana, peeled and chopped
- ½ cup frozen pineapple chunks
- Two teaspoons chia seeds
- one tablespoon matcha green tea powder
- 1½ cups chilled unsweetened almond milk

Directions
1. In a blender, place all the ingredients and pulse until smooth.
2. Place the smoothie into glasses and serve immediately

Nutrition: Calories: 165; Total Fat: 3.8g; Saturated Fat: 0.4g; Protein: 3.6g; Carbs: 33.6g; Fiber: 4.6g; Sugar: 20.2g

Fruit Cocktail

Servings: 2 | Preparation: 10 min

Ingredients
- ½ cup frozen mango, peeled, pitted, and chopped
- One frozen banana, peeled and sliced

- One teaspoon maple syrup
- ½ teaspoon organic vanilla extract
- Three tablespoons coconut yogurt
- ½ cup fresh orange juice
- one teaspoon fresh lime juice
- One teaspoon fresh lemon juice
- ¾ cup chilled filtered water
- One tablespoon coconut oil, melted

Directions
1. In a high-speed blender, add all ingredients except coconut oil and pulse until smooth.
2. While the motor is running, slowly add coconut oil and pulse until creamy.
3. Transfer into two large glasses and serve immediately.

Nutrition: Calories: 189; Total Fat: 7.6g; Saturated Fat: 6.2g; Protein: 1.6g; Carbs: 30.2g; Fiber: 2.4g; Sugar: 21g

Oats & Fruit Smoothie Bowl

Servings: 3 | Preparation: 10 min

Ingredients
- 1 cup rolled oats, uncooked
- two ripe peaches, pitted and chopped
- One large orange, peeled, seeded, and sectioned
- One large frozen banana, peeled and sliced
- 1 cup frozen mixed berries
- One tablespoon raw honey
- 1 cup unsweetened almond milk
- 1 cup mixed fruit
- ¼ cup raw pumpkin seeds, shelled

Directions
1. In a high-speed blender, add all the ingredients except the fruit and pumpkin seeds and pulse until smooth.
2. Transfer the mixture into three bowls evenly.
3. Top with the mixed fruit and pumpkin seeds and serve.

Nutrition: Calories: 412; Total Fat: 9g; Saturated Fat: 1.5g; Protein: 10.2g; Carbs: 78g; Fiber: 10.8g; Sugar: 10.8g

Chia Seed Pudding

Servings: 2 | Preparation: 10 min

Ingredients
- 1 cup unsweetened almond milk
- two tablespoons maple syrup
- ¼ cup chia seeds
- ¼ teaspoon organic vanilla extract
- ½ of a small apple, cored and sliced
- two tablespoons almonds, chopped

Directions
1. In a large bowl, add all ingredients except apple and almonds and stir to combine well.
2. Cover and refrigerate for at least 30-40 min.
3. Top with apple and almonds and serve.

Nutrition: Calories: 195; Total Fat: 9.9g; Saturated Fat: 0.8g; Protein: 4.9g; Carbs: 29.5g; Fiber: 7.6g; Sugar: 18g

Fruity Chia Seed Pudding

Servings: 4 | Preparation: 10 min

Ingredients
- 2/3 cup unsweetened almond milk
- 2 cups frozen blueberries
- ½ of a frozen banana, peeled and sliced
- 5 large soft dates, pitted and chopped
- ½ cup chia seeds

Directions
1. In a food processor, add all ingredients except chia seeds and pulse until smooth.
2. Transfer the mixture into a bowl.
3. Add chia seeds and stir to combine well.
4. Refrigerate for 30 min, stirring after every 5 min.

Nutrition: Calories: 149; Total Fat: 5.9g; Saturated Fat: 0.5g; Protein: 4.1g; Carbs: 28g; Fiber: 8.1g; Sugar: 15.6g

Apple Porridge

Servings: 4 | Preparation: 15 min | Cooking time: 5 min

Ingredients
- 2 cups unsweetened almond milk
- 2 large apples, peeled, cored and grated
- 3 tablespoons walnuts, chopped and divided
- 3 tablespoons pumpkin seeds, shelled
- ½ teaspoon organic vanilla extract
- Pinch of ground cinnamon
- ½ small apple, cored and sliced

Directions

1. In a large pan, add the milk, grated apple, 2 tablespoons of walnuts, pumpkin seeds, vanilla extract, cinnamon, and mix well.
2. Place the pan over medium-low heat and cook for about 3-4 min, stirring occasionally.
3. Transfer the porridge into the serving bowls.
4. Top with the remaining walnuts and apple slices and serve.

Nutrition: Calories: 165; Total Fat: 8.4g; Saturated Fat: 0.9g; Protein: 3.9g; Carbs: 22.1g; Fiber: 4.6g; Sugar: 14.7g

Banana Porridge

Servings: 6 | Preparation: 15 min | Cooking time: 20 min

Ingredients

- 2 cups apple, peeled, cored and shredded
- ½ cup cauliflower rice
- ½ cup unsweetened coconut, shredded
- 1¾ cups unsweetened coconut milk
- 1 teaspoon organic vanilla extract
- ¾ cup fresh strawberries, hulled and sliced

Directions

1. In a large pan, add all ingredients except strawberries over medium heat and bring to gentle simmer.
2. Reduce the heat to low and simmer for about 15-20 min.
3. Serve warm with the topping of strawberries.

Nutrition: Calories: 177; Total Fat: 12.1g; Saturated Fat: 10.7g; Protein: 1.6g; Carbs: 14.9g; Fiber: 3g; Sugar: 11g

Overnight Oatmeal

Servings: 3 | Preparation: 10 min

Ingredients

- 1 cup rolled oats
- 2 tablespoons chia seeds
- 2 bananas, peeled and mashed
- 2 teaspoons matcha green tea powder
- 1½ cups unsweetened coconut milk
- Pinch of sea salt
- 2 tablespoons almonds, chopped

Directions

1. In a large bowl, add all ingredients except almonds and mix till well combined.
2. Cover the bowl and refrigerate overnight.
3. In the morning, remove from refrigerator.
4. Top with almonds and serve.

Nutrition: Calories: 396; Total Fat: 22.2g; Saturated Fat: 15.7g; Protein: 7.8g; Carbs: 42g; Fiber: 7g; Sugar: 13.1g

Quinoa & Orange Porridge

Servings: 4 | Preparation: 10 min | Cooking: 20 min

Ingredients

- 2 cups water
- 1 cup dry red quinoa
- ½ cup unsweetened coconut milk
- 2 tablespoons maple syrup
- ¼ teaspoon fresh orange peel, grated finely
- 1 cup banana, peeled and sliced

Directions

1. In a pan, mix water and quinoa over medium heat and bring to boil.
2. Reduce the heat to low and cook for about 10-15 min or until all liquid is absorbed, stirring occasionally.
3. Stir in remaining ingredients and immediately, remove from heat.
4. Top with banana slices serve.

Nutrition: Calories: 285; Total Fat: 9.9g; Saturated Fat: 6.7g; Protein: 7.1g; Carbs: 44.2g; Fiber: 4.6g; Sugar: 11.5g

Vanilla Crepes

Servings: 4 | Preparation: 10 min | Cooking time: 8 min

Ingredients

- 2 tablespoons arrowroot powder
- 2 tablespoons almond flour
- ½ teaspoon ground cinnamon
- Salt, as required
- 4 organic eggs
- 1 teaspoon organic vanilla extract
- 1 tablespoon olive oil

Directions

1. In a bowl, add arrowroot powder, almond flour, cinnamon, salt, and mix well.

2. In another bowl, add the eggs and vanilla and beat until well combined.
3. Add egg mixture into flour mixture and mix until well combined.
4. In a non-stick frying pan, heat the oil over medium heat.
5. Add desired sized mixture and swirl to coat the pan evenly in a thin layer
6. Cook for about 1 minute per side.
7. Repeat with the remaining mixture.

Nutrition: Calories: 137; Total Fat: 9.8g; Saturated Fat: 2g; Protein: 5.6g; Carbs: 5.3g; Fiber: 0.5g; Sugar: 0.6g

Egg White Waffles

Servings: 2 | Preparation: 10 min | Cooking time: 8 min

Ingredients

- ¼ cup coconut flour
- 1 teaspoon organic baking powder
- ¼ cup unsweetened almond milk
- 6 organic egg whites
- 1 tablespoon maple syrup
- Dash of organic vanilla extract

Directions

1. Preheat the waffle iron and lightly grease it.
2. In a large bowl, add the flour and baking powder and mix well.
3. Add the remaining ingredients and mix until well combined.
4. Place half of the mixture in preheated waffle iron.
5. Cook for about 3-4 min or until waffles become golden brown.
6. Repeat with the remaining mixture.
7. Serve warm.

Nutrition: Calories: 156; Total Fat: 3.1g; Saturated Fat: 2g; Protein: 13.9g; Carbs: 17.9g; Fiber: 6.2g; Sugar: 7.7g

Blueberry Pancakes

Servings: 4 | Preparation: 10 min | Cooking time: 20 min

Ingredients

- ½ cup coconut flour
- 1 teaspoon baking soda
- 2 drops liquid stevia
- Pinch of salt
- 4 organic eggs
- 1 cup unsweetened almond milk
- 1 teaspoon organic vanilla extract
- 2 tablespoons fresh blueberries
- 2 tablespoons olive oil
- 2 tablespoons maple syrup

Directions

1. In a large bowl, mix the flour, baking soda and salt.
2. In another bowl, add the egg, milk and vanilla extract and beat until well combined.
3. Add the egg mixture into flour mixture and mix until well combined.
4. Gently, fold in blueberries.
5. In a large skillet, heat the oil over medium heat.
6. Add the desired amount of mixture and spread evenly with the back of a wooden spoon.
7. Cook for about 2-3 min.
8. Carefully, flip the side and cook for about 1-2 min.
9. Repeat with the remaining mixture.
10. Serve warm with the drizzling of maple syrup.

Nutrition: Calories: 172; Total Fat: 12.5g; Saturated Fat: 2.7g; Protein: 6.1g; Carbs: 9.3g; Fiber: 1g; Sugar: 7g

Chicken & Zucchini Pancakes

Servings: 4 | Preparation: 15 min | Cooking time: 40 min

Ingredients

- 4 cups zucchinis, shredded
- Salt, as required
- ¼ cup grass-fed cooked chicken, shredded
- ¼ cup scallion, chopped finely
- 1 organic egg, beaten
- ¼ cup coconut flour
- Ground black pepper, as required
- 2 tablespoons olive oil

Directions

1. In a colander, add the zucchini and sprinkle with salt.
2. Set aside for about 10-15 min.
3. Then squeeze the zucchini well.
4. In a bowl, add the zucchini and remaining ingredients and mix until we combined.
5. In a large nonstick skillet, heat desired oil over medium-low heat.
6. Add ¼ cup of the zucchini mixture and spread evenly with the back of a wooden spoon.

7. Cook for 3-5 min per side.
8. Repeat with the remaining mixture.
9. Serve warm.

Nutrition: Calories: 113; Total Fat: 8.7g; Saturated Fat: 1.6g; Protein: 5.5g; Carbs: 4.9g; Fiber: 1.7g; Sugar: 2.2g

Pumpkin Muffins

Servings: 5 | Preparation: 15 min | Cooking time: 25 min

Ingredients
- 1 cup almond flour
- ½ cup coconut flour
- 1 teaspoon baking soda
- 1 teaspoon pumpkin pie spice
- Salt, as required
- ¼ cup raw honey
- 3 tablespoons coconut oil, melted
- 3 organic eggs
- 1 teaspoon organic vanilla extract
- ¾ cup homemade pumpkin puree
- ¼ cup pecans, chopped

Directions
1. Preheat the oven to 325 degrees F. Grease 10 cups of a muffin pan.
2. In a large bowl, mix flours, baking soda and salt.
3. In another bowl, add the remaining ingredients except pecans and beat until well combined.
4. Add the egg mixture into flour mixture and mix until just combined.
5. Fold in the pecans.
6. Place the mixture into prepared muffin cups evenly.
7. Bake for about 20-25 min or until a toothpick inserted in the center comes out clean.
8. Remove from the oven and place the muffin pan onto a wire rack to cool for about 5 min.
9. Carefully invert the muffins onto the wire rack to cool completely before serving.

Nutrition: Calories: 372; Total Fat: 27.8g; Saturated Fat: 9.4g; Protein: 4.7g; Carbs: 23.2g; Fiber: 4.8g; Sugar: 16.6g

Chicken & Veggie Muffins

Servings: 6 | Preparation: 20 min | Cooking time: 40 min

Ingredients
- 8 large organic eggs, beaten
- 2 tablespoons olive oil, divided
- 1 small red onion, chopped
- 2 small garlic cloves, minced
- 1 teaspoon fresh rosemary, minced
- ¼ teaspoon red pepper flakes, crushed
- 1 pound grass-fed ground chicken
- Salt and ground black pepper, as required
- 2 small carrots, peeled and grated
- 1 small red bell pepper, seeded and chopped
- 1 small green bell pepper, seeded and chopped
- 4 fresh mushrooms, chopped

Directions
1. Preheat the oven to 355 degrees F. Lightly, grease a large 12 cups muffin pan.
2. In a bowl, crack the eggs and beat well. Set aside.
3. In a large skillet, heat 1 tablespoon of oil over medium heat and sauté the onion for about 5-6 min.
4. Add the garlic, rosemary and red pepper flakes and sauté for about 1 minute.
5. Add the chicken with a bit of salt and black pepper and cook for about 5-6 min.
6. Transfer the chicken mixture into a bowl.
7. In the same skillet, heat the remaining oil over medium heat and cook the carrot for about 2-3 min.
8. Add the bell peppers and mushrooms and cook for about 1 minute.
9. Stir in the salt and black pepper and cook for 2-3 min more.
10. Transfer the vegetable mixture into the bowl with chicken mixture and mix until well.
11. Add the beaten eggs and stir to combine well.
12. Transfer the mixture into prepared muffin cups evenly.
13. Bake for about 15-20 min or until top of muffins become golden brown.
14. Remove from the oven and place the muffin pan onto a wire rack to cool for about 5 min.
15. Carefully invert the muffins onto a platter and serve warm.

Nutrition: Calories: 308; Total Fat: 17.1g; Saturated Fat: 4.3g; Protein: 31.4g; Carbs: 7.1g; Fiber: 1.4g; Sugar: 4.1g

Zucchini Bread

Servings: 6 | Preparation: 15 min | Cooking time: 45 min

Ingredients

- ½ cup coconut flour
- 1½ teaspoons baking soda
- Pinch of salt
- ¼ cup coconut oil, softened
- 2 teaspoons organic vanilla extract
- 1½ cups bananas, peeled and mashed
- 1 cup zucchini, grated and squeezed
- 1 teaspoon orange zest, grated freshly

Directions

1. Preheat the oven to 350 degrees F. Grease a loaf pan.
2. In a large bowl, mix the flour, baking soda and salt.
3. In another bowl, add the coconut oil and vanilla extract and beat well.
4. Add the banana and beat until well combined.
5. Add the oil mixture into flour mixture and mix until just combined.
6. Fold in zucchini and orange zest.
7. Place the mixture into prepared loaf pan evenly.
8. Bake for about 40-45 min or until a toothpick nested in the center comes out clean.
9. Remove the loaf pan from oven and place onto a wire rack to cool for about 15-20 min.
10. Carefully, remove the bread from the loaf pan and place onto the wire rack to cool completely before slicing.
11. With a sharp knife, cut the bread loaf into desired sized slices and serve.

Nutrition: Calories: 124; Total Fat: 9.4g; Saturated Fat: 8.1g; Protein: 0.8g; Carbs: 10.1g; Fiber: 1.6g; Sugar: 5.2g

Banana Bread

Servings: 10 | Preparation: 15 min | Cooking time: 1 h

Ingredients

- ½ cup almond meal
- ½ cup coconut flour
- ¾ teaspoon baking soda
- 1 teaspoon ground cinnamon
- Pinch of salt 4 organic eggs
- ¼ cup maple syrup
- 3½ tablespoons coconut oil, melted
- 2 teaspoons organic vanilla extract
- 2 medium bananas, peeled and mashed

Directions

1. Preheat the oven to 340 degrees F. Grease a loaf pan.

2. In a large bowl, mix flours, baking soda, cinnamon and salt.
3. In another bowl, add eggs, maple syrup, coconut oil and vanilla and beat until well combined.
4. Add bananas and beat until well combined.
5. Add the egg mixture into flour mixture and mix until just combined.
6. Place the mixture into prepared loaf pan evenly.
7. Bake for about 40-60 min or until a toothpick inserted in the center comes out clean.
8. Remove bread from oven and let it cool slightly before slicing.
9. Remove the loaf pan from oven and place onto a wire rack to cool for about 15-20 min.
10. Carefully, remove the bread from the loaf pan and place onto the wire rack to cool completely before slicing.
11. With a sharp knife, cut the bread loaf into desired sized slices and serve.

Nutrition: Calories: 146; Total Fat: 9.5g; Saturated Fat: 5g; Protein: 3.8g; Carbs: 12.7g; Fiber: 1.6g; Sugar: 8.1g

Caraway Seed Bread

Servings: 10 | Preparation: 15 min | Cooking time: 35 min

Ingredients

- 1 1|3 cups almond flour
- 1 tablespoon caraway seeds
- 1 teaspoon organic baking powder
- ½ teaspoon garlic powder
- ½ teaspoon onion powder
- ¼ teaspoon salt
- 3 organic eggs
- ¼ cup olive oil
- ¼ cup water
- 1 tablespoon maple syrup
- ¼ teaspoon white vinegar

Directions

1. Preheat oven to 350 degrees F. Line a loaf pan with parchment paper.
2. In a large bowl, mix almond flour, baking powder, caraway seeds, garlic powder, onion powder and salt.
3. In another bowl, add the remaining ingredients and beat until well combined.
4. Add the egg mixture into flour mixture and mix until just combined.
5. Place the mixture into prepared loaf pan evenly.

6. Bake for about 35 min or until a toothpick inserted in the center comes out clean.
7. Remove the loaf pan from oven and place onto a wire rack to cool for about 15-20 min.
8. Carefully, remove the bread from the loaf pan and place onto the wire rack to cool completely before slicing.
9. With a sharp knife, cut the bread loaf into desired sized slices and serve.

Nutrition: Calories: 167; Total Fat: 14.5g; Saturated Fat: 1.7g; Protein: 1.8g; Carbs: 4.9g; Fiber: 1.9g; Sugar: 1.9g

Eggs in Avocado Cups

Servings: 4 | Preparation: 10 min | Cooking time: 22 min

Ingredients

- 2 medium avocados, halved and pitted
- 4 small organic eggs
- 6 cherry tomatoes, sliced
- ¼ cup fresh basil leaves, chopped
- Salt and ground black pepper, as required

Directions

1. Preheat the oven to 450 degrees F. Lightly, grease a baking dish.
2. Scoop out some flesh from each avocado half to create a cup.
3. Arrange avocado halves into the prepared baking dish, cut side up.
4. Carefully, crack each egg into each avocado half.
5. Divide tomato slices over eggs evenly.
6. Bake for about 20-22 min.
7. Sprinkle with salt, and black pepper.
8. Garnish with basil and serve.

Nutrition: Calories: 291; Total Fat: 123.7g; Saturated Fat: 5.3g; Protein: 8.2g; Carbs: 16.1g; Fiber: 9g; Sugar: 5.6g

Apple Omelet

Servings: 2 | Preparation: 10 min | Cooking time: 10 min

Ingredients

- 4 teaspoons olive oil, divided
- 2 small green apples, cored and sliced thinly
- ¼ teaspoon ground cinnamon
- Pinch of ground cloves

- Pinch of ground nutmeg
- 4 large organic eggs
- ¼ teaspoon organic vanilla extract
- Pinch of salt

Directions

1. In a large nonstick frying pan, heat 1 teaspoon of oil over medium-low heat and cook the apple slices with spices for about 4-5 min, flipping once halfway through.
2. Meanwhile, in a bowl, add the eggs, vanilla extract, salt, and beat until fluffy.
3. Add the remaining oil in the pan and let it heat.
4. Place the egg mixture over apple slices evenly and cook for about 3-5 min or until desired doneness.
5. Carefully, turn the pan over a serving plate and immediately, fold the omelet.
6. Serve immediately.

Nutrition: Calories: 342; Total Fat: 19.8g; Saturated Fat: 4.5g; Protein: 13.2g; Carbs: 32g; Fiber: 5.6g; Sugar: 24.1g

Herbed Tomato Frittata

Servings: 6 | Preparation: 15 min | Cooking time: 35 min

Ingredients

- 8 organic eggs, beaten
- 1 teaspoon red pepper flakes, crushed
- Salt and ground black pepper, as required
- 4 tomatoes, chopped
- 2 garlic cloves, minced
- 2 tablespoons fresh chives, chopped
- 2 tablespoons fresh dill, chopped

Directions

1. Preheat the oven to 325 degrees F. Grease a baking dish.
2. In a large bowl, add eggs, salt and black pepper and beat well.
3. Stir in tomatoes and herbs.
4. Place the mixture into the prepared baking dish evenly.
5. Bake for about 30-35 min.
6. Remove from oven and set aside to cool for about 5-10 min before serving.

Nutrition: Calories: 104; Total Fat: 6.1g; Saturated Fat: 1.9g; Protein: 8.4g; Carbs: 4.8g; Fiber: 1.3g; Sugar: 2.7g

Chicken & Veggie Casserole

Servings: 6 | Preparation: 20 min | Cooking time: 55 min

Ingredients
- 6 organic eggs
- 2 tablespoons fresh cilantro, minced
- ¼ teaspoon red pepper flakes, crushed
- Salt and ground black pepper, as required
- 1 cup fresh kale, trimmed and chopped
- 3 medium zucchinis, grated
- 1 cup fresh mushrooms, chopped
- 1 medium onion, chopped
- 1 cup grass-fed cooked chicken, shredded
- 2 tablespoons almond flour

Directions
1. Preheat the oven to 400 degrees F. Lightly, grease an 8x8-inch casserole dish.
2. In a medium bowl, add eggs, cilantro, red pepper flakes, salt and black pepper and beat until well combined.
3. In another large bowl, mix all vegetables.
4. Place the vegetable mixture into prepared casserole dish evenly and top with the shredded chicken, followed by
5. Sprinkle with almond flour evenly.
6. Top with egg mixture evenly.
7. Bake for about 45-55 min or until top is golden brown.
8. Remove from oven and set aside to cool for about 5-10 min before serving.

Nutrition: Calories: 144; Total Fat: 6.6g; Saturated Fat: 1.7g; Protein: 14.4g; Carbs: 7.4g; Fiber: 2g; Sugar: 3.1g

Veggies Quiche

Servings: 4 | Preparation: 15 min | Cooking time: 20 min

Ingredients
- 6 organic eggs
- ½ cup unsweetened almond milk
- Salt and ground black pepper, as required
- 1 cup fresh baby spinach, chopped
- 1 cup fresh baby kale, chopped
- ¼ cup fresh mushrooms, sliced
- 2 tablespoons red bell pepper, seeded and chopped
- 2 tablespoons green bell pepper, seeded and chopped
- 1 scallion, chopped
- ¼ cup fresh cilantro, chopped
- 1 tablespoon fresh chives, minced

Directions
1. Preheat the oven to 400 degrees F. Lightly grease a pie dish.
2. In a large bowl, add eggs, almond milk, salt and black pepper and beat well. Keep aside.
3. In another bowl, add remaining ingredients.
4. Place the veggie mixture in the bottom of prepared pie dish evenly and top with the egg mixture over vegetable mixture evenly.
5. Bake for about 20 min or until a toothpick inserted in the center comes out clean.
6. Remove from oven and set aside to cool for about 5-10 min before slicing before serving.

Nutrition: Calories: 114; Total Fat: 7.1g; Saturated Fat: 2.1g; Protein: 9.5g; Carbs: 3.7g; Fiber: 0.9g; Sugar: 1g

Zucchini with Eggs

Servings: 2 | Preparation: 10 min | Cooking time: 5 min

Ingredients
- 1 tablespoon olive oil
- 2 small garlic clove, minced
- 2 large zucchinis, spiralized with blade C
- Salt and ground black pepper, as required
- 2 organic eggs

Directions
1. In a large skillet, heat the oil over medium heat and sauté the garlic for about 1 minute.
2. Add the zucchini, salt and black pepper and cook for about 3-4 min.
3. Transfer the zucchini mixture onto 2 large serving plates.
4. Meanwhile, in a large pan, add 2-3-inches water over high heat and bring to a gentle simmer.
5. Carefully, crack the eggs in water one by one.
6. Cover the pan and turn off the heat.
7. Place the pan covered for about 4 min or until desired doneness.
8. Place the eggs over zucchini.
9. Sprinkle the eggs with salt and black pepper and serve.

Sweet Potato & Bell Pepper Hash

Servings: 4| Preparation: 15 min | Cooking time: 32 min

Ingredients

- 1 tablespoon olive oil
- 1 medium onion, chopped
- 1 large sweet potato, peeled and cubed into ½-inch size
- 1 small green bell pepper, seeded and chopped
- 1 small red bell pepper, seeded and chopped
- Salt and ground black pepper, as required
- 2 tablespoons water
- ¼ cup scallion (green part), chopped

Directions

1. In a large skillet, heat oil over medium heat and sauté onion for about 4-5 min.
2. Add the sweet potato and cook for about 4-5 min, stirring occasionally.
3. Add the bell peppers and cook for about 1 minute.
4. Add the salt, black pepper and water and stir to combine.
5. Cover the skillet and cook for about 15-20 min, stirring occasionally.
6. Stir in scallion and immediately remove from heat.
7. Serve hot.

Nutrition: Calories: 96; Total Fat: 3.8g; Saturated Fat: 0.5g; Protein: 1.8g; Carbs: 15.3g; Fiber: 2.8g; Sugar: 6.8g

Quinoa & Coconut Granola

Servings: 4 | Preparation: 15 min | Cooking time: 15 min

Ingredients

- ¾ cup uncooked red quinoa
- ½ cup coconut flakes
- ¼ cup almonds, chopped
- ¼ cup cashews, chopped
- 2 tablespoons raw pumpkin seeds, shelled
- 2 tablespoons chia seeds
- ½ teaspoon ground cinnamon
- Pinch of ground ginger
- Pinch of ground nutmeg Pinch of ground cloves
- Pinch of salt 3 tablespoons raw honey
- 2 tablespoons coconut oil, melted
- ½ cup raisins
- 1 medium banana, peeled and sliced
- 1 medium apple, cored and sliced

Directions

1. Preheat the oven to 350 degrees F. Lightly grease a large baking sheet.
2. In a large bowl, add quinoa, almonds, coconut flakes, seeds, spices, salt, and mix well.
3. Add the honey and oil and stir until well combined.
4. Transfer the quinoa mixture onto the prepared baking sheet and spread into an even layer.
5. Bake for about 12-15 min, tossing occasionally.
6. Remove from the oven and immediately, stir in the raisins.
7. Set aside for about 10 min before serving.
8. Serve with your choice of non-dairy milk and fruit's topping.

Nutrition: Calories: 492; Total Fat: 22.6g; Saturated Fat: 10.6g; Protein: 10.3g; Carbs: 70.4g; Fiber: 8.6g; Sugar: 34.4g

Banana Pancakes

Servings: 4 | Preparation: 10 min | Cooking: 20 min
Ingredients

- 1 cup whole wheat flour
- ¼ tsp baking soda
- ¼ tsp baking powder
- 1 cup mashed banana
- 2 eggs
- 1 cup milk
Directions

1. In a bowl combine all ingredients and mix well
2. In a skillet heat olive oil
3. Pour ¼ of the batter and cook each pancake for 1 2 min per side
4. When ready remove from heat and serve

Buckwheat Pancakes

Servings: 6 | Preparation: 5 min | Cooking: 10 min
Ingredients

- 1 cup buckwheat flour
- 1 tablespoon brown sugar
- ¼ tsp salt
- 1 tsp baking powder
- 1 cup almond milk
- 1 tablespoon canola oil

- 2 bananas

Directions
1. In a bowl combine dry ingredients
2. Add wet ingredients and mix well
3. In a skillet pour ¼ cup batter and cook for 1 2 min per side
4. When ready remove and serve with syrup

Berry Power Smoothie

Preparation: 5 min| Cooking: 0 min| Servings: 1

Ingredients
- ¼ cup frozen blueberries
- ¼ cup frozen strawberries
- ½ cup baby spinach
- 2 tablespoons unsalted almond butter
- 1½ cups coconut milk or unsweetened nut milk
- 1/8 teaspoon ground cinnamon (optional)

Directions
Place all of the ingredients into a blender and pulse until well combined, about 1 minute.
Pour into a glass and enjoy immediately.

Nutrition: Calories 359; Total fat: 27g; Total carbs: 19g; Fiber: 7g; Sugar: 8g; Protein: 11g; Sodium: 129mg

Grain-Free Nutty Granola

Preparation: 7 min| Cooking: 25 min| Servings: 6

Ingredients
- 1½ cups chopped raw walnuts or pecans
- 1 cup raw almonds, sliced
- ½ cup seeds, toasted or roasted unsalted sunflower, sesame, or shelled pumpkin
- ¼ cup unsweetened coconut flakes
- ½ cup coconut oil or unsalted grass-fed butter, melted
- 1 tablespoon maple syrup
- 1 teaspoon alcohol-free vanilla extract
- 1 teaspoon ground cinnamon, or to taste
- ¼ teaspoon sea salt or Himalayan salt

Directions
1. Preheat oven to 300°F.
2. Line a rimmed baking sheet with parchment paper or foil.
3. Add the walnuts, almonds, seeds, and coconut flakes to a large bowl. In a separate bowl, mix the

oil with the maple syrup, vanilla, cinnamon, and salt. Pour over the nut mixture, tossing to coat.
4. Spread the mixture evenly on the prepared baking sheet and bake until golden brown, about 25 min, stirring once halfway through. Cool completely.

Nutrition: Calories 248; Total fat: 25g; Total carbs: 6g; Fiber: 3g; Sugar: 2g; Protein: 4g; Sodium: 40mg

Overnight Chia Seed Pudding

Preparation: 5 min| Cooking: 0 min| Servings: 1

Ingredients
- 3 tablespoons chia seeds
- 1 cup coconut milk or unsweetened nut milk
- 1 teaspoon alcohol-free vanilla extract
- 1 teaspoon maple syrup (optional)

Directions
1. In a large jar or bowl, combine all the ingredients, stirring to mix. Close or cover and refrigerate overnight.
2. The next day, add your preferred toppings and enjoy.

Nutrition: Calories 293; Total fat: 19g; Total carbs: 21g; Fiber: 17g; Sugar: 1g; Protein: 10g; Sodium: 367mg

Mini Pegan Pancakes with Blueberry Syrup

Preparation: 5 min| Cooking: 15 min| Servings: 4

Ingredients
- 1 very ripe banana
- 2 large eggs
- 1 tablespoon alcohol-free vanilla extract
- 1 teaspoon ground cinnamon
- Pinch sea salt or Himalayan salt
- ¼ cup coconut oil or clarified butter, divided
- 2 cups fresh or frozen blueberries

Directions
1. In a medium bowl, mash the banana until softened. Add the eggs and continue to mash until smooth and most of the chunks are blended. Stir in the vanilla, cinnamon, and salt.
2. Heat 1 tablespoon of the coconut oil in a large skillet or flat cast iron pan over medium heat. Pour in 2 to 3 tablespoons of the batter to form 3-

inch rounds. Cook the pancakes four simultaneously until set and golden brown, 2 to 4 min total, flipping once. Transfer to a plate to cool. Repeat until the remaining batter is used up, adding 1 tablespoon coconut oil between each batch.

3. In a separate, small saucepan, add the blueberries and remaining 1 tablespoon coconut oil. Cook over medium heat, constantly mashing berries with a wooden spoon, until juices reduce to a syrup-like consistency, 3 to 5 min. Set aside to cool.

4. Serve pancakes with the blueberry syrup on the side.

Nutrition: Calories 224; Total fat: 17g; Total carbs: 18g; Fiber: 3g; Sugar: 12g; Protein: 4g; Sodium: 48mg

Easy Avocado-Baked Eggs

Preparation: 5 min| Cooking: 15 min| Servings: 4

Ingredients

- 2 medium or large avocados, halved and pitted
- 4 large eggs
- ¼ teaspoon freshly ground black pepper

Directions

1. Preheat the oven to 425°F.
2. Scoop out some of the pulp from the avocado halves, leaving enough space to fit an egg, reserving the pulp for Easy Guacamole (see the recipe Ceviche Fish Tacos with Easy Guacamole).
3. Line an 8-by-8-inch baking pan with foil. Place the avocado halves in the pan to fit snugly in a single layer, folding the foil around the outer avocados to prevent tipping.
4. Crack 1 egg into each avocado half; season with pepper. Bake, uncovered, until the whites are set and the egg yolks are cooked to your desired doneness, 12 to 15 min. Remove from the oven and let rest for 5 min before serving.

Nutrition: Calories 433; Total fat: 37g; Total carbs: 16g; Fiber: 12g; Sugar: 1g; Protein: 16g; Sodium: 154mg

Veggie-Eggy Muffins

Preparation: 10 min| Cooking: 20 min| Servings: 6

Ingredients

- Extra-virgin olive oil, coconut oil, or clarified butter, for greasing (optional)

- 12 large eggs
- 2 teaspoons sea salt or Himalayan salt
- 2 teaspoons freshly ground black pepper
- 1 medium red bell pepper, seeded and diced
- 1 medium orange, yellow, or green bell pepper, seeded and diced
- 1 cup packed baby spinach, finely chopped
- ½ cup thinly sliced scallions
- 1 small jalapeño pepper, seeded and minced (optional)

Directions

1. Preheat the oven to 350°F. Grease a 12-hole muffin pan or use paper muffin liners.
2. Place the eggs, salt, and pepper in a large bowl and beat until fluffy. Add the peppers, spinach, scallions, and jalapeño, stirring to combine.
3. Spoon the egg mixture evenly into the prepared muffin pan.
4. Bake until a toothpick or paring knife comes out clean when inserted, about 20 min. Let the muffins cool in the pan about 10 min before serving.

Nutrition: Calories 83; Total fat: 5g; Total carbs: 3g; Fiber: 1g; Sugar: 1g; Protein: 7g; Sodium: 385mg

Meat-Free Eggs Benedict with Lemon Hollandaise Sauce

Preparation: 12 min| Cooking: 6 min| Servings: 2

Ingredients

Hollandaise sauce:

- 3 large egg yolks (save whites for other use)
- ½ cup extra-virgin olive oil, ghee, or clarified butter
- 1 tablespoon lemon juice (from about ½ lemon)
- Pinch salt
- Pinch cayenne pepper

Eggs:

- 2 teaspoons apple cider vinegar or white vinegar
- 4 large eggs
- 1 large ripe beefsteak or heirloom tomato, ends removed, cut into 4 thick slices
- 1 cup baby spinach
- Freshly ground black pepper

Directions

1. For the hollandaise sauce, bring a pot of water, filled to about 4 inches up the sides, to a boil. Set

aside 2 tablespoons of the hot water. In a medium metal bowl, whisk the egg yolks.

2. Add in the olive oil, hot water, lemon juice, salt, and cayenne and continue whisking. Hover the bowl over the pot of boiling water.

3. Whisk constantly until the sauce thickens, 1 to 2 min, keeping the bowl from touching the boiling water, to prevent the eggs from curdling.

4. Remove the bowl of hollandaise sauce from the pot of water, and set it aside on another part of the stovetop.

5. To poach the eggs, reduce the heat under the pot of boiling water to a simmer and add the vinegar. Prepare a paper-towel lined plate.

6. One at a time, carefully crack the eggs into a small bowl, then use the bowl to slowly slide 2 of the eggs into the water. Simmer for 2 min.

7. Using a slotted spoon, transfer the eggs to the paper towel-lined plate. Repeat the process with the remaining 2 eggs.

8. To serve, divide the tomato slices between two plates. Top each tomato with a few spinach leaves, 1 poached egg, and 2 heaping tablespoons of the warm hollandaise. Season with black pepper and serve immediately.

Nutrition: Calories 423; Total fat: 39g; Total carbs: 6g; Fiber: 2g; Sugar: 4g; Protein: 16g; Sodium: 242mg

Breakfast "Burritos" with Avocado and Pico de Gallo

Preparation: 10 min | Cooking: 5 min | Servings: 2

Ingredients

Pico de gallo:

- 4 very ripe medium plum tomatoes, diced
- ½ red onion, cut into ½-inch pieces
- 1 small serrano pepper, seeded and minced
- ¼ cup chopped fresh cilantro
- Juice from 1 lime

Burritos:

- 6 large eggs
- ½ teaspoon sea salt or Himalayan salt
- ½ teaspoon freshly ground black pepper
- 2 tablespoons unsalted grass-fed butter
- 1 large or 2 small avocados, peeled, pitted, and cut lengthwise into 1-inch slices

Directions

1. Make the pico de gallo first to allow the flavors to meld. In a medium bowl, toss together all the ingredients until well combined. Set aside.

2. In a large bowl, beat the eggs with the salt and pepper until fluffy. Heat the butter in a large skillet over medium-low heat until melted, then spoon in half of the egg mixture. Using a rubber spatula, spread out the egg mixture in a thin layer and allow to set on the bottom, about 1 minute.

3. Gently flip the egg "tortilla" and continue to cook, about 30 seconds. Transfer to a plate.

4. Repeat the process with the remaining eggs.

5. To roll the burritos, spread about 2 to 3 tablespoons of the pico de gallo down the center of each of the "tortillas," forming a line from top to bottom. Roll, starting with the filled side closest to you. Top with avocado and additional salsa, if desired, before serving.

Nutrition: Calories 528; Total fat: 39g; Total carbs: 25g; Fiber: 9g; Sugar: 10g; Protein: 24g

Blueberry Pancakes (Version 2)

Servings: 4 | Preparation: 10 min | Cooking: 20 min

Ingredients

- 1 cup whole wheat flour
- ¼ tsp baking soda
- ¼ tsp baking powder
- 1 cup blueberries
- 2 eggs
- 1 cup milk

Directions

1. In a bowl combine all ingredients and mix well
2. In a skillet heat olive oil
3. Pour ¼ of the batter and cook each pancake for 1 2 min per side
4. When ready remove from heat and serve

Apple Pancakes

Servings: 4 | Preparation: 10 min | Cooking: 30 min

Ingredients

- 1 cup whole wheat flour
- ¼ tsp baking soda
- ¼ tsp baking powder
- 1 cup apples
- 2 eggs
- 1 cup milk

Directions

1. In a bowl combine all ingredients and mix well
2. In a skillet heat olive oil
3. Pour ¼ of the batter and cook each pancake for 1 2 min per side
4. When ready remove from heat and serve

Apricots Pancakes

Servings: 4 | Preparation: 10 min | Cooking: 20 min

Ingredients

- 1 cup whole wheat flour
- ¼ tsp baking soda
- ¼ tsp baking powder
- 1 cup apricots
- 2 eggs
- 1 cup milk

Directions

1. In a bowl combine all ingredients and mix well
2. In a skillet heat olive oil
3. Pour ¼ of the batter and cook each pancake for 1 2 min per side
4. When ready remove from heat and serve

Pancakes

Servings: 4 | Preparation: 10 min | Cooking: 30 min

Ingredients

- 1 cup whole wheat flour
- ¼ tsp baking soda
- ¼ tsp baking powder
- 2 eggs
- 1 cup milk

Directions

1. In a bowl combine all ingredients and mix well
2. In a skillet heat olive oil
3. Pour ¼ of the batter and cook each pancake for 1 2 min per side
4. When ready remove from heat and serve

Durian Muffins

Servings: 8 12 | Preparation: 10 min | Cooking: 20 min

Ingredients

- 2 eggs
- 1 tablespoon olive oil
- 1 cup milk
- 2 cups whole wheat flour
- 1 tsp baking soda
- ¼ tsp baking soda
- 1 tsp cinnamon
- 1 cup durian

Directions

1. In a bowl combine all wet ingredients
2. In another bowl combine all dry ingredients
3. Combine wet and dry ingredients
4. Pour mixture into 8 12 prepared muffin cups, fill 2/3 of the cups
5. Bake for 18-20 min at 375 F
6. When ready remove from the oven and serve

Blueberry Muffins

Servings: 8 12 | Preparation: 10 min | Cooking: 20 min

Ingredients

- 2 eggs
- 1 tablespoon olive oil
- 1 cup milk
- 2 cups whole wheat flour
- 1 tsp baking soda
- ¼ tsp baking soda
- 1 tsp cinnamon
- 1 cup blueberries

Directions

1. In a bowl combine all wet ingredients
2. In another bowl combine all dry ingredients
3. Combine wet and dry ingredients
4. Fold in blueberries and mix well
5. Pour mixture into 8 12 prepared muffin cups, fill 2/3 of the cups
6. Bake for 18-20 min at 375 F

Feijoa Muffins

Servings: 8 12 | Preparation: 10 min | Cooking: 20 min

Ingredients

- 2 eggs
- 1 tablespoon olive oil
- 1 cup milk
- 2 cups whole wheat flour
- 1 tsp baking soda
- ¼ tsp baking soda
- 1 tsp cinnamon
- 1 cup feijoa

Directions

1. In a bowl combine all wet ingredients
2. In another bowl combine all dry ingredients
3. Combine wet and dry ingredients
4. Pour mixture into 8 12 prepared muffin cups, fill 2/3 of the cups
5. Bake for 18-20 min at 375 F
6. When ready remove from the oven and serve

Kiwi Muffins

Servings: 8 12 | Preparation: 10 min | Cooking: 20 min

Ingredients

- 2 eggs
- 1 tablespoon olive oil
- 1 cup milk
- 2 cups whole wheat flour
- 1 tsp baking soda
- ¼ tsp baking soda
- 1 tsp cinnamon
- 1 cup kiwi

Directions

1. In a bowl combine all wet ingredients
2. In another bowl combine all dry ingredients
3. Combine wet and dry ingredients
4. Pour mixture into 8 12 prepared muffin cups, fill 2/3 of the cups
5. Bake for 18-20 min at 375 F
6. When ready remove from the oven and serve

Muffins

Servings: 8 12 | Preparation: 10 min | Cooking: 20 min

Ingredients

- 2 eggs
- 1 tablespoon olive oil
- 1 cup milk
- 2 cups whole wheat flour
- 1 tsp baking soda
- ¼ tsp baking soda
- 1 tsp cinnamon

Directions

1. In a bowl combine all wet ingredients
2. In another bowl combine all dry ingredients
3. Combine wet and dry ingredients
4. Pour mixture into 8 12 prepared muffin cups, fill 2/3 of the cups

5. Bake for 18-20 min at 375 F
6. When ready remove from the oven and serve

Goat Cheese Omelette

Servings: 1 | Preparation: 5 min | Cooking: 10 min

Ingredients

- 2 eggs
- ¼ tsp salt
- ¼ tsp black pepper
- 1 tablespoon olive oil
- ¼ cup goat cheese
- ¼ tsp basil

Directions

1. In a bowl combine all ingredients and mix well
2. In a skillet heat olive oil and pour the egg mixture
3. Cook for 1-2 min per side
4. When ready remove omelette from the skillet and serve

Bacon Omelette

Servings: 1 | Preparation: 5 min | Cooking: 10 min

Ingredients

- 2 eggs
- ¼ tsp salt
- ¼ tsp black pepper
- 1 tablespoon olive oil
- ½ cup bacon
- ¼ tsp basil
- 1 cup zucchini

Directions

1. In a bowl combine all ingredients and mix well
2. In a skillet heat olive oil and pour the egg mixture
3. Cook for 1-2 min per side
4. When ready remove omelette from the skillet and serve

Onion Omelette

Servings: 1 | Preparation: 5 min | Cooking: 10 min

Ingredients

- 2 eggs
- ¼ tsp salt
- ¼ tsp black pepper
- 1 tablespoon olive oil
- ¼ cup cheese
- ¼ tsp basil

- 1 cup red onion

Directions

1. In a bowl combine all ingredients and mix well
2. In a skillet heat olive oil and pour the egg mixture
3. Cook for 1-2 min per side
4. When ready remove omelette from the skillet and serve

Feta Cheese Omelette

Servings: 1 | Preparation: 5 min | Cooking: 10 min

Ingredients

- 2 eggs
- ¼ tsp salt
- ¼ tsp black pepper
- 1 tablespoon olive oil
- ¼ cup cheese
- ¼ tsp basil
- ½ cup feta cheese

Directions

1. In a bowl combine all ingredients and mix well
2. In a skillet heat olive oil and pour the egg mixture
3. Cook for 1-2 min per side
4. When ready remove omelette from the skillet and serve

Tomato Omelette

Servings: 1 | Preparation: 5 min | Cooking: 10 min

Ingredients

- 2 eggs
- ¼ tsp salt
- ¼ tsp black pepper
- 1 tablespoon olive oil
- ¼ cup cheese
- ¼ tsp basil
- 1 cup tomatoes

Directions

1. In a bowl combine all ingredients and mix well
2. In a skillet heat olive oil and pour the egg mixture
3. Cook for 1-2 min per side
4. When ready remove omelette from the skillet and serve

Beans Omelette

Servings: 1 | Preparation: 5 min | Cooking: 10 min

Ingredients

- 2 eggs
- ¼ tsp salt
- ¼ tsp black pepper
- 1 tablespoon olive oil
- ¼ cup cheese
- ¼ tsp basil
- 1 cup beans

Directions

1. In a bowl combine all ingredients and mix well
2. In a skillet heat olive oil and pour the egg mixture
3. Cook for 1 2 min per side
4. When ready remove omelette from the skillet and serve

Breakfast Granola

Servings: 2 | Preparation: 5 min | Cooking: 30 min

Ingredients

- 1 tsp vanilla extract
- 1 tablespoon honey
- 1 lb. rolled oats
- 2 tablespoons sesame seeds
- ¼ lb. almonds
- ¼ lb. berries

Directions

1. Preheat the oven to 325 F
2. Spread the granola onto a baking sheet
3. Bake for 12-15 min, remove and mix everything
4. Bake for another 12-15 min or until slightly brown
5. When ready remove from the oven and serve

Raisin Breakfast Mix

Servings: 1 | Preparation: 5 min | Cooking: 5 min

Ingredients

- ½ cup dried raisins
- ½ cup dried pecans
- ¼ cup almonds
- 1 cup coconut milk
- 1 tsp cinnamon

Directions

1. In a bowl combine all ingredients
2. Serve with milk

Sausage Breakfast Sandwich

Servings: 2 | Preparation: 5 min | Cooking: 15 min

Ingredients

- ¼ cup egg substitute
- 1 muffin
- 1 turkey sausage patty
- 1 tablespoon cheddar cheese

Directions

1. In a skillet pour egg and cook on low heat
2. Place turkey sausage patty in a pan and cook for 4 5 min per side
3. On a toasted muffin place the cooked egg, top with a sausage patty and cheddar cheese
4. Serve when ready

Morning Cookies

Servings: 6 | Preparation: 10 min | Cooking: 15 min

Ingredients

- 3 bananas
- ¼ cup peanut butter
- ¼ cup cocoa powder
- handful of salt

Directions

1. Preheat oven to 325 F
2. In a bowl mix all ingredients
3. Form small cookies and place them onto a greased cookie sheet
4. Sprinkle with salt and bake for 12-15 min
5. Remove and serve

Blueberry Bites

Servings: 8 | Preparation: 5 min | Cooking: 30 min

Ingredients

- 2 cups oats
- ½ tsp cinnamon
- 1 cup blueberries
- ½ cup honey
- ½ cup almond butter
- 1 tsp vanilla

Directions

1. Mix all of the ingredients, except for the blueberries.
2. Fold in the blueberries and refrigerate for 30 min.
3. Form balls from the mixture and serve.

Ginger Lemonade

Servings: 8 | Preparation: 5 min | Cooking: 10 min

Ingredients

- 1/3 cup honey
- 4 lemons juice
- Ice
- 4 strips of lemon peel
- 2 tbs ginger root
- 2 sprigs rosemary

Directions

1. Mix the honey, ginger, lemon peel and 2 sprigs rosemary in a pot with 2 cups water.
2. Bring to a boil, then simmer for 10 min.
3. Remove from heat and allow to cool for 15 min.
4. Strain into a pitcher.
5. Discard the ginger and rosemary.
6. Add 6 cups of cold water and lemon juice to the pitcher.
7. Stir to combine and serve with ice.

Lime Grilled Corn

Servings: 4 | Preparation: 5 min | Cooking: 15 min

Ingredients

- 4 corns
- 2 tbs mayonnaise
- Salt
- Pepper
- 2 tbs lime juice
- ¼ tsp chili powder

Directions

1. Preheat the grill.
2. Cook the shucked corn onto the grill for 5 min.
3. Turn every few min until all sides are charred.
4. Mix the mayonnaise, chili powder, and lime juice in a bowl.
5. Season with salt and pepper and add lime juice and chili powder.
6. Serve coated with the mayonnaise mixture.

Apple Crumble

Servings: 6 | Preparation: 10 min | Cooking: 30 min

Ingredients

- 4 apples
- 2 tsp cinnamon
- 1 cup flour
- ½ cup walnuts
- 2 cups quinoa
- 1/3 cup ground almonds

Directions

1. Preheat the oven to 350F.
2. Oil a baking dish.
3. Place the apples into prepared dishes.
4. Mix the remaining ingredients in a bowl.
5. Crumble over the apples.
6. Bake for 30 min.
7. Serve immediately.

Gingersnaps

Servings: 18 | Preparation: 10 min | Cooking: 10 min

Ingredients

- 1 ¾ cups flour
- 1 ¾ ground ginger
- ¼ tsp ground cinnamon
- 1/8 tsp nutmeg
- 1/8 tsp cloves
- 1 ½ tsp cornstarch
- ¼ cup milk
- ¼ cup molasses
- 3 tbs Swerve
- ¼ tsp salt
- 2 tbs butter
- 1 egg white
- 2 ¼ tsp vanilla
- 2 tsp stevia
- 1 tsp baking powder

Directions

1. Preheat the oven to 325F.
2. Mix the cornstarch, nutmeg, flour, cloves, ginger, cinnamon, baking powder, and salt in a bowl.
3. In another bowl, whisk the butter, egg, vanilla, and stevia.
4. Stir in the molasses and milk.
5. Incorporate the flour mixture.
6. Divide into 18 portions and roll into balls.
7. Roll in the Swerve until coated.
8. Place on a lined baking sheet.
9. Sprinkle with Swerve and bake for 10 min.
10. Allow to cool, then serve.

Rice Krispies

Servings: 16 | Preparation: 10 min | Cooking: 60 min

Ingredients

- 4 cups rice cereal
- 2 tbs dark chocolate
- 2/3 cup honey

- ½ cup peanut butter
- Salt
- 1 tsp vanilla

Directions

1. Combine all of the ingredients except for the dark chocolate in a bowl.
2. Spread the mixture on a lined baking pan.
3. Drizzle the melted chocolate on top.
4. Refrigerate for 1 h.
5. Cut into bars and serve.

Breakfast Cookies

Servings: 8 12 | Preparation: 5 min | Cooking: 15 min

Ingredients

- 1 cup rolled oats
- ¼ cup applesauce
- ½ tsp vanilla extract
- 3 tablespoons chocolate chips
- 2 tablespoons dried fruits
- 1 tsp cinnamon

Directions

1. Preheat the oven to 325 F
2. In a bowl combine all ingredients and mix well
3. Scoop cookies using an ice cream scoop
4. Place cookies onto a prepared baking sheet
5. Place in the oven for 12-15 min or until the cookies are done
6. When ready remove from the oven and serve

Sweet Potato & Bell Pepper Hash (Version 2)

Preparation: 10 min | Cooking: 17 min | Servings: 4

Ingredients

- 1 tablespoon olive oil or edible coconut oil
- 1 medium onion, chopped
- 1 large sweet potato, peeled and cubed into ½-inch size
- 1 small green bell pepper, seeded and chopped
- 1 small red bell pepper, seeded and chopped
- Salt and freshly ground black pepper, to taste
- 2 tablespoons water
- ¼ cup scallion (green part), chopped

Directions

1. In a large skillet, heat oil on medium heat. Add onion and sauté for about 2 min.
2. Add sweet potato and cook, stirring occasionally for about 4-5 min.

3. Add bell peppers and cook for about 1 minute.
4. Add salt, black pepper and water and stir to combine.
5. Cover the skillet. Cook, stirring occasionally for about 10 min.
6. Stir in scallion and immediately remove from heat. Serve hot.

Nutrition: Calories: 95; Fat: 3.7g; ; Sodium: 20mg; Carbohydrates: 14.6g; Fiber: 3g; Sugar: 5.8g; Protein: 1.7g

Chicken & Mixed Vegetables Casserole

Preparation: 10 min | Cooking: 55 min | Servings: 6

Ingredients

- 6 organic eggs
- 2 tablespoons fresh cilantro, minced
- ¼ teaspoon red pepper flakes, crushed
- Salt and freshly ground black pepper, to taste
- 1 cup fresh kale, trimmed and chopped
- 3 medium zucchinis, grated
- 1 cup fresh mushrooms, chopped
- 1 medium onion, chopped
- 1 cup cooked organic chicken, shredded
- 2 tablespoons almond flour

Directions

1. Preheat the oven to 400 degrees F.
2. Lightly, grease an 8x8-inch casserole dish.
3. In a medium bowl, add eggs, cilantro, red pepper flakes, salt and black pepper and beat till well combined. Keep aside.
4. In another large bowl, mix together all vegetables.
5. Transfer the vegetable mixture into prepared casserole dish evenly.
6. Place shredded chicken over vegetable mixture evenly.
7. Sprinkle with almond flour evenly.
8. Top with egg mixture evenly.
9. Bake for about 45-55 min or till top is golden brown.

Nutrition: Calories: 141; Fat: 6.3g; ; Sodium: 93mg; Carbohydrates: 7.3g; Fiber: 2g; Sugar: 3.1g; Protein: 14.8g

Superfood Smoothie

Preparation: 10 min | Cooking: 0 min | Servings: 2

Ingredients

- 1½ cups chilled unsweetened almond milk
- 1 cup fresh baby spinach, chopped
- 1 cup fresh kale, trimmed and chopped
- 1 frozen banana, peeled and chopped
- ½ cup frozen pineapple chunks
- 2 teaspoons chia seeds
- 1 tablespoon matcha green tea powder

Directions

1. In a high speed blender, add all ingredients and pulse till smooth.
2. Transfer into 2 large serving glasses and serve immediately.

Nutrition: Calories: 188; Fat: 3.8g; ; Sodium: 163mg; Carbohydrates: 40.6g; Fiber: 6.2g; Sugar: 25.6g; Protein: 3.6g

Sweet Potato & Rosemary Waffles

Preparation: 10 min | Cooking: 10 min | Servings: 2

Ingredients

- 2 medium sweet potatoes, peeled, grated and squeezed finely
- 1½ teaspoons fresh rosemary, minced
- Salt and freshly ground black pepper, to taste

Directions

1. Preheat the waffle iron and lightly grease it.
2. In a large bowl, mix all ingredients.
3. Place half of the sweet potato mixture in preheated waffle iron.
4. Cook for 8-10 min or till waffles become golden brown.
5. Repeat with the remaining mixture.

Nutrition: Calories: 180; Fat: 0.4g; Sodium: 14mg; Carbohydrates: 42.4g; Fiber: 6.5g; Sugar: 0.8g; Protein: 2.3g

Citrus Apple Smoothie

Preparation: 10 min| Cooking: 0 min | Servings: 2

Ingredients

- 1½ cups chilled unsweetened almond milk
- 1 cup fresh baby spinach, chopped
- 1 cup fresh kale, trimmed and chopped
- 1 frozen banana, peeled and chopped
- ½ cup frozen pineapple chunks

- 2 teaspoons chia seeds
- 1 tablespoon matcha green tea powder

Directions

1. In a high speed blender, add all ingredients and pulse till smooth.
2. Transfer into 2 large serving glasses and serve immediately.

Nutrition: Calories: 188; Fat: 3.8g; Sodium: 163mg; Carbohydrates: 40.6g; Fiber: 6.2g; Sugar: 25.6g; Protein: 3.6g

Apple Smoothie (Version 2)

Preparation: 10 min| Cooking: 0 min | Servings: 2

Ingredients

- 1½ cups chilled filtered water
- 1 large apple, peeled, cored and chopped
- 1 large orange, peeled, seeded and sectioned
- ½ teaspoon lemon zest, grated freshly
- ½ tablespoon fresh lemon juice

Directions

1. In a high speed blender, add all ingredients and pulse till smooth.
2. Transfer into 2 large serving glasses and serve immediately.

Nutrition: Calories: 102; Fat: 0.3g; Sodium: 2mg; Carbohydrates: 26.4g; Fiber: 5g; Sugar: 20.3g; Protein: 1.2g

Tropical Fruit Smoothie

Preparation: 10 min| Cooking: 0 min | Servings: 2

Ingredients

- 1½ cups chilled unsweetened almond milk
- ½ cup frozen pineapple chunks
- ½ cup papaya, peeled and chopped
- 1 frozen banana, peeled and sliced

Directions

1. In a high speed blender, add all ingredients and pulse till smooth.
2. Transfer into 2 large serving glasses and serve immediately.

Nutrition: Calories: 151; Fat: 3g; Sodium: 140mg; Carbohydrates: 32.5g; Fiber: 3.6g; Sugar: 23g; Protein: 1.8g

Breakfast Salad

Preparation: 10 min| Cooking: 0 min | Servings: 4

Ingredients

- ½ cup banana, peeled and sliced
- ½ cup kiwi, peeled and chopped
- ½ cup fresh strawberries, hulled and sliced
- ¼ cup seedless red grapes, halved
- ¼ cup seedless green grapes, halved
- ½ cup apple, cored and chopped
- 2 tablespoons extra virgin olive oil coconut oil
- 2 tablespoons fresh lemon juice
- Salt and freshly ground black pepper, to taste
- 4 cups fresh baby spinach

Directions

1. In a large salad bowl, add all ingredients except baby spinach and toss to coat well.
2. Serve immediately over the bed of baby spinach.

Nutrition: Calories: 123; Fat: 7.4g; Sodium: 27mg; Carbohydrates: 14.8g; Fiber: 2.7g; Sugar: 9.3g; Protein: 1.7g

Healthy Breakfast Bowl

Preparation: 5 min| Cooking: 5 min | Servings: 4

Ingredients

- 2 cups unsweetened almond milk
- 2 large delicious red apples, peeled, cored and grated
- 3 tablespoons sunflower seeds
- ½ teaspoon organic vanilla extract
- ¼ teaspoon ground cinnamon
- 1 medium banana, peeled and sliced
- 3 tablespoons almonds, toasted and chopped

Directions

1. In a large pan, mix almond milk, grated apples sunflower seeds, vanilla extract and cinnamon on medium-low heat.
2. Cook gently, stirring occasionally for about 3-4 min.
3. Remove from heat and transfer into serving bowls.
4. Let it cool slightly.
5. Top with banana slices and almonds.
6. Serve.

Nutrition: Calories: 145; Fat: 5.4g; Sodium: 92mg; Carbohydrates: 24.7g; Fiber: 6.5g; Sugar: 15.5g; Protein: 2.5g

Egg Filled Avocado

Preparation: 10 min| Cooking: 22 min| Servings: 4

Ingredients

- 2 medium avocados, halved and pitted
- 4 small organic eggs
- 6 cherry tomatoes, sliced
- ¼ cup fresh basil leaves, chopped
- Salt and freshly ground black pepper, to taste

Directions

1. Preheat the oven to 450 degrees F.
2. Lightly grease a baking dish.
3. Scoop out some flesh from each avocado half to create a cup.
4. Arrange avocado halves, cut side up in prepared baking dish.
5. Carefully, crack each egg into each avocado half.
6. Divide tomato slices over eggs evenly.
7. Bake for about 20-22 min.
8. Sprinkle with salt, and black pepper.
9. Garnish with basil and Serve.

Nutrition: Calories: 239; Fat: 19.5g; Sodium: 63mg; Carbohydrates: 12g; Fiber: 6.9g; Sugar: 3.9g; Protein: 7.3g

Blueberry & Pumpkin Muffins

Preparation: 5 min| Cooking: 18 min| Servings: 5

Ingredients

- 2½ cups almond flour
- ¾ teaspoon baking soda
- ½ teaspoon ground cinnamon
- ¼ teaspoon salt
- 3 large organic eggs
- 1½ tablespoons pure maple syrup
- 2 tablespoons coconut oil, melted
- 1 teaspoon organic vanilla extract
- 1/3 cup homemade pumpkin puree
- 1 cup fresh blueberries

Directions

1. Preheat the oven to 350 degrees F.
2. Line 10 muffin cups with lightly, greased paper liners.
3. In a large bowl, mix flour, baking soda, cinnamon and salt.
4. In another bowl, add eggs, maple syrup, coconut oil and vanilla extract and beat till well combined.
5. Stir in pumpkin puree and beat till well combined.
6. Add egg mixture into flour mixture and mix till well combined.
7. Gently, fold in fresh blueberries.
8. Divide the mixture into prepared muffin cups evenly.
9. Bake for about 14-18 min or till a toothpick inserted in the center comes out clean.

Nutrition: Calories: 211; Fat: 15.6g; Sodium: 354mg; Carbohydrates: 10.1g; Fiber: 2.8g; Sugar: 7.8g; Protein: 7.2g

Zucchini & Scallion Pancakes

Preparation: 5 min| Cooking: 5 min| Servings: 4

Ingredients

- 1/3 cup filtered water
- 2 tablespoons ground flax seeds
- 1 teaspoon coconut oil
- 3 large zucchinis, grated
- Salt and freshly ground black pepper, to taste
- ¼ cup scallion, chopped finely

Directions

1. In a bowl, mix ground flax seeds and water and set aside.
2. In a large skillet, heat oil on medium heat.
3. Add zucchini and cook, stirring occasionally for about 2-3 min.
4. Stir in salt and black pepper and immediately, remove from heat.
5. Transfer the zucchini into a large bowl and let it cool slightly.
6. Add flax seed mixture and scallion and mix till well combined.
7. Preheat a grill and grease it.
8. Add ¼ of the zucchini mixture into preheated skillet.
9. Cook for 2-3 min. Carefully flip the side and cook for 1-2 min further.
10. Repeat with the remaining mixture.

Nutrition: Calories: 69; Fat: 2.7g; Sodium: 27mg; Carbohydrates: 9.6g; Fiber: 3.8g; Sugar: 4.4g; Protein: 3.7g

Garlicky Zucchini with Poached Eggs

Preparation: 10 min | Cooking: 10 min | Servings: 2

Ingredients

- 1 tablespoon olive oil

- 2 small garlic cloves, minced
- 2 large zucchinis, spiralized with blade C
- Salt and freshly ground black pepper, to taste
- 2 organic eggs

Directions

1. In a large skillet, heat oil on medium heat.
2. Add garlic and sauté for about 1 minute.
3. Add zucchini, salt and black pepper and cook for about 3-4 min.
4. Transfer the zucchini mixture into 2 large serving plates.
5. Meanwhile in a large pan, bring 2-3-inches water to a simmer on high heat.
6. Carefully, crack the eggs in water one by one. Cover the pan and turn off the heat.
7. Keep, covered for about 4 min or till desired cooking of the egg is reached..
8. Place the eggs over zucchini.
9. Sprinkle the eggs with salt and black pepper and serve.

Nutrition: Calories: 179; Fat: 12g; Sodium: 94mg; Carbohydrates: 12.2g
Fiber: 3.6g; Sugar: 6g; Protein: 9.6g

Chia Seed Pudding (Version 2)

Preparation: 15 min| Cooking: 0 min| Servings: 2

Ingredients

- 1 cup unsweetened almond milk
- 2 tablespoons maple syrup
- ¼ cup chia seeds
- ¼ teaspoon organic vanilla extract
- ½ of small apple, cored and sliced
- 2 tablespoons almonds, chopped

Directions

1. In a large bowl, add all ingredients except apple and almonds and stir to combine well.
2. Cover and refrigerate for at least 30-40 min.
3. Top with apple and almonds and serve.

Nutrition: Calories: 185; Fat: 9.8g; Sodium: 92mg; Carbohydrates: 26.9g; Fiber: 7.1g; Sugar: 16.1g; Protein: 4.9g

Zucchini & Banana Bread

Preparation: 10 min| Cooking: 45 min| Servings: 6

Ingredients

- ½ cup coconut flour

- 1½ teaspoons baking soda
- Pinch of salt
- ¼ cup coconut oil, softened
- 2 teaspoons vanilla extract
- 1½ cups ripe bananas, peeled and mashed
- 1 cup zucchini, grated and squeezed
- 1 teaspoon orange zest, grated freshly

Directions

1. Preheat the oven to 350 degrees F.
2. Grease a loaf pan.
3. In a large bowl, mix flour, baking soda and salt.
4. In another bowl, add oil and vanilla and beat well.
5. Add banana and beat till well combined.
6. Mix oil mixture into flour mixture.
7. Fold in zucchini and orange zest. Transfer the mixture into prepared loaf pan evenly.
8. Bake for about 40-45 min or till a toothpick nested in the center comes out clean.

Nutrition: Calories: 166; Fat: 10.9g; Sodium: 364mg; Carbohydrates: 15.5g; Fiber: 5.2g; Sugar: 5.8g; Protein: 2.6g

Fruity Breakfast Bowl

Preparation: 5 min| Cooking: 25 min| Servings: 2

Ingredients

- 1 cup kiwi, sliced
- 1 cup fresh cherries, pitted and halved
- ½ cup fresh blueberries
- ½ cup fresh blackberries
- 1 tablespoon fresh lime juice
- 2 tablespoons maple syrup
- 2 tablespoons coconut cream
- ¼ cup pistachios, chopped

Directions

1. In a large bowl, mix fruit, maple syrup and lime juice.
2. Divide fruit mixture in 2 bowls.
3. Top with coconut cream and garnish with pistachios before serving.

Nutrition: Calories: 265; Fat: 7.7g; Sodium: 19mg; Carbohydrates: 48.3g
Fiber: 5.4g; Sugar: 18g; Protein: 3.9g

Cauliflower, Apple & Coconut Porridge

Preparation: 5 min| Cooking: 20 min| Servings: 6

Ingredients

- ½ cup cauliflower
- 2 cups apple, peeled, cored and shredded
- ½ cup coconut, shredded
- 1¾ cups fat-free coconut milk
- 1 teaspoon organic vanilla extract
- ½ cup banana, peeled and sliced
- ½ cup blueberries

Directions

1. In a large pan, add all ingredients except blueberries and mix.
2. Bring to gentle simmer on medium heat.
3. Reduce the heat to low. Simmer, stirring occasionally for about 15 to 20 min.
4. Serve warm with the topping of blueberries.

Nutrition: Calories: 222; Fat: 19g; Sodium: 28mg; Carbohydrates: 13.7g; Fiber: 3.7g; Sugar: 8.5g; Protein: 2.4g

Avocado Pancakes

Servings: 4 | Preparation: 10 min | Cooking: 20 min

Ingredients

- 1 cup whole wheat flour
- ¼ tsp baking soda
- ¼ tsp baking powder
- 1 avocado
- 2 eggs
- 1 cup milk

Directions

1. In a bowl combine all ingredients and mix well
2. In a skillet heat olive oil
3. Pour ¼ of the batter and cook each pancake for 1 2 min per side
4. When ready remove from heat and serve

Mushrooms Pancakes

Servings: 4 | Preparation: 10 min | Cooking: 30 min

Ingredients

- 1 cup whole wheat flour
- ¼ tsp baking soda
- ¼ tsp baking powder
- 1 cup mushrooms
- 2 eggs
- 1 cup milk

Directions

1. In a bowl combine all ingredients and mix well
2. In a skillet heat olive oil
3. Pour ¼ of the batter and cook each pancake for 1 2 min per side
4. When ready remove from heat and serve

Lime Pancakes

Servings: 4 | Preparation: 10 min | Cooking: 20 min

Ingredients

- 1 cup whole wheat flour
- ¼ tsp baking soda
- ¼ tsp baking powder
- 2 lime slices
- 2 eggs
- 1 cup milk

Directions

1. In a bowl combine all ingredients and mix well
2. In a skillet heat olive oil
3. Pour ¼ of the batter and cook each pancake for 1 2 min per side
4. When ready remove from heat and serve

Ginger Puffins

Servings: 8 12 | Preparation: 10 min | Cooking: 20 min

Ingredients

- 2 eggs
- 1 tablespoon olive oil
- 1 cup milk
- 2 cups whole wheat flour
- 1 tsp baking soda
- ¼ tsp baking soda
- 1 tsp ginger
- 1 tsp cinnamon
- ¼ cup molasses

Directions

1. In a bowl combine all dry ingredients
2. In another bowl combine all dry ingredients
3. Combine wet and dry ingredients
4. Fold in ginger and mix well
5. Pour mixture into 8 12 prepared muffin cups, fill 2/3 of the cups
6. Bake for 18 20 min at 375 F
7. When ready remove from the oven and serve

Lemon Muffins

Servings: 8 12 | Preparation: 1 min | Cooking: 20 min

Ingredients

- 2 eggs
- 1 tablespoon olive oil
- 1 cup milk
- 2 cups whole wheat flour
- 1 tsp baking soda
- ¼ tsp baking soda
- Lemon slices
- 1 cup mashed banana

Directions

1. In a bowl combine all dry ingredients
2. In another bowl combine all dry ingredients
3. Combine wet and dry ingredients
4. Pour mixture into 8 12 prepared muffin cups, fill 2/3 of the cups
5. Bake for 18 20 min at 375 F
6. When ready remove from the oven and serve

Mango Muffins

Servings: 8 12 | Preparation: 10 min | Cooking: 20 min

Ingredients

- 2 eggs
- 1 tablespoon olive oil
- 1 cup milk
- 2 cups whole wheat flour
- 1 tsp baking soda
- ¼ tsp baking soda
- 1 tsp cinnamon
- 1 cup mango

Directions

1. In a bowl combine all dry ingredients
2. In another bowl combine all dry ingredients
3. Combine wet and dry ingredients
4. Pour mixture into 8 12 prepared muffin cups, fill 2/3 of the cups
5. Bake for 18 20 min at 375 F
6. When ready remove from the oven and serve

Chocolate Muffins

Servings: 8 12 | Preparation: 10 min | Cooking: 20 min

Ingredients

- 2 eggs
- 1 tablespoon olive oil
- 1 cup milk
- 2 cups whole wheat flour
- 1 tsp baking soda
- ¼ tsp baking soda
- 1 tsp cinnamon
- 1 cup chocolate chips

Directions

1. In a bowl combine all dry ingredients
2. In another bowl combine all dry ingredients
3. Combine wet and dry ingredients
4. Fold in chocolate chips and mix well
5. Pour mixture into 8 12 prepared muffin cups, fill 2/3 of the cups
6. Bake for 18 20 min at 375 F
7. When ready remove from the oven and serve

Apricot Muffins

Servings: 8 12 | Preparation: 10 min | Cooking: 20 min

Ingredients

- 2 eggs
- 1 tablespoon olive oil
- 1 cup milk
- 2 cups whole wheat flour
- 1 tsp baking soda
- ¼ tsp baking soda
- 1 cup apricots

Directions

1. In a bowl combine all dry ingredients
2. In another bowl combine all dry ingredients
3. Combine wet and dry ingredients
4. Pour mixture into 8 12 prepared muffin cups, fill 2/3 of the cups
5. Bake for 18 20 min at 375 F
6. When ready remove from the oven and serve

Omelette

Servings: 1 | Preparation: 5 min | Cooking: 10 min

Ingredients

- 2 eggs
- ¼ tsp salt
- ¼ tsp black pepper
- 1 tablespoon olive oil
- ¼ cup cheese

- ¼ tsp basil

Directions

1. In a bowl combine all ingredients and mix well
2. In a skillet heat olive oil and pour the egg mixture
3. Cook for 1 2 min per side
4. When ready remove omelette from the skillet and serve

Mushroom Omelette

Servings: 1 | Preparation: 5 min | Cooking: 10 min

Ingredients

- 2 eggs
- ¼ tsp salt
- ¼ tsp black pepper
- 1 tablespoon olive oil
- ¼ cup cheese
- ¼ tsp basil
- 1 cup mushrooms

Directions

1. In a bowl combine all ingredients and mix well
2. In a skillet heat olive oil and pour the egg mixture
3. Cook for 1 2 min per side
4. When ready remove omelette from the skillet and serve

Corn Omelette

Servings: 1 | Preparation: 5 min | Cooking: 10 min

Ingredients

- 2 eggs
- ¼ tsp salt
- ¼ tsp black pepper
- 1 tablespoon olive oil
- ¼ cup cheese
- ¼ tsp basil
- 1 cup corn

Directions

1. In a bowl combine all ingredients and mix well
2. In a skillet heat olive oil and pour the egg mixture
3. Cook for 1 2 min per side
4. When ready remove omelette from the skillet and serve

Basil Omelette

Servings: 1 | Preparation: 5 min | Cooking: 10 min

Ingredients

- 2 eggs
- ¼ tsp salt
- ¼ tsp black pepper
- 1 tablespoon olive oil
- ¼ cup cheese
- ¼ tsp basil
- 1 cup mushrooms

Directions

1. In a bowl combine all ingredients and mix well
2. In a skillet heat olive oil and pour the egg mixture
3. Cook for 1 2 min per side
4. When ready remove omelette from the skillet and serve

Tuna Sandwich

Servings: 4 | Preparation: 5 min | Cooking: 5 min

Ingredients

- 1 tablespoon mayonnaise
- ¼ tsp salt
- 2 bread slices
- 1 tuna tin

Directions

1. Mix the tuna, mayonnaise and celery then season
2. Toast the bread
3. Spread the tuna mixture over the bread and serve

Eggs and Vegetables

Servings: 4 | Preparation: 10 min | Cooking: 10 min

Ingredients

- 2 3 tbs oil
- 1 garlic clove
- Pepper
- 1 cup green beans
- 2 lb potatoes
- Salt
- 4 eggs

Directions

1. Peel and dice the potatoes then boil until starting to soften
2. Dice the green beans and cook for almost 5 min then drain
3. Cook the potatoes in hot oil until crispy then add the green beans and the garlic

French Toast

Servings: 4 | Preparation: 10 min | Cooking: 20 min

Ingredients
- 3 tbs honey
- 1 cup milk
- 4 slices of bread
- 2 eggs
- 2 tsp vanilla

Directions
1. Preheat the oven to 350 F
2. Whisk together the milk, vanilla, eggs, and honey
3. Place the bread into a dish and pour the egg mixture over
4. Bake for at least 20 min
5. Serve drizzled with honey

Simple Pancake

Servings: 4 | Preparation: 10 min | Cooking: 30 min

Ingredients
- 1 cup whole wheat flour
- ¼ tsp baking soda
- ¼ tsp baking powder
- 2 eggs
- 1 cup milk

Directions
- In a bowl combine all ingredients and mix well
- In a skillet heat olive oil
- Pour ¼ of the batter and cook each pancake for 1 2 min per side
- When ready remove from heat and serve

Ginger Muffins

Servings: 8 12 | Preparation: 10 min | Cooking: 20 min

Ingredients
- 2 eggs
- 1 tablespoon olive oil
- 1 cup milk
- 2 cups whole wheat flour
- 1 tsp baking soda
- ¼ tsp baking soda
- 1 tsp ginger
- 1 tsp cinnamon
- ¼ cup molasses

Directions
1. In a bowl combine all dry ingredients
2. In another bowl combine all dry ingredients
3. Combine wet and dry ingredients
4. Fold in ginger and mix well
5. Pour mixture into 8 12 prepared muffin cups, fill 2/3 of the cups
6. Bake for 18 20 min at 375 F
7. When ready remove from the oven and serve

Omelette

Servings: 1 | Preparation: 5 min | Cooking: 10 min

Ingredients
- 2 eggs
- ¼ tsp salt
- ¼ tsp black pepper
- 1 tablespoon olive oil
- ¼ cup cheese
- ¼ tsp basil

Directions
1. In a bowl combine all ingredients and mix well
2. In a skillet heat olive oil and pour the egg mixture
3. Cook for 1 2 min per side
4. When ready remove omelette from the skillet and serve

Cranberries Pancakes

Servings: 4 | Preparation: 10 min | Cooking: 30 min

Ingredients
- 1 cup whole wheat flour
- ¼ tsp baking soda
- ¼ tsp baking powder
- 1 cup cranberries
- 2 eggs
- 1 cup milk

Directions
1. In a bowl combine all ingredients and mix well
2. In a skillet heat olive oil
3. Pour ¼ of the batter and cook each pancake for 1 2 min per side
4. When ready remove from heat and serve

Date Pancakes

Servings: 4 | Preparation: 10 min | Cooking: 20 min

Ingredients
- 1 cup whole wheat flour

- ¼ tsp baking soda
- ¼ tsp baking powder
- 1 tablespoons date fruit
- 2 eggs
- 1 cup milk

Directions

1. In a bowl combine all ingredients and mix well
2. In a skillet heat olive oil
3. Pour ¼ of the batter and cook each pancake for 1 2 min per side
4. When ready remove from heat and serve

Strawberry Pancakes

Servings: 4 | Preparation: 10 min | Cooking: 20 min

Ingredients

- 1 cup whole wheat flour
- ¼ tsp baking soda
- ¼ tsp baking powder
- 1 cup strawberries
- 2 eggs
- 1 cup milk

Directions

1. In a bowl combine all ingredients and mix well
2. In a skillet heat olive oil
3. Pour ¼ of the batter and cook each pancake for 1 2 min per side
4. When ready remove from heat and serve

Jujabe Pancakes

Servings: 4 | Preparation: 10 min | Cooking: 30 min

Ingredients

- 1 cup whole wheat flour
- ¼ tsp baking soda
- ¼ tsp baking powder
- 2 eggs
- 1 cup milk
- 2 tablespoons jujabe fruit

Directions

1. In a bowl combine all ingredients and mix well
2. In a skillet heat olive oil
3. Pour ¼ of the batter and cook each pancake for 1 2 min per side
4. When ready remove from heat and serve

Nectarine muffins

Servings: 8 12 | Preparation: 10 min | Cooking: 20 min

Ingredients

- 2 eggs
- 1 tablespoon olive oil
- 1 cup milk
- 2 cups whole wheat flour
- 1 tsp baking soda
- ¼ tsp baking soda
- 1 cup nectarine
- 1 tsp cinnamon
- ¼ cup molasses

Directions

1. In a bowl combine all wet ingredients
2. In another bowl combine all dry ingredients
3. Combine wet and dry ingredients
4. Pour mixture into 8 12 prepared muffin cups, fill 2/3 of the cups
5. Bake for 18 20 min at 375 F, when ready remove and serve

Banana muffins

Servings: 8 12 | Preparation: 10 min | Cooking: 20 min

Ingredients

- 2 eggs
- 1 tablespoon olive oil
- 1 cup milk
- 2 cups whole wheat flour
- 1 tsp baking soda
- ¼ tsp baking soda
- 1 tsp cinnamon
- 1 cup mashed banana

Directions

1. In a bowl combine all wet ingredients
2. In another bowl combine all dry ingredients
3. Combine wet and dry ingredients
4. Fold in mashed banana and mix well
5. Pour mixture into 8 12 prepared muffin cups, fill 2/3 of the cups
6. Bake for 18 20 min at 375 F, when ready remove and serve

Papaya muffins

Servings: 8 12 | Preparation: 10 min | Cooking: 20 min

Ingredients

- 2 eggs
- 1 tablespoon olive oil
- 1 cup milk
- 2 cups whole wheat flour
- 1 tsp baking soda
- ¼ tsp baking soda
- 1 tsp cinnamon
- 1 cup papaya

Directions

1. In a bowl combine all wet ingredients
2. In another bowl combine all dry ingredients
3. Combine wet and dry ingredients
4. Fold in papaya and mix well
5. Pour mixture into 8 12 prepared muffin cups, fill 2/3 of the cups
6. Bake for 18 20 min at 375 F, when ready remove and serve

Pear muffins

Servings: 8 12 | Preparation: 10 min | Cooking: 20 min

Ingredients

- 2 eggs
- 1 tablespoon olive oil
- 1 cup milk
- 2 cups whole wheat flour
- 1 tsp baking soda
- ¼ tsp baking soda
- 1 tsp cinnamon
- 1 cup pear

Directions

1. In a bowl combine all wet ingredients
2. In another bowl combine all dry ingredients
3. Combine wet and dry ingredients
4. Fold in pear and mix well
5. Pour mixture into 8 12 prepared muffin cups, fill 2/3 of the cups
6. Bake for 18 20 min at 375 F

Peaches muffins

Servings: 8 12 | Preparation: 10 min | Cooking: 20 min

Ingredients

- 2 eggs
- 1 tablespoon olive oil
- 1 cup milk
- 2 cups whole wheat flour
- 1 tsp baking soda
- ¼ tsp baking soda
- 1 tsp cinnamon
- 1 cup peaches

Directions

1. In a bowl combine all wet ingredients
2. In another bowl combine all dry ingredients
3. Combine wet and dry ingredients
4. Pour mixture into 8 12 prepared muffin cups, fill 2/3 of the cups
5. Bake for 18 20 min at 375 F
6. When ready remove from the oven and serve

Asparagus omelette

Servings: 1 | Preparation: 5 min | Cooking: 10 min

Ingredients

- 2 eggs
- ¼ tsp salt
- ¼ tsp black pepper
- 1 tablespoon olive oil
- ¼ cup cheese
- ¼ tsp basil
- 1 cup asparagus

Directions

1. In a bowl combine all ingredients and mix well
2. In a skillet heat olive oil and pour the egg mixture
3. Cook for 1 2 min per side
4. When ready remove omelette from the skillet and serve

Zucchini omelette

Servings: 1 | Preparation: 5 min | Cooking: 10 min

Ingredients

- 2 eggs
- ¼ tsp salt
- ¼ tsp black pepper
- 1 tablespoon olive oil
- ¼ cup cheese
- ¼ tsp basil
- 1 cup zucchini

Directions

1. In a bowl combine all ingredients and mix well

2. In a skillet heat olive oil and pour the egg mixture
3. Cook for 1 2 min per side
4. When ready remove omelette from the skillet and serve

Broccoli omelette

Servings: 1 | Preparation: 5 min | Cooking: 10 min

Ingredients

- 2 eggs
- ¼ tsp salt
- ¼ tsp black pepper
- 1 tablespoon olive oil
- ¼ cup cheese
- ¼ tsp basil
- 1 cup red onion
- 1 cup broccoli

Directions

1. In a bowl combine all ingredients and mix well
2. In a skillet heat olive oil and pour the egg mixture
3. Cook for 1 2 min per side
4. When ready remove omelette from the skillet and serve

Brussels sprouts omelette

Servings: 1 | Preparation: 5 min | Cooking: 10 min

Ingredients

- 2 eggs
- ¼ tsp salt
- ¼ tsp black pepper
- 1 tablespoon olive oil
- ¼ cup cheese
- ¼ tsp basil
- 1 cup brussels sprouts

Directions

1. In a bowl combine all ingredients and mix well
2. In a skillet heat olive oil and pour the egg mixture
3. Cook for 1 2 min per side
4. When ready remove omelette from the skillet and serve

Arugula omelette

Servings: 1 | Preparation: 5 min | Cooking: 10 min

Ingredients

- 2 eggs
- ¼ tsp salt
- ¼ tsp black pepper
- 1 tablespoon olive oil
- ¼ cup cheese
- ¼ tsp basil
- 1 cup arugula

Directions

1. In a bowl combine all ingredients and mix well
2. In a skillet heat olive oil and pour the egg mixture
3. Cook for 1 2 min per side
4. When ready remove omelette from the skillet and serve

Cinnamon & yoghurt breakfast bowls

Servings: 1 2 | Preparation: 10 min | Cooking: 20 min

Ingredients

- ¼ tsp cinnamon
- 6 figs
- 2 tablespoons orange juice
- 2 tablespoons honey
- ¼ lb. blackberries
- ½ lb. Greek yogurt
- 2 tablespoons granola

Directions

1. In a bowl combine cinnamon, orange juice, honey and mix well
2. Add figs and mix well
3. Roast at 375 F for 18 20 min
4. When ready remove from the oven
5. Add remaining ingredients and mix well

Oatmeal with raisins

Servings: 1 | Preparation: 5 min | Cooking: 5 min

Ingredients

- 1 cup oats
- ¼ cup coconut milk
- 1 tablespoon raisins
- 1 tablespoon apricots
- 1 tablespoon almonds

Directions

1. In a bowl combine all ingredients
2. Refrigerate overnight
3. Serve in the morning

Egg tacos

Servings: 2 | Preparation: 10 min | Cooking: 10 min

Ingredients

- 2 tablespoons olive oil
- 1 clove garlic
- 2 cups baby spinach
- 4 eggs
- 4 tortillas
- ¼ tsp cumin
- 1 can black beans

Directions

1. In a skillet heat olive oil
2. Add garlic, beans and cook until golden brown
3. Add spinach, cumin, baby spinach and eggs
4. When ready pour mixture into prepared tortillas and serve

Walnut oatmeal

Servings: 2 | Preparation: 10 min | Cooking: 20 min

Ingredients

- 2 cups oats
- 2 cups pineapple
- 1 cup walnuts
- 1 cup coconut milk
- 1 cup almond milk
- ¼ cup maple syrup
- 2 tablespoons honey
- ¼ tsp cinnamon
- 1 tsp vanilla extract

Directions

1. In a bowl combine all ingredients and mix well
2. Mix well and transfer mixture to a baking sheet
3. Press the mixture on the baking sheet and bake at 425 F for 18 20 min
4. When ready remove from the oven and serve

Skinny omelette

Servings: 2 | Preparation: 10 min | Cooking: 10 min

Ingredients

- 2 eggs
- pinch of salt
- 1 tablespoon chives
- 1 tablespoon pesto
- bit of goat cheese
- handful of salad greens

Directions

1. In a bowl beat eggs and pour in a skillet over medium heat, sprinkle with chives, and spread the pesto across the omelette
2. Sprinkle salad greens, cheese and season with salt

Veggie quinoa cups

Servings: 6 | Preparation: 10 min | Cooking: 10 min

Ingredients

- ½ cup quinoa
- 1 tablespoon olive oil
- 1 onion
- 3 cups spinach leaves
- 1 garlic clove
- ¼ shallot
- salt
- ¼ cup cheddar cheese
- ¼ cup parmesan cheese
- 1 egg

Directions

1. Preheat oven to 350 F and line a six cup muffin pan
2. Combine water and quinoa in a saucepan and bring to boil
3. Lower the heat and cook for 12 15 min, remove from heat and allow to cool
4. In a skillet heat oil, add onion and cook for 4 5 min
5. Stir in shallot, garlic and spinach and season with salt and pepper
6. Remove the pan from heat and mix with quinoa, pour in the eggs
7. Divide the batter into muffin cups and bake for 30 35 min

Cranberry stuffing

Servings: 4 | Preparation: 10 min | Cooking: 10 min

Ingredients

- 10 cups
- ½ cup butter
- 1 cup diced celery
- ¼ cup onion
- 1 cup chopped cranberries
- ½ cup sugar
- 1 tsp sage
- 1 tsp rosemary
- 1 tsp sage

- 1 tsp rosemary
- 1 tsp thyme
- ½ cup parsley
- salt
- 1 lb. ground sausage
- 1 cup chicken broth

Directions
1. In a saucepan heat butter over medium heat, add onion, celery and cook, add cranberries, sage, sugar, rosemary, parsley, thyme
2. Season with salt and pepper
3. Brown the sausage in a skillet, drain off fat
4. Toss the ingredients in the bowl and add chicken broth
5. Serve when ready

Crustless quiche cups

Servings: 6 | Preparation: 10 min | Cooking: 10 min

Ingredients
- 10 oz. chopped kale
- 2 eggs
- 2 egg whites
- ½ cup leek
- ½ cup chopped tomato
- ½ cup bell pepper

Directions
1. Preheat oven to 325 F and line a muffin pan with paper liners
2. In a bowl leek, egg whites, tomatoes, kale, eggs and bell pepper
3. Divide mixture into muffin cups and bake for 15 20 min
4. Remove and serve

Quinoa with scallions

Servings: 6 | Preparation: 10 min | Cooking: 10 min

Ingredients
- 3 ears corn
- 1 tablespoon lemon zest
- 1 tablespoon lemon juice
- ½ cup butter
- 1 tablespoon honey
- ¼ tsp salt
- ½ tsp pepper
- 1 cup quinoa
- 3 scallions

Directions
1. In a pot place the corn and fill the pan with water, bring to boil and cover for 5 6 min
2. Remove from pot and let it cool
3. In a bowl mix the rest of the ingredients for dressing: lemon juice, melted butter, lemon zest, honey, pepper
4. Cook the quinoa in a pot, add scallions in a bowl with the dressing and toss well
5. Season with salt and serve

Berry granola

Servings: 4 | Preparation: 10 min | Cooking: 10 min

Ingredients
- 2 tablespoons chia
- ¾ cup rolled oats
- 1 cup vanilla cashewmilk
- ½ cup fresh blueberries
- 2 strawberries
- ½ raspberries
- sprinkle of granola

Directions
1. In a bowl mix cashewmilk, oats, chia and divide into 2 servings
2. Refrigerate overnight, remove top with berries and serve

Overnight oats

Servings: 2 | Preparation: 5 min | Cooking: 5 min

Ingredients
- 2 tablespoons chia
- ¾ cup rolled oats
- 1 cup vanilla cashewmilk
- ¼ cup peach
- ¼ plum
- 3 basil leaves
- 1 tsp pumpkin seeds
- 1 tsp hemp seeds

Directions
1. In a bowl mix cashewmilk, oats, chia and oats, divide into 2 3 servings
2. Refrigerate overnight
3. Remove and serve

Avocado brownie

Servings: 4 | Preparation: 10 min | Cooking: 30 min

Ingredients

- 1 ripe avocado
- 3 tablespoons melted butter
- 1 egg
- ¼ cup brown sugar
- ¼ maple syrup
- 1 tablespoon vanilla extract
- ¾ cup cocoa powder
- ½ tsp salt
- ½ cup gluten free flour
- ¼ cup dark chocolate chips

Directions

1. Preheat the oven to 325 F
2. In a bowl mash the avocado, brown sugar, maple syrup, vanilla, sugar, water, butter, add cocoa powder
3. In a bowl mix salt and flour and stir in avocado mixture, spread bake in the pan and bake for 35 min
4. Remove and cool before serving

Breakfast mix

Servings: 1 | Preparation: 5 min | Cooking: 5 min

Ingredients

- 1 cup corn cereal
- 1 cup rice cereal
- ¼ cup cocoa cereal
- ¼ cup rice cakes

Directions

1. In a bowl combine all ingredients
2. Serve with milk

Raspberry crumble

Servings: 4 | Preparation: 10 min | Cooking: 50 min

Ingredients

- 2 eggs
- 1 cup raspberries
- 1 cup apple juice
- 1 cup oats
- 1 tablespoon butter
- 1 tablespoon brown sugar
- 1 tablespoon cinnamon
- ¼ tsp cloves

Directions

1. Preheat oven to 375 F

2. In a bowl combine raspberries, apple slices and apple juice
3. In another bowl combine sugar, spices, oats, butter and mix well
4. Cover apple slices with crumble topping
5. Bake for 45 50 min
6. When ready remove and serve

Quinoa crepes with applesauce

Servings: 4 | Preparation: 10 min | Cooking: 30 min

Ingredients

- 1 cup quinoa flour
- ½ cup tapioca flour
- 1 tsp baking soda
- 1 tsp cinnamon
- 1 cup water
- 2 tablespoons canola oil
- 2 cups organic apple sauce

Directions

1. In a bowl combine quinoa flour, baking soda, cinnamon, tapioca flour, water, oil and whisk well
2. Preheat a skillet over medium heat and pour ¼ cup batter into skillet
3. Cook each crepe on low heat for 1 2 min per side
4. When ready remove and serve with apple sauce

Cheese omelette

Servings: 1 | Preparation: 5 min | Cooking: 10 min

Ingredients

- 2 eggs
- ¼ tsp salt
- ¼ tsp black pepper
- 1 tablespoon olive oil
- ¼ cup cheese
- ¼ tsp basil
- 1 cup low fat cheese

Directions

1. In a bowl combine all ingredients and mix well
2. In a skillet heat olive oil and pour the egg mixture
3. Cook for 1 2 min per side
4. When ready remove omelette from the skillet and serve

Cucumber omelette

Servings: 1 | Preparation: 5 min | Cooking: 10 min

Ingredients

- 2 eggs
- ¼ tsp salt
- ¼ tsp black pepper
- 1 tablespoon olive oil
- ¼ cup cheese
- ¼ tsp basil
- 1 cup cucumber

Directions

1. In a bowl combine all ingredients and mix well
2. In a skillet heat olive oil and pour the egg mixture
3. Cook for 1 2 min per side
4. When ready remove omelette from the skillet and serve

Baked eggs in zoodles nests

Preparation: 10 min | Cooking: 11 min | Servings: 2

Ingredients

- 3 spiralized zucchini
- 2 tablespoons extra-virgin avocado oil
- 1 teaspoon kosher salt
- ½ teaspoon black pepper
- 1 teaspoon dried or fresh basil
- ½ teaspoon paprika
- 4 large eggs

Directions

- Program the oven to 350°F, then spray a cookie sheet lightly with nonstick spray.
- Place the spiralized zucchini noodles in a large bowl, add the avocado oil, salt, pepper, basil, and paprika and toss to coat the zoodles in the seasoning.
- Divide the zoodles into 4 even portions, then arrange each pile on the baking sheet into a nest.
- Careful y crack a large egg into each zucchini nest, then bake for 9-11
- min until the eggs are set.
- Set and enjoy!

Nutrition; Carbohydrates: 17.7g; Protein: 18.6g; Fat: 24.9g; Saturated Fat: 6.3g; Cholesterol: 372mg; ; Sodium: 1352mg; Potassium: 1424mg; Sugar: 9.2g;

Butternut squash breakfast porridge

Preparation: 5 min | Cooking: 20 min

Ingredients

- 1/4 cup roasted pumpkin seeds
- 2 tablespoon unsweetened shredded coconut
- 1 tablespoon ground flaxseed meal
- 1 teaspoon cinnamon
- ¼ teaspoon nutmeg
- ¼ teaspoon ground ginger
- 1/8 teaspoon ground cloves
- 1 teaspoon sea salt
- ½ cup coconut milk,
- 1 cup butternut squash, chopped cooked
- 1 tablespoon pure maple syrup

Directions

1. Add the pumpkin seeds, coconut, flax seeds, cinnamon, nutmeg, ginger, cloves, and sea salt to a spice grinder and blend the mixture into a fine powder.
2. Add the spice mixture to a bowl with the coconut milk and allow it to sit for 5 min until it gelatinizes. Add the spice and coconut milk mixture and the cooked butternut squash to a high-speed blender and blend until smooth.
3. Add the butternut squash porridge to a saucepan and heat it over medium-low heat, stirring every so often until bubbles start to appear.
4. Remove the butternut squash porridge from the stove, pour it into a bowl, drizzle with maple syrup, and top with your favorite.
5. Serve and enjoy.

Nutrition; Carbohydrates: 24.9g; Protein: 8.7g; Fat: 32.3g; Saturated Fat: 21.3g; Cholesterol: 0mg; ; Sodium: 971mg; Potassium: 419mg; Sugar: 11.2g;

Spinach Mushroom Hash With Eggs

Preparation: 5 min | Cooking: 20 min | Servings: 4

Ingredients

- 1 tablespoon extra-virgin olive oil
- 1 cup baby Portobello mushrooms, sliced
- 1 lb. button mushrooms, sliced
- 1 small onion, diced
- 3 cloves garlic, minced
- 4 heaping cups of spinach
- 1 teaspoon salt
- ½ teaspoon black pepper
- ½ teaspoon red pepper flakes
- 4 large eggs

Directions

1. Place the olive oil in a skillet, then add the mushrooms and onions once the pan is hot. Cook the mushrooms on medium-high heat for 3-5 min until the vegetables have softened.
2. Stir in the spinach, garlic, salt, pepper, and red pepper flakes and cook for 1-2 min until the spinach has wilted.
3. Decrease the heat to medium-low, then make 4 holes in the spinach and mushroom mixture. Crack the eggs into the wels, then cover the pan with the lid so the eggs can cook evenly. Cook the eggs for 3-4 min before removing spinach mushroom and egg skillet from the heat.
4. Serve and enjoy.

Nutrition; Carbohydrates: 13.9g; Protein: 17.1g; Fat: 9g; Saturated Fat: 2.1g; Cholesterol: 186mg; ; Sodium: 693mg; Potassium: 878mg; Sugar: 3.2g;

Sweet Potato Breakfast Bowl

Preparation: 10 min | Cooking: 55 min | 1 h 5 min | Servings: 4

Ingredients

- 2 medium sweet potatoes
- ¼ cup unsweetened coconut milk
- 1 teaspoon pure vanila extract
- 2 tablespoon unsalted natural cashew butter
- 1 tablespoon pure maple syrup
- 1 teaspoon cinnamon
- ½ teaspoon nutmeg
- 2 tablespoon ground flaxseed meal
- 4 kiwis
- 1 cup blueberries
- ½ cup sugar-free granola

Directions

1. Program the oven to 400F, then wash the sweet potatoes well and place them on a parchment-lined cookie sheet. Roast the sweet potatoes for about 45-50 min until they are tender when penetrated with a fork. Set the potatoes aside to cool.
2. Remove the flesh of the sweet potatoes from the skins and add it to a large bowl.
3. Add the coconut milk, vanila extract, cashew butter, cinnamon, nutmeg, and flaxseed meal to the bowl. Beat the sweet potatoes with an electric hand mixer until it is fluffy.
4. Place the sweet potatoes into 4 bowls, top with kiwi, granola, and blueberries. Serve and enjoy!

Nutrition; Carbohydrates: 48.8g; Protein: 17.6g; Fat: 15.7g; Saturated Fat: 5.3g; Cholesterol: 0mg; ; Sodium: 49mg; Potassium: 627mg; Sugar: 20.4g;

Yellow Superfood Smoothie Bowl

Preparation: 5 min | Cooking: 0 min | 5 min | Servings: 2

Ingredients

- 1 ½ cup frozen mango
- 1 ½ cup frozen pineapple
- 1 banana, sliced
- 2/3 cup almond milk
- ½ teaspoon turmeric

Directions

1. Add the mango, pineapple, banana, almond milk, and turmeric to a high-speed blender and blend until it is smooth.
2. Pour the yellow superfood smoothie into a bowl, top with kiwi, berries, fruit, granola, or coconut flakes.
3. Serve and enjoy!

Nutrition; Carbohydrates: 75.3g; Protein: 1.8g; Fat: 1.3g; Saturated Fat: 0.1g; Cholesterol: 0mg; ; Sodium: 51mg; Potassium: 574mg; Sugar: 63.8g;

Vegetable Frittata

Preparation: 5 min | Cooking: 30 min | Servings: 6

Ingredients

- 1 tablespoon olive oil
- 1 medium red bell pepper
- 1 red onion
- 1 zucchini diced
- 2 cloves garlic, minced
- 1 cup spinach
- 1 tomato, diced
- 1 cup green peas
- 6 eggs
- ¼ cup dairy-free heavy whipping cream
- 1 teaspoon kosher salt
- ½ teaspoon black pepper
- 1 teaspoon smoked paprika

Directions

1. Arrange your oven rack in the oven center, then program your oven to 350°F.

2. Add the olive oil to an 8-inch oven-safe cast-iron skillet over medium-high heat. Saute the bell pepper, onion, zucchini, and garlic for 6-10 min until the vegetables have softened and most of the moisture has evaporated.
3. Stir in the spinach and saute for 1-2 min until the spinach wilts.
4. Add the eggs to a bowl, along with the dairy-free cream, salt, pepper, and smoked paprika, then whisk the eggs until smooth.
5. Stir the green peas into the vegetables, then pour in the eggs. Stir the egg mixture for 30 seconds to distribute the vegetables and help the frittata set.
6. Bake the frittata in the oven for 16-20 min until the eggs are set. Let the frittata cool for 5 min. Serve and enjoy!

Nutrition; Carbohydrates: 11.3g; Protein: 8.3g; Fat: 7.3g; Saturated Fat: 1.9g; Cholesterol: 165mg; ; Sodium: 461mg; Potassium: 373mg; Sugar: 4.4g;

Sweet Potato Avocado Toast With Tomato Red Onions And Cilantro

Preparation: 15 min | Cooking: 30 min | Servings: 2

Ingredients
- 1 large sweet potato scrubbed clean and sliced lengthwise
- 1 tablespoon olive oil, melted
- 1 avocado, sliced
- ½ cup red onion, diced
- ½ cup cherry tomatoes
- ½ tablespoon lemon juice
- ¼ teaspoon kosher salt
- ¼ teaspoon black pepper
- 2 tablespoons freshly chopped cilantro

Directions
1. Program your oven to 400F, arrange the sliced sweet potato disc onto a parchment-lined baking sheet and brush both sides with olive oil.
2. Bake the sweet potato discs for 20 min, remove them from the oven, flip them over and bake for 10 min until tender. Let the sweet potato discs cool slightly before transferring them to your serving dish.
3. Top each disc with sliced avocadoes, cherry tomatoes, and red onions.
4. Sprinkle the avocado toast with lemon juice, then with salt and pepper.

5. Garnish the sweet potato avocado toast with the chopped cilantro.
6. Serve and enjoy!

Nutrition; Carbohydrates: 26.4g; Protein: 4g; Fat: 26.8g; Saturated Fat: 5.2g; Cholesterol: 0mg; ; Sodium: 337mg; Potassium: 877mg; Sugar: 5.6g;

Citrus Flavored Fruit Salad

Preparation: 10 min | Cooking: 0 min | Servings: 6

Ingredients
- juice from 2 large oranges
- juice from 1 lemon juice
- ½ teaspoon lime zest
- juice from ½ lime juice
- 1 cup blueberries
- 2 cup strawberries, quartered
- 2 cups fresh mango
- 2 oranges, peeled and segmented
- 4 kiwis, peeled and sliced
- 1 cup seedless grapes

Directions
1. Place the blueberries, strawberries, mangoes, oranges, kiwi, grapes, and lime zest into a large bowl.
2. To make the citrus marinade, squeeze the juice from the oranges, lemon, and lime into a bowl and stir to combine.
3. Pour the citrus marinade over the fruit and stir to combine 4. Serve and enjoy!

Nutrition; Carbohydrates: 40.3g; Protein: 2.7g; Fat: 1g; Saturated Fat: 0.1g; Cholesterol: 0mg; ; Sodium: 4mg; Potassium: 618mg; Sugar: 32.2g;

Spiced Peanut Butter Banana Smoothie Bowl

Preparation: 5 min | Cooking: 0 min | Calories: 491 kcal

Ingredients
- 3 ripe frozen bananas
- 3 tablespoon natural creamy peanut butter
- 2 tablespoon flaxseed meal
- ½ cup light coconut milk
- ½ teaspoon ground cinnamon
- ¼ teaspoon nutmeg
- 1/8 teaspoon ground ginger

Directions

1. Add the bananas, peanut butter, flaxseeds, coconut milk, cinnamon, nutmeg, and ginger to a high-speed blender and blend until the peanut butter banana smooth and creamy.
2. Divide the peanut butter smoothie between two bowls and top with coconut, peanuts, raisins, bananas, or your favorite toppings.
3. Serve and enjoy!

Nutrition; Carbohydrates: 53.3g; Protein: 15.6g; Fat: 28.1g; Saturated Fat: 6.5g; Cholesterol: 0mg; ; Sodium: 17mg; Potassium: 1007mg; Sugar: 26.3g;

Sweet Potato Hash With Eggs

Preparation: 10 min | Cooking: 20 min | Servings: 4

Ingredients

- 2 tablespoons extra virgin avocado oil
- 1 small yellow onion, diced
- 2 cloves garlic, minced
- 4 sweet potatoes, washed diced into 1/2-inch chunks
- 1 teaspoon kosher salt
- ½ teaspoon black pepper
- ½ teaspoon fresh or dried thyme
- 1 medium yellow pepper, diced
- ½ teaspoon smoked paprika
- ¼ teaspoon cayenne pepper
- 4 large eggs

Directions

1. Program your oven to 425°F, then heat a large cast-iron skillet on medium-high heat. Add the avocado oil, and add the chopped onion once the pan is hot.
2. Stir in the minced garlic, then cook for 1 minute, then add the sweet potatoes, salt, black pepper, thyme, stir to combine, and cook for 4 min until the sweet potatoes are lightly browned.
3. Cook the potatoes for 5-7 min until the potatoes are tender, then add the bell pepper and cook for 2 min. Remove the sweet potatoes from the burner and stir in the smoked paprika and cayenne pepper.
4. Turn off heat, add smoked paprika and cayenne pepper and stir to combine. Use a cooking spoon to make holes in the sweet potato, then crack an egg into each wel .
5. Place the sweet potato hash into the oven and bake for 7-8 min until the egg whites set and the yolk moves slightly when shaking the pan.

Nutrition; Carbohydrates: 31.9g; Protein: 9.7g; Fat: 12.1g; Saturated Fat: 2.5g; Cholesterol: 186mg; ; Sodium: 725mg; Potassium: 665mg; Sugar: 6.4g;

Eggs in a Portobello Hole

Preparation: 5 min | Cooking: 15 min | Servings: 2

Ingredients

- 4 Portobello mushrooms caps, cleaned, stems removed
- 4 large eggs
- 1 cup arugula
- ½ teaspoon kosher salt
- ¼ teaspoon black pepper
- 2 tablespoon freshly minced parsley

Directions

1. Program the oven to 400F, then divide the arugula between the 4
2. mushroom caps.
3. Gently crack the eggs into each mushroom and sprinkle with salt and pepper.
4. Bake the mushrooms and eggs for 12-15 min until the whites are set, then garnish the egg mushrooms with parsley.
5. Serve and enjoy!

Nutrition; Carbohydrates: 10.3g; Protein: 17.3g; Fat: 10.4g; Saturated Fat: 3.2g; Cholesterol: 372mg; ; Sodium: 737mg; Potassium: 1028mg; Sugar: 4.1g;

Pumpkin cupcakes

Servings: 4 | Preparation: 10 min | Cooking: 30 min

Ingredients

- 1 cup pumpkin puree
- 1 tsp cinnamon
- ½ tsp mixed spice
- 1 tsp ginger
- ¼ lb. butter
- 1 cups brown sugar
- 2 eggs
- 2 cups flour
- 3 tsp baking powder

Directions

1. Boil the pumpkin and then puree in a food processor
2. Cream butter and sugar, add the eggs and beat well, stir in pureed pumpkin and dry ingredients

3. Combine all ingredients and spoon mixture into a muffin tin
4. Bake at 300 F for 20 min, remove and serve

Buckwheat pancakes (Version 2)

Servings: 2 | Preparation: 10 min | Cooking: 10 min

Ingredients
- 1 cup buckwheat mix
- 1 egg
- 1 cup milk
- 1 tablespoon butter

Directions
1. In a bow mix all ingredients, add olive oil and pour batter
2. Cook for 1 2 min per side
3. Remove and serve

Carrot cake

Servings: 4 | Preparation: 10 min | Cooking: 40 min

Ingredients
- 1 cup whole meal self raising flour
- 1 cup brown sugar
- 1 cup self raising flour
- 1 tsp salt
- 1 tsp cinnamon
- 1 tsp ginger
- 1 cup olive oil
- 2 cups carrots
- 3 eggs
- ½ tsp allspice

Directions
1. Preheat oven to 275 F and place all ingredients in a bowl except eggs
2. In another bowl mix eggs and add to the mixture
3. Pour into cake in
4. For carrot cake pour batter into cupcake molds
5. Bake for 40 min
6. Remove and serve

Russian fudge

Servings: 2 | Preparation: 10 min | Cooking: 30 min

Ingredients
- ½ butter
- 1 can condensed milk
- ¾ cup milk
- 2 tablespoons golden syrup
- 3 cups sugar
- 1 tablespoon vanilla essence

Directions
1. In a pot place all the ingredients except vanilla essence and bring to boil
2. Boil for 15 20 min and in another bowl drop some fudge mixture
3. Add vanilla essence and beat with a mixer for 5 6 min
4. Pour into greased tin and place in fridge
5. Cut into pieces and serve

Ginger beer

Servings: 2 | Preparation: 10 min | Cooking: 20 min

Ingredients
- 1 inch ginger
- 4 tablespoons brown sugar
- 1 tsp citric acid
- 1 L soda water
- fresh mint

Directions
1. Grate ginger and mix with the rest of ingredients and let them sit for 10 12 min
2. Serve when ready

Cinnamon scones

Servings: 4 | Preparation: 10 min | Cooking: 30 min

Ingredients
- 2 cups self raising flour
- 2 tablespoons butter
- 2/3 cups milk

Filling:

- 1/3 cup butter
- ¾ cup brown sugar
- 1 tsp cinnamon

Directions
1. Preheat oven to 350 F
2. In a blender add butter, flour and blend until smooth
3. Add milk and blend or another 1 2 min
4. Remove mixture onto floured surface
5. In the blender put all ingredients for the filling and blend until smooth
6. Spread the filling into the dough

Mac and cheeseless

Servings: 4 | Preparation: 10 min | Cooking: 30 min

Ingredients

- 1 leek
- 1 clove garlic
- sat
- citric acid
- 1 tsp turmeric
- 1 tsp cumin
- 1 tsp coriander powder
- ½ cup roasted sunflower seeds
- 1 tablespoon rice flour
- 1 tsp arrowroot
- 1 cup broccoli
- 2 tablespoons butter
- 1 cup milk
- macaroni pasta

Directions

1. Cook pasta, add leek and sauté with butter, citric acid and pepper
2. Add butter, cumin, coriander powder, turmeric, sunflower seeds
3. Add arrowroot and rice flour and cook for 2 3 min
4. Add broccoli, pasta and stir
5. Cook for 20 min at 350 F, remove and serve

Ginger crunch

Servings: 4 | Preparation: 10 min | Cooking: 30 min

Ingredients

- ¼ lb. butter
- ½ cup sugar
- 1 cup plain flour
- ½ whole meal flour
- 1 tsp baking powder
- 1 tsp ginger

Directions

1. In a food processor add butter and soon and blend until smooth
2. Add the rest of ingredients and blend
3. Remove from blender and bake for 20 min at 350 F
4. Cut into cookie shape and serve

Cornmeal waffels

Servings: 2 | Preparation: 10 min | Cooking: 10 min

Ingredients

- 1 cup corn flour
- 1 egg
- 1 cup milk
- 1 tablespoon butter
- 2 tablespoons honey
- ½ cup rice flour
- 1 tsp baking powder
- ½ tsp salt

Directions

1. Let sit for 8 10 min
2. Place in the waffle iron and cook
3. Remove and serve

Cheese cake

Servings: 4 | Preparation: 10 min | Cooking: 30 min

Ingredients

- ½ lb. gingernut biscuits
- ½ lb. blueberries
- 1 tsp vanilla extract
- 1 tsp acid
- ¼ lb. butter
- ¼ lb. caster sugar
- 2 tablespoons arrowroot
- ¼ lb. full fat Philadelphia
- 2 eggs

Directions

1. Preheat oven to 350 F
2. In a bowl mix butter and biscuits and press into the base of the tin
3. Bake for 10 12 min
4. In a saucepan cook blueberry with sugar and milk for 10 12 min
5. Take off heat add citric acid and vanilla
6. Bake for 40 min remove and let it chill

Basic waffles

Servings: 2 | Preparation: 10 min | Cooking: 10 min

Ingredients

- 2 eggs
- 1 tablespoon sugar
- 1 tablespoon baking powder
- 1 cup flour
- 1/8 cup milk
- ½ tsp vanilla essence

Directions

1. In a food processor add all the ingredients and blend until smooth
2. Heat the waffle iron pour in the batter
3. Cook until golden
4. Serve with maple syrup

Caramel popcorn

Servings: 4 | Preparation: 10 min | Cooking: 20 min

Ingredients

- 1 tablespoon olive oil
- 4 tablespoons popcorn kernels

Caramel sauce:

- 1 tablespoon butter
- 1 tablespoon brown sugar
- 1 tablespoon golden syrup

Directions

1. In a saucepan pour olive oil and popcorn kernels over medium heat and cover
2. Shake the saucepan to distribute evenly
3. In another saucepan melt the caramel sauce ingredients
4. Remove from heat and pour over your popcorn

Onion pancakes

Servings: 4 | Preparation: 10 min | Cooking: 10 min

Ingredients

- ½ tsp salt
- 1 cup plain flour
- 1 tsp olive oil
- 1 onion
- ½ cup hot water
- 1 tablespoon cold water

Directions

1. In a bowl mix all ingredients
2. Pour mixture into a pan and cook for 1 2 min per side
3. Remove and serve

Toasted muesli

Servings: 4 | Preparation: 10 min | Cooking: 60 min

Ingredients

- 2 cups oats
- 1 cup oat mix
- ½ cup sunflower seeds

- ½ cup sunflower oil

Directions

1. In a bowl mix all ingredients
2. Bake for 60 min at 275 F
3. Garnish with blueberries and serve

Gingerbread biscuits

Servings: 4 | Preparation: 10 min | Cooking: 30 min

Ingredients

- 2 oz. butter
- 1 cup self raising flour
- ½ tsp salt
- 3 tablespoons ginger
- ½ cup milk
- 1 egg beaten
- 1 tablespoon vanilla extract
- ½ cup golden syrup
- ½ cup maple syrup
- ½ cup honey

Directions

1. Preheat oven to 300 F
2. In a pan melt honey, butter, syrup and set aside
3. White syrup mixture is cooling, grate the ginger and add to the syrup mixture
4. Add flour, salt, milk, egg and vanilla extract
5. Form small cookies and bake for 15 18 min at 300 F
6. Remove and serve

Vanilla chia pudding

Servings: 4 | Preparation: 10 min | Cooking: 10 min

Ingredients

- 2 cups hemp milk
- 2 packets stevia
- ½ tsp cinnamon
- ½ cup chia seeds
- 1 tablespoon vanilla extract

Directions

1. In a bowl whisk all ingredients together
2. Let it chill overnight and serve

Acerola pancakes

Servings: 4 | Preparation: 10 min | Cooking: 20 min

Ingredients

- 1 cup whole wheat flour

- ¼ tsp baking soda
- ¼ tsp baking powder
- 1 cup acerola
- 2 eggs
- 1 cup milk

Directions

1. In a bowl combine all ingredients and mix well
2. In a skillet heat olive oil
3. Pour ¼ of the batter and cook each pancake for 1 2 min per side
4. When ready remove from heat and serve

Java plum muffins

Servings: 8 12 | Preparation: 10 min | Cooking: 20 min

Ingredients

- 2 eggs
- 1 tablespoon olive oil
- 1 cup milk
- 2 cups whole wheat flour
- 1 tsp baking soda
- ¼ tsp baking soda
- 1 tsp cinnamon
- 1 cup java plum

Directions

1. In a bowl combine all wet ingredients
2. In another bowl combine all dry ingredients
3. Combine wet and dry ingredients
4. Pour mixture into 8 12 prepared muffin cups, fill 2/3 of the cups
5. Bake for 18 20 min at 375 F
6. When ready remove from the oven and serve

Bok choy omelette

Servings: 1 | Preparation: 5 min | Cooking: 10 min

Ingredients

- 2 eggs
- ¼ tsp salt
- ¼ tsp black pepper
- 1 tablespoon olive oil
- ¼ cup cheese
- ¼ tsp basil
- 1 cup bok choy

Directions

1. In a bowl combine all ingredients together and mix well
2. In a skillet heat olive oil and pour the egg mixture
3. Cook for 1 2 min per side

4. When ready remove omelette from the skillet and serve

Brussel sprouts omelette

Servings: 1 | Preparation: 5 min | Cooking: 10 min

Ingredients

- 2 eggs
- ¼ tsp salt
- ¼ tsp black pepper
- 1 tablespoon olive oil
- ¼ cup cheese
- ¼ tsp basil
- 1 cup Brussel sprouts

Directions

1. In a bowl combine all ingredients together and mix well
2. In a skillet heat olive oil and pour the egg mixture
3. Cook for 1 2 min per side
4. When ready remove omelette from the skillet and serve

Carrot omelette

Servings: 1 | Preparation: 5 min | Cooking: 10 min

Ingredients

- 2 eggs
- ¼ tsp salt
- ¼ tsp black pepper
- 1 tablespoon olive oil
- ¼ cup cheese
- ¼ tsp basil
- 1 cup carrot

Directions

1. In a bowl combine all ingredients together and mix well
2. In a skillet heat olive oil and pour the egg mixture
3. Cook for 1 2 min per side
4. When ready remove omelette from the skillet and serve

Eggplant omelette

Servings: 1 | Preparation: 5 min | Cooking: 10 min

Ingredients

- 2 eggs
- ¼ tsp salt
- ¼ tsp black pepper

- 1 tablespoon olive oil
- ¼ cup cheese
- ¼ tsp basil
- 1 cup eggplant

Directions

1. In a bowl combine all ingredients together and mix well
2. In a skillet heat olive oil and pour the egg mixture
3. Cook for 1 2 min per side
4. When ready remove omelette from the skillet and serve

Chapter 2: Lunch Recipes

Beet & Orange Salad

Servings: 3 | Preparation: 15 min

Ingredients
- 2 oranges, peeled, seeded and sectioned
- 2 beets, trimmed, peeled and sliced
- 4 cups fresh arugula
- 3 tablespoons olive oil
- 2 tablespoon balsamic vinegar
- Salt, as required

Directions
1. In a large bowl, add all ingredients and gently, toss to coat.
2. Serve immediately.

Nutrition: Calories: 216; Total Fat: 14.5g; Saturated Fat: 2.1g; Protein: 3g; Carbs: 22.1g; Fiber: 4.7g; Sugar: 17.4g

Broccoli & Carrot Salad

Servings: 2 | Preparation: 15 min

Ingredients
- 1 small head broccoli with stem
- 2 medium carrots, peeled and spiralized with Blade C
- ¼ cup red onion, chopped
- 3 hard-boiled organic eggs, chopped
- ¼ cup fresh basil, chopped
- 1 garlic clove, minced
- ½ teaspoon lime zest, grated freshly
- 2 tablespoons extra-virgin olive oil
- 1 tablespoon fresh lime juice
- Water, as required
- Salt and ground black pepper, as required
- 2 tablespoons pumpkin seeds, roasted

Directions
1. Cut the broccoli florets into bite-sized pieces.
2. Spiralized the stem with Blade C.
3. Transfer the chopped broccoli florets and spiralized stem into a large serving bowl.
4. Add the carrot, onion and egg into the bowl with broccoli and mix.
5. In a food processor, add remaining ingredients except pumpkin seeds and pulse until well combined.
6. Pour mixture over vegetables and gently, toss to coat.
7. Garnish with pumpkin seeds and serve.

Nutrition: Calories: 329; Total Fat: 24.9g; Saturated Fat: 8.6g; Protein: 14.1g; Carbs: 16.7g; Fiber: 4.9g; Sugar: 6g

Zoodles & Radish Salad

Servings: 4 | Preparation: 15 min

Ingredients
- 2 tablespoons fresh lemon juice
- 2 teaspoons fresh lemon zest, grated
- ½ teaspoon Dijon mustard
- ½ teaspoon garlic powder
- Salt and ground black pepper, as required
- 1|3 cup olive oil
- 3 medium zucchinis, spiralized with Blade C
- 1 bunch radishes, thinly sliced

Directions
1. For dressing: in a small bowl, add the lemon juice, lemon zest, Dijon mustard, garlic powder, salt and black pepper and beat until well combined.
2. Slowly, add the oil, beating continuously until well combined.
3. In a large bowl, add the zucchini noodles, radishes and dressing and toss to coat well.
4. Serve immediately.

Nutrition: Calories: 178; Total Fat: 17.2g; Saturated Fat: 2.5g; Protein: 2.2g; Carbs: 6.9g; Fiber: 2.4g; Sugar: 3.6g

Greens Salad

Servings: 4| Preparation: 20 min | Cooking time: 6 min

Ingredients
- 1½ teaspoons fresh ginger, grated finely
- 2 tablespoons apple cider vinegar
- 3 tablespoons olive oil
- 1 teaspoon sesame oil, toasted
- 3 teaspoons raw honey, divided
- ½ teaspoon red pepper flakes, divided
- Salt, as required
- 1 tablespoon water
- 2 tablespoons raw sunflower seeds
- 1 tablespoon raw pumpkin seeds, shelled
- 1 tablespoon raw sesame seeds
- 10 ounces mixed salad greens

Directions

1. For dressing: in a bowl, add the ginger, vinegar, both oils, 1 teaspoon of honey, ¼ teaspoon of the red pepper flakes and salt and beat until well combined.
2. Set aside.
3. In another bowl, add the remaining honey, remaining red pepper flakes and water and mix until well combined.
4. Heat a medium nonstick skillet over medium heat and cook all the seeds for about 3 min, stirring continuously.
5. Stir in the honey mixture and cook for about 3 min, stirring continuously.
6. Transfer the seeds mixture onto a parchment paper and set aside to cool completely.
7. Break the seeds mixture into small pieces.
8. In a large bowl, add the greens, 2 teaspoons of the dressing and a little salt and toss to coat well.
9. With your hands, rub the greens for about 30 seconds.
10. Add the remaining dressing and seeds pieces and toss to coat well.
11. Serve immediately.

Nutrition: Calories: 153; Total Fat: 14.6g; Saturated Fat: 2.1g; Protein: 2.2g; Carbs: 8.4g; Fiber: 0.6g; Sugar: 4.4g

Quinoa & Mango Salad

Servings: 2 | Preparation: 15 min

Ingredients

- 1 large cucumber, spiralized with Blade C
- ½ cup mango, peeled, pitted and cubed
- ½ cup cooked quinoa
- ¼ cup dried cranberries
- 3 tablespoons raw pumpkin seeds, shelled
- ½ teaspoon fresh ginger, grated
- 1-2 fresh basil leaves, chopped
- Salt and ground black pepper, as required
- 3 teaspoons balsamic vinegar
- 3 teaspoons extra-virgin olive oil

Directions

- In a large serving bowl, add all the ingredients and toss to coat well.
- Serve immediately.

Nutrition: Calories: 345; Total Fat: 15.9g; Saturated Fat: 2.5g; Protein: 10.6g; Carbs: 42.9g; Fiber: 5.5g; Sugar: 8.8g

Chilled Zucchini Soup

Servings: 4 | Preparation: 15 min | Cooking time: 26 min

Ingredients

- 2 tablespoons extra-virgin coconut oil
- 1 small onion, chopped
- 2 small garlic cloves, minced
- 1 teaspoon dried oregano, crushed
- ¼ teaspoon red pepper flakes, crushed
- 2 large zucchinis, chopped
- Salt and ground black pepper, as required
- 2|3 cup homemade vegetable broth
- 1½ cups water
- 1 small zucchini, spiralized with Blade C

Directions

1. In a large pan, heat the oil over medium heat and sauté the onion for about 8- 9 min.
2. Add the garlic, oregano and red pepper flakes and sauté for about 1 minute.
3. Add the chopped zucchini, salt and black pepper and cook for about 8-10 min, stirring occasionally.
4. Add the broth and water and bring to a boil over high heat.
5. Reduce the heat to medium-low and simmer for about 10 min.
6. Remove from the heat and set aside to cool slightly.
7. In a blender, add the soup in batches and pulse until smooth.
8. Transfer the soup into a large bowl and season with required salt and black pepper.
9. Cover the bowl and refrigerate to chill.
10. Top with spiralized zucchini and serve.

Nutrition: Calories: 112; Total Fat: 7.7g; Saturated Fat: 6.9g; Protein: 3.6g; Carbs: 9.3g; Fiber: 2.8g; Sugar: 4.4g

Egg Drop Soup

Servings: 6 | Preparation: 10 min | Cooking time: 20 min

Ingredients

- 1 tablespoon olive oil
- 1 tablespoon garlic, minced
- 6 cups homemade chicken broth, divided
- 2 organic eggs
- 1 tablespoon arrowroot powder

- 1|3 cup fresh lemon juice
- Freshly ground white pepper, as required
- ¼ cup scallion (green part), chopped

Directions

1. In a large soup pan, heat oil over medium-high heat and sauté garlic for about 1 minute.
2. Add 5½ cups of broth and bring to a boil over high heat.
3. Reduce the heat to medium and simmer for about 5 min.
4. Meanwhile, in a bowl, add eggs, arrowroot powder, lemon juice, white pepper and remaining broth and beat until well combined.
5. Slowly, add egg mixture in the pan, stirring continuously.
6. Simmer for about 5-6 min or until desired thickness of soup , stirring continuously
7. Serve hot with the garnishing of scallion.

Nutrition: Calories: 92; Total Fat: 5.3g; Saturated Fat: 1.3g; Protein: 7g; Carbs: 3.4g; Fiber: 0.2g; Sugar: 1.2g

Broccoli Soup

Servings: 4 | Preparation: 15 min | Cooking time: 35 min

Ingredients

- 1 tablespoon coconut oil
- 1 celery stalk, chopped
- ½ cup white onion, chopped
- Salt, as required
- 1 teaspoon ground turmeric
- 2 garlic cloves, minced
- 1 large head broccoli, cut into florets
- ¼ teaspoon fresh ginger, grated
- 1 bay leaf
- 1|8 teaspoon cayenne pepper
- Ground black pepper, as required
- 5 cups homemade vegetable broth
- 1 small avocado, peeled, pitted and chopped
- 1 tablespoon fresh lemon juice

Directions

1. In a large soup pan, heat oil over medium heat and sauté celery, onion and some salt for about 3-4 min.
2. Add turmeric and garlic and sauté for about 1 minute.
3. Add desired mount of salt and remaining ingredients except avocado and lemon juice and bring to a boil

4. Reduce the heat to medium-low and simmer, covered for about 25-30 min.
5. Remove from heat and keep aside to cool slightly.
6. In a blender, add soup and avocado in batches and pulse until smooth.
7. Serve immediately with the drizzling of lemon juice.

Nutrition: Calories: 184; Total Fat: 13.5g; Saturated Fat: 5.1g; Protein: 3.1g; Carbs: 14.8g; Fiber: 6.9g; Sugar: 4.6g

Pumpkin Soup

Servings: 4 | Preparation: 15 min | Cooking time: 25 min

Ingredients

- 2 teaspoons olive oil
- 1 onion, chopped
- 1 teaspoon fresh ginger, chopped
- 2 garlic cloves, chopped
- 2 tablespoons fresh cilantro, chopped
- 3 cups pumpkin, peeled, seeded and cubed
- 4¼ cups homemade vegetable broth
- Salt and ground black pepper, as required
- ¾ cup coconut cream
- 2 tablespoons fresh lime juice

Directions

1. In a large soup pan, heat the oil over medium heat and sauté the onion, ginger, garlic and cilantro for about 4-5 min.
2. Add the pumpkin and broth and bring to a boil
3. Reduce the heat to low and simmer, covered for about 15 min.
4. Remove from the heat and set aside to cool slightly.
5. Transfer the mixture into a high-speed blender in batches with ½ cup of the coconut cream and pulse until smooth.
6. Return the soup into the pan over medium heat and cook for about 3-5 min or until heated through.
7. Serve hot with the topping of the remaining coconut cream.

Nutrition: Calories: 216; Total Fat: 13.6g; Saturated Fat: 10.1g; Protein: 3.5g; Carbs: 23.8g; Fiber: 8g; Sugar: 10.9g

Meatballs with Apple Chutney

Servings: 6 | Preparation: 20 min | Cooking time: 20 min

Ingredients

For Meatballs:

- 1 pound ground turkey
- 1 tablespoon olive oil
- 1 teaspoon dehydrated onion flakes, crushed
- ½ teaspoon granulated garlic
- ½ teaspoon ground cumin
- ½ teaspoon red pepper flakes, crushed
- Salt, as required

For Chutney:

- 3 medium tart apples, peeled, cored and chopped
- ½ handful of golden raisins
- 3 tablespoons maple syrup
- 2 tablespoons almond butter
- 1 tablespoon apple cider vinegar
- ¼ cup water
- ¼ teaspoon ground cumin
- Pinch of red pepper flakes, crushed
- Salt, as required

Directions

1. Preheat the oven to 400 degrees F. Line a large baking sheet with parchment paper.
2. For meatballs in a large mixing bowl, add all ingredients and mix until well combined.
3. Make equal-sized balls from the mixture.
4. Arrange the meatballs onto prepared baking sheet in a single layer.
5. Bake for about 15-20 min or until done completely.
6. Meanwhile, for chutney in a medium pan, mix together all ingredients over medium-high heat.
7. Cover the pan and cook for about 6-8 min, stirring occasionally.
8. Uncover and cook for 2-3 min or until desired thickness.
9. Remove from heat and let it cool slightly.
10. With a potato masher, mash the apple pieces slightly to form a chunky mixture forms.
11. Serve meatballs with chutney.

Nutrition: Calories: 306; Total Fat: 14g; Saturated Fat: 1.9g; Protein: 22.4g; Carbs: 28.5g; Fiber: 3.6g; Sugar: 21.6g

Black Beans Meatballs

Servings: 8 | Preparation: 20 min | Cooking time: 19 min

Ingredients

- 1 pound ground turkey breast
- 1 cup cooked black beans, mashed roughly
- 1 small yellow bell pepper, seeded and chopped finely
- 1 small green bell pepper, seeded and chopped finely
- ½ cup fresh parsley, chopped
- Salt and ground black pepper, as required
- ¼ cup olive oil
- 4 cups cherry tomatoes, halved

Directions

1. For meatballs: in a large bowl, add all ingredients and mix until well combined.
2. Make equal-sized balls from the mixture.
3. In a skillet, heat oil over medium heat and cook the meatballs for about 5-7 min or until golden brown from all sides.
4. Cover the skillet and cook for about 5 min more.
5. Divide the cherry tomatoes and meatballs onto serving plates and serve.

Nutrition: Calories: 271; Total Fat: 11.1g; Saturated Fat: 2.2g; Protein: 22.7g; Carbs: 21.1g; Fiber: 5.3g; Sugar: 4.4g

Veggie Meatballs

Servings: 6 | Preparation: 15 min | Cooking time: 30 min

Ingredients

- ½ cup carrot, peeled and grated
- ½ cup zucchini, grated
- ½ cup yellow squash, grated
- Salt, as required
- 1 pound grass-fed ground beef
- 1 organic egg, beaten
- ¼ of a small onion, chopped finely
- 1 garlic clove, minced
- 8 cups lettuce, torn

Directions

1. Preheat the oven to 400 degrees F. Line a large baking sheet with parchment paper.
2. Set a large colander over the sink.
3. In the sink, place the carrot, zucchini and yellow squash and sprinkle with 2 pinches of salt.

4. Set aside for at least 10 min.
5. Transfer the veggies onto a paper towel and squeeze out all the moisture of veggies.
6. In a large bowl, add the squeezed vegetables, beef, egg, onion, garlic, herbs and desired amount of salt and mix until well combined.
7. Make equal-sized balls from the mixture.
8. Arrange the meatballs onto prepared baking sheet in a single layer.
9. Bake for about 25-30 min or until done completely.
10. Divide the lettuce and meatballs onto serving plates and serve.

Nutrition: Calories: 163; Total Fat: 8.3g; Saturated Fat: 3.3g; Protein: 17g; Carbs: 4.2g; Fiber: 1g; Sugar: 1.7g

Oats & Black Beans Burgers

Servings: 6 | Preparation: 20 min | Cooking time: 40 min

Ingredients

- ½ cup rolled oats
- ¼ cup raw pumpkin seeds, shelled
- 2 (15-ounce) cans black beans, rinsed, drained and divided
- 2 cups carrots, peeled and grated
- ½ teaspoon ground coriander
- ½ teaspoon ground cumin
- ½ teaspoon red pepper flakes, crushed
- ¼ teaspoon cayenne pepper
- ¼ teaspoon onion powder
- ¼ teaspoon garlic powder
- Salt and ground black pepper, as required
- 1 tablespoon olive oil 8 cups fresh baby greens

Directions

1. Preheat the oven to 300 degrees F. Line a large baking sheet with parchment paper.
2. In a food processor, add the pumpkin seeds and oats and pulse until chopped roughly.
3. Add ¾ of the beans, carrots, spices and oil and pulse until well combined.
4. Transfer the mixture into a large bowl.
5. Fold in remaining beans.
6. With your wet hands, make 6 equal-sized patties from the mixture.
7. Arrange the patties onto the prepared baking sheet in a single layer.
8. Bake for about 20 min per side.
9. Divide the greens onto serving plates.
10. Top each with 1 burger and serve.

Nutrition: Calories: 227; Total Fat: 6.6g; Saturated Fat: 0.9g; Protein: 11.4g; Carbs: 31.4g; Fiber: 9.3g; Sugar: 2.5g

Salmon & Quinoa Burgers

Servings: 6 | Preparation: 20 min | Cooking time: 20 min

Ingredients

- 2 tablespoons ground flax seeds
- 5 tablespoons hot water
- 1 cooked large beet, peeled and chopped
- 2 (6-ounce) cans salmon
- ½ cup cooked quinoa
- ½ cup fresh kale, chopped
- ½ cup fresh parsley, chopped
- 2 garlic cloves, peeled
- Salt and ground black pepper, as required
- 8 cups fresh baby spinach

Directions

1. Preheat the oven to 350 degrees F. Line a baking sheet with parchment paper.
2. In a bowl, add the flaxseeds and water and mix well.
3. In a food processor, add the beet and pulse until chopped.
4. Add the flax seeds mixture and remaining ingredients a chucky mixture is formed.
5. With your wet hands, make 6 equal-sized patties from the mixture.
6. Arrange the patties onto the prepared baking sheet in a single layer.
7. Bake for about 15-20 min, flipping once halfway through.
8. Divide the spinach onto serving plates.
9. Top each with 1 burger and serve.

Nutrition: Calories: 162; Total Fat: 5.3g; Saturated Fat: 0.7g; Protein: 15.2g; Carbs: 14.1g; Fiber: 3.1g; Sugar: 1.6g

Beef & Veggie Burgers

Servings: 4 | Preparation: 15 min | Cooking time: 8 min

Ingredients

- 1 pound grass-fed ground beef
- 1 medium raw beetroot, trimmed, peeled and chopped finely

- 1 carrot, peeled and chopped finely
- 1 small brown onion, chopped finely
- 1 tablespoon fresh rosemary, chopped finely
- Salt and ground black pepper, as required
- 2-3 tablespoons coconut oil
- 6 cups salad greens

Directions

1. In a large mixing bowl, add all ingredients except oil and mix until well combined.
2. Make 12 equal-sized patties from mixture.
3. In a large skillet, heat the oil over medium heat and cook the patties for about 3-4 min per side or until golden brown.
4. Divide the greens onto serving plates.
5. Top each with 1 burger and serve.

Nutrition: Calories: 198; Total Fat: 12g; Saturated Fat: 7g; Protein: 16.4g; Carbs: 5.6g; Fiber: 1.6g; Sugar: 2.3g

Turkey & Apple Burgers

Servings: 4 | Preparation: 15 min | Cooking time: 12 min

Ingredients

- 12 ounces lean ground turkey
- ½ of apple, peeled, cored and grated
- ½ of red bell pepper, chopped finely
- ¼ cup red onion, minced
- 2 small garlic cloves, minced
- 1 tablespoon fresh ginger, minced
- 2½ tablespoons fresh cilantro, chopped
- 2 tablespoons curry paste
- 1 teaspoon ground cumin
- 1 teaspoon olive oil
- 6 cups fresh baby spinach

Directions

1. Preheat the grill to medium heat. Grease the grill grate.
2. For burgers: in a large bowl, add all ingredients and mix until well combined.
3. Make 4 equal-sized burgers from mixture. Brush the burgers with olive oil evenly.
4. Grill the burgers for about 5-6 min per side.
5. Divide the spinach onto serving plates.
6. Top each with 1 burger and serve.

Nutrition: Calories: 223; Total Fat: 12.1g; Saturated Fat: 2.1g; Protein: 19g; Carbs: 11.1g; Fiber: 2.3g; Sugar: 4.2g

Veggies Burgers

Servings: 4 | Preparation: 15 min | Cooking time: 40min

Ingredients

- 1 large organic egg
- ¼ teaspoon ground cumin
- ½ teaspoon red pepper flakes, crushed
- Salt and ground black pepper, as required
- ¼ cup coconut oil, melted
- 2 tablespoons almond flour
- 1 large zucchini, spiralized with Blade C and chopped
- 1 large sweet potato, peeled, spiralized with Blade C and chopped
- 2 tablespoons fresh cilantro leaves, chopped
- 6 cups lettuce, torn

Directions

1. Preheat the oven to 375 degrees F. Line 2 baking sheets with greased parchment papers.
2. In a large bowl, add the egg and spices and beat well.
3. Add the butter and flour and mix until well combined.
4. Add the remaining ingredients and mix until well combined.
5. Make equal sized patties from the mixture.
6. Arrange the patties onto prepared baking sheets in a single layer.
7. Bake for about 10 min.
8. Now, reduce the temperature of oven to 350 degrees F.
9. Bake for about 15 min.
10. Carefully, flip the side of patties and bake for about 15 min.
11. Divide the lettuce onto serving plates.
12. Top each with 1 burger and serve.

Nutrition: Calories: 217; Total Fat: 17.2g; Saturated Fat: 12.3g; Protein: 3.8g; Carbs: 13.9g; Fiber: 3.1g; Sugar: 4.9g

Turkey & Beans Lettuce Wraps

Servings: 2 | Preparation: 15 min | Cooking time: 13 min

Ingredients

- 4 ounces lean ground turkey
- ¼ cup onion, minced
- 2 tablespoons sugar-free tomato sauce

- 1|8 teaspoon garlic powder
- 1|8 teaspoon ground cumin
- 2 teaspoons extra-virgin olive oil
- Salt and ground black pepper, as required
- 1|3 cup cooked black beans
- 1 cup tomato, chopped
- 4 large lettuce leaves
- 4 tablespoons avocado, peeled, pitted and chopped

Directions

1. In a bowl, add turkey, onion, tomato sauce and spices and mix until well combined.
2. In a large skillet, heat the oil over medium heat and cook the turkey mixture for about 8-10 min.
3. Add the beans and tomato and stir to combine.
4. Reduce the heat to low and cook for about 2-3 min.
5. Remove from the heat and set aside to cool.
6. Arrange the lettuce leaves onto serving plates.
7. Divide turkey mixture onto each lettuce leaf and top with avocado pieces.
8. Serve immediately.

Nutrition: Calories: 297; Total Fat: 13g; Saturated Fat: 2.8g; Protein: 19.7g; Carbs: 27.9g; Fiber: 7.8g; Sugar: 4.6g

Shrimp Lettuce Wraps

Servings: 6 | Preparation: 20 min | Cooking time: 4 min

Ingredients

For Salsa:

- 1 mango, peeled, pitted and chopped
- ¼ cup red onion, chopped finely
- ½ cup red bell pepper, seeded and chopped finely
- ¼ cup fresh cilantro, chopped
- 1 jalapeño pepper, chopped finely
- 2 tablespoons fresh lime juice
- Salt and ground black pepper, as required

For Wraps:

- 1 teaspoon olive oil
- 2 pounds large shrimp, peeled, deveined and chopped
- ½ teaspoon ground cumin
- 1 tablespoon red chili powder
- Salt and ground black pepper, as required
- 12 lettuce leaves

Directions

1. For salsa: in a large bowl, add all the ingredients and gently, stir to combine.
2. Set aside until using.
3. In a large skillet, heat the oil over medium heat and cook the shrimp with spices for about 3-4 min.
4. Remove from the heat and set aside to cool slightly.
5. Arrange the lettuce leaves onto serving plates.
6. Divide the shrimp mixture onto each lettuce leaf and top with mango salsa.
7. Serve immediately.

Nutrition: Calories: 170; Total Fat: 1g; Saturated Fat: 0.2g; Protein: 29.1g; Carbs: 12.8g; Fiber: 1.3g; Sugar: 8.5g

Chicken & Pineapple Kabobs

Servings: 6 | Preparation: 15 min | Cooking time: 22 min

Ingredients

For Sauce:

- 3 cups pineapple, chopped
- ¼ cup coconut aminos
- 2 tablespoons cashew butter
- 1 tablespoon maple syrup
- 1 tablespoon fresh lime juice
- ½ teaspoon red pepper flakes, crushed
- ¼ teaspoon garlic powder
- ¼ teaspoon onion powder
- Salt and ground black pepper, as required

For Kabobs:

- 2 pounds grass-fed skinless, boneless chicken thighs, cubed
- 2 cups fresh pineapple, cubed

Directions

1. For sauce: in a food processor, add all the ingredients and pulse until smooth.
2. Transfer the sauce into a pan over medium heat and cook for about 10-12 min, stirring occasionally.
3. Remove from the heat and set aside.
4. Preheat the grill to medium-high heat. Grease the grill grate.
5. Thread the chicken and pineapple cubes onto the metal skewers.
6. Place the skewers onto the grill and cook for about 8-10 min, flipping after every 2-3 min.

7. In the last 2 min of cooking, coat the kabobs with sauce evenly.
8. Serve with remaining sauce as a dipping sauce.

Nutrition: Calories: 309; Total Fat: 8.2g; Saturated Fat: 2.6g; Protein: 35.5g; Carbs: 24g; Fiber: 2.1g; Sugar: 15.6g

Chicken & Veggie Kabobs

Servings: 4 | Preparation: 15 min | Cooking time: 8 min

Ingredients

- 1 teaspoon paprika
- ¼ teaspoon cayenne pepper
- ½ teaspoon ground coriander
- 1 teaspoon ground cumin
- Pinch of ground ginger
- Pinch of ground cumin
- Salt and ground black pepper, as required
- 2 teaspoons fresh lemon juice
- ½ tablespoon extra-virgin olive oil
- 1 pound grass-fed boneless, skinless chicken breast, cubed
- 1 large green bell pepper, seeded and cut into 1-inch pieces
- 12 cherry tomatoes, halved
- 1 medium red onion, cut into 1-inch pieces

Directions

1. Preheat the oven to 425 degrees F. Lightly, grease a large baking sheet.
2. For marinade: in a large bowl, mix together spices, lemon juice and oil.
3. Add chicken cubes and coat with marinade generously.
4. Cover and refrigerate for about 20 min.
5. Remove chicken from marinade and thread onto skewers with bell pepper, tomato and onion.
6. Place the skewers in prepared baking sheet in a single layer.
7. Bake for about 10 min or until desired doneness.
8. Serve warm.

Nutrition: Calories: 176; Total Fat: 5g; Saturated Fat: 0.3g; Protein: 25.2g; Carbs: 6.8g; Fiber: 1.7g; Sugar: 3.7g

Veggie Kabobs

Servings: 4 | Preparation: 15 min | Cooking time: 10 min

Ingredients

For Marinade:

- 2 garlic cloves, chopped
- 2 tablespoons fresh ginger, chopped
- 1 teaspoon fresh oregano
- 1 teaspoon fresh basil
- ½ teaspoon cayenne pepper
- Salt and ground black pepper, as required
- ¼ cup olive oil

For Veggies:

- ½ head of cauliflower, cut into large florets
- 1 large zucchinis, cut into thick slices
- 4 large button mushrooms, quartered
- 1 medium red bell pepper, seeded and cut into large cubes
- 1 medium onion, cut into large cubes
- Salt and ground black pepper, as required

Directions

1. For marinade: in a food processor, add all the ingredients and pulse until well combined.
2. In a large bowl, add all the vegetables.
3. Pour marinade mixture over vegetables and toss to coat well.
4. Cover and refrigerate to marinate for at least 6-8 h.
5. Preheat the grill to medium-high heat. Grease the grill grate.
6. Remove vegetables from marinade and thread onto pre-soaked wooden skewers.
7. Place the skewers onto the grill and cook for about 8-10 min or until done completely, flipping occasionally.
8. Serve warm.

Nutrition: Calories: 168; Total Fat: 13.2g; Saturated Fat: 1.9g; Protein: 3.4g; Carbs: 12.9g; Fiber: 3.5g; Sugar: 5.4g

Shrimp Kabobs

Servings: 4 | Preparation: 15 min | Cooking time: 8 min

Ingredients

- 1 jalapeño pepper, chopped
- 1 large garlic clove, chopped
- 1 (1-inch) fresh ginger, minced
- 1|3 cup fresh mint leaves
- 1 cup unsweetened coconut milk

- ¼ cup fresh lime juice
- 1½ pounds medium shrimp, peeled and deveined

Directions

1. In a food processor, add jalapeño, garlic, ginger, mint, coconut milk, lime juice and fish sauce and pulse until smooth.
2. Add the shrimp and coat with marinade generously.
3. Cover and refrigerate to marinate for at least 1-2 h.
4. Preheat the grill to medium-high heat. Grease the grill grate.
5. Remove shrimp from marinade and thread onto pre-soaked wooden skewers with avocado and watermelon.
6. Grill, turning once for about 6-8 min or until done completely.
7. Serve warm.

Nutrition: Calories: 307; Total Fat: 16.4g; Saturated Fat: 12.7g; Protein: 38.2g; Carbs: 4.6g; Fiber: 2g; Sugar: 2.1g

Shrimp & Watermelon Kabobs

Servings: 4 | Preparation: 15 min | Cooking time: 4 min

Ingredients

- 1|3 cup plus 1 tablespoon olive oil, divided
- 3 tablespoons fresh lime juice
- 1|3 cup fresh mint leaves, chopped
- 1 tablespoon fresh thyme leaves
- 2 garlic cloves, minced
- 2-3 teaspoons lime zest, grated
- ½ teaspoon red pepper flakes
- Salt and ground black pepper, as required
- 1 pound jumbo shrimp, peeled and deveined
- 3 cups seedless watermelon, peeled and cubed into 1-inch size

Directions

1. In a small bowl, add 1|3 cup of oil, lime juice, 1|3 cup of mint, thyme, garlic, lime zest, red pepper flakes, salt and black pepper and beat until well combined.
2. In a large bowl, add the shrimp and half of the marinade and toss to coat well.
3. Cover the bowl and refrigerate for about 1 h.
4. Reserve remaining marinade in refrigerator until using.
5. Preheat the grill to high heat. Grease the grill grate.

6. Thread the watermelon onto metal skewers and coat with the remaining oil.
7. Place the skewers onto the grill and cook for about 1-2 min, flipping occasionally.
8. Coat the shrimp with some of the reserved marinade and thread onto skewers.
9. Place the skewers onto the grill and cook for about 1 minute per side.
10. Arrange the watermelon and shrimp onto a platter.
11. Drizzle with the remaining marinade and serve.

Nutrition: Calories: 335; Total Fat: 24.8g; Saturated Fat: 3.6g; Protein: 21.4g; Carbs: 10.5g; Fiber: 1.4g; Sugar: 9.1g

Spinach in Creamy Sauce

Servings: 4 | Preparation: 10 min | Cooking time: 15 min

Ingredients

- 2 tablespoons coconut oil
- 1 small onion, chopped
- 1 garlic clove, minced
- Salt and ground black pepper, as required
- 1 small head cauliflower, chopped roughly
- 1 cup homemade vegetable broth
- 1 tablespoon fresh lemon zest, grated
- 1 tablespoon Dijon mustard
- 1|8 teaspoon ground cinnamon
- 1 cup unsweetened coconut milk
- 2 pounds fresh spinach, chopped roughly

Directions

1. In a large skillet, melt the coconut oil over medium heat and sauté the onion and garlic for about 2 min.
2. Add the cauliflower and cook for about 1-2 min.
3. Stir in the broth and bring to a boil.
4. Reduce the heat to low and simmer, covered for about 5-7 min.
5. Remove from heat and stir in remaining ingredients except spinach.
6. With a giant blender, blend the spinach until a smooth puree forms.
7. Meanwhile, in a large microwave-safe bowl, add spinach and cook on high for about 4 min.
8. Remove from microwave and set aside to cool completely.
9. Then squeeze the spinach thoroughly.
10. Add spinach in creamy sauce and stir to combine.
11. Serve immediately.

Nutrition: Calories: 287; Total Fat: 22.6g; Saturated Fat: 18.8g; Protein: 10.8g; Carbs: 17.8g; Fiber: 8.6g; Sugar: 5.6g

Broccoli with Kale

Servings: 6 | Preparation: 15 min | Cooking time: 20 min

Ingredients

- 2 tablespoons olive oil
- 1 onion, chopped
- 2 garlic cloves, minced
- 1 cup fresh kale, tough ribs removed and chopped
- 1 head broccoli, cut into florets
- 2 cups cherry tomatoes, halved
- 1 teaspoon ground cumin
- 1 teaspoon red chili powder
- Salt, as required

Directions

1. In a large skillet, heat the oil over medium heat and sauté onion for about 4-5 min.
2. Add garlic and sauté for about 1 minute.
3. Add the kale, broccoli florets, tomatoes, cumin, chipotle powder and salt and cook for about 10 min, stirring occasionally.
4. Serve warm.

Nutrition: Calories: 82; Total Fat: 5.1g; Saturated Fat: 0.7g; Protein: 2.4g; Carbs: 8.8g; Fiber: 2.6 g; Sugar: 3.1g

Cabbage with Apple

Servings: 4 | Preparation: 15 min | Cooking time: 12 min

Ingredients

- 2 teaspoons coconut oil
- 1 large apple, cored and sliced thinly
- 1 onion, sliced thinly
- 1½ pounds cabbage, chopped finely
- 1 tablespoon fresh thyme, chopped
- 1 fresh red chili, chopped
- 1 tablespoon apple cider vinegar

Directions

1. In a nonstick skillet, melt 1 teaspoon of coconut oil over medium heat and stir fry apple for about 2-3 min.
2. Transfer the apple into a bowl.
3. In the same skillet, melt 1 teaspoon of coconut oil over medium heat and sauté onion for about 2-3 min.

4. Add cabbage and stir fry for about 4-5 min.
5. Add apple, thyme and vinegar and cook, covered for about 1 minute.
6. Serve warm.

Nutrition: Calories: 105; Total Fat: 2.6g; Saturated Fat: 2g; Protein: 2.7g; Carbs: 20.7g; Fiber: 6.5g; Sugar: 12.5g

Kale with Cranberries

Servings: 4 | Preparation: 15 min | Cooking time: 5 min

Ingredients

- 1 tablespoon extra-virgin olive oil
- 1 small garlic cloves, chopped
- 1 large shallot, sliced thinly
- 1 teaspoon fresh orange zest, grated
- 12-16 fresh kale leaves, trimmed and torn
- 2 tablespoons water
- 2 tablespoons dried unsweetened cranberries
- ½ tablespoon balsamic vinegar
- 2 tablespoons fresh orange juice
- Salt and ground black pepper, as required
- 2 tablespoons pumpkin seeds, toasted
- ¼ cup pine nuts

Directions

1. In a large skillet, heat the oil over medium heat and sauté the garlic and shallots for about 2 min.
2. Add the orange zest, kale and water and cook for about 2-3 min.
3. Stir in the cranberries, vinegar and orange juice and cook, covered for about 1-2 min.
4. Uncover the skillet and cook for about 1-2 min or until all the liquid is absorbed.
5. Remove from the heat and stir in the salt and black pepper.
6. Stir in the pumpkin seeds and pine nuts and serve.

Nutrition: Calories: 191; Total Fat: 11.3g; Saturated Fat: 1.3g; Protein: 6.7g; Carbs: 19g; Fiber: 2.8g; Sugar: 1.2g

Sweet & Sour Shrimp

Servings: 3 | Preparation: 15 min | Cooking time: 10 min

Ingredients

For Sauce:

- 3 tablespoons fresh orange juice
- 1 tablespoon raw honey
- 1 tablespoon coconut aminos
- ½ tablespoon balsamic vinegar

For Shrimp:

- ¾ pound shrimp, peeled and deveined
- ½ tablespoons arrowroot powder
- 1 tablespoon extra-virgin olive oil
- 2 garlic cloves, minced
- 1 teaspoon fresh ginger, minced

Directions

1. For sauce: in a bowl, all ingredients and mix well. Keep aside.
2. In another bowl, add shrimp and arrowroot powder and toss to coat well.
3. In a large skillet, heat oil over medium-high heat and sauté garlic and ginger for about 1 minute
4. Add shrimp and cook for about 3 min.
5. Add sauce and cook for about 2 min, stirring continuously.
6. With a slotted spoon, transfer the shrimp into a bowl.
7. Cook for about 2-4 min or until desired thickness, stirring continuously.
8. Serve shrimp with the topping of sauce.

Nutrition: Calories: 219; Total Fat: 6.7g; Saturated Fat: 1.3g; Protein: 26.1g; Carbs: 12.5g; Fiber: 0.2g; Sugar: 7.1g

Quinoa with Green Peas

Servings: 4 | Preparation: 15 min | Cooking time: 15 min

Ingredients

- 2 cups plus 1 tablespoon water, divided
- 1 cup dry quinoa, rinsed
- Salt, as required
- 1 cup fresh green peas, shelled
- ¼ cup fresh basil, chopped finely
- 2 tablespoons fresh lemon juice
- 2 tablespoons olive oil
- 2 teaspoons Dijon mustard
- 1 teaspoon maple syrup
- Ground black pepper, as required

Directions

1. In a pan, add 2 cups of the water, quinoa and a pinch of salt over medium-high heat and bring to a boil.
2. Reduce the heat to low and simmer, partially covered for about 15 min or until all the liquid is absorbed.
3. Meanwhile, in a microwave-safe dish, add the peas and remaining water.
4. Cover the bowl and microwave on high for about 3-4 min.
5. Stir the peas and microwave for about 3-5 min more.
6. Remove from the microwave and drain any liquid from the dish.
7. Remove the pan of the quinoa from the heat and set aside, covered for about 5 min.
8. Uncover the pan and with a fork, fluff the quinoa.
9. In a large bowl, add the quinoa, peas and basil and mix.
10. In another bowl, add the lemon juice, oil, maple syrup, mustard, salt and black pepper and beat until well combined.
11. Pour the oil mixture over the quinoa mixture and toss to coat well.
12. Serve warm.

Nutrition: Calories: 254; Total Fat: 9.9g; Saturated Fat: 1.4g; Protein: 8.2g; Carbs: 34g; Fiber: 5g; Sugar: 3.2g

Simple pizza recipe

Servings: 6 8 | Preparation: 10 min | Cooking: 15 min

Ingredients

- 1 pizza crust
- ½ cup tomato sauce
- ¼ black pepper
- 1 cup pepperoni slices
- 1 cup mozzarella cheese
- 1 cup olives

Directions

1. Spread tomato sauce on the pizza crust
2. Place all the toppings on the pizza crust
3. Bake the pizza at 425 F for 12 15 min
4. When ready remove pizza from the oven and serve

Zucchini pizza

Servings: 6 8 | Preparation: 10 min | Cooking: 15 min

Ingredients

- 1 pizza crust
- ½ cup tomato sauce
- ¼ black pepper
- 1 cup zucchini slices
- 1 cup mozzarella cheese
- 1 cup olives

Directions

1. Spread tomato sauce on the pizza crust
2. Place all the toppings on the pizza crust
3. Bake the pizza at 425 F for 12 15 min
4. When ready remove pizza from the oven and serve

Butternut frittata

Servings: 2 | Preparation: 10 min | Cooking: 20 min

Ingredients

- ½ lb. butternut
- 1 tablespoon olive oil
- ½ red onion
- 2 eggs
- ¼ tsp salt
- 2 oz. cheddar cheese
- 1 garlic clove
- ¼ tsp dill

Directions

1. In a bowl whisk eggs with salt and cheese
2. In a frying pan heat olive oil and pour egg mixture
3. Add remaining ingredients and mix well
4. Serve when ready

Coriander frittata

Servings: 2 | Preparation: 10 min | Cooking: 20 min

Ingredients

- ½ lb. spinach
- 1 tablespoon olive oil
- ½ red onion
- 2 eggs
- ¼ tsp salt
- 2 oz. cheddar cheese
- 1 garlic clove
- ¼ tsp dill
- 1 tablespoon coriander

Directions

1. In a bowl whisk eggs with salt and cheese

2. In a frying pan heat olive oil and pour egg mixture
3. Add remaining ingredients and mix well
4. Serve when ready

Dill frittata

Servings: 2 | Preparation: 10 min | Cooking: 20 min

Ingredients

- 1 tablespoon olive oil
- ½ red onion
- ¼ tsp salt
- 2 eggs
- 2 oz. cheddar cheese
- 1 garlic clove
- 1 tsp dill

Directions

1. In a bowl whisk eggs with salt and cheese
2. In a frying pan heat olive oil and pour egg mixture
3. Add remaining ingredients and mix well
4. Serve when ready

Prosciutto frittata

Servings: 2 | Preparation: 10 min | Cooking: 20 min

Ingredients

- 8 10 slices prosciutto
- 1 tablespoon olive oil
- ½ red onion
- ¼ tsp salt
- 2 eggs
- 2 oz. parmesan cheese
- 1 garlic clove
- ¼ tsp dill

Directions

1. In a bowl whisk eggs with salt and parmesan cheese
2. In a frying pan heat olive oil and pour egg mixture
3. Add remaining ingredients and mix well
4. When prosciutto and eggs are cooked remove from heat and serve

Pea frittata

Servings: 2 | Preparation: 10 min | Cooking: 20 min

Ingredients

- ½ lb. pea

- 1 tablespoon olive oil
- ½ red onion
- ¼ tsp salt
- 2 oz. cheddar cheese
- 1 garlic clove
- 2 eggs
- ¼ tsp dill

Directions
1. In a bowl whisk eggs with salt and cheese
2. In a frying pan heat olive oil and pour egg mixture
3. Add remaining ingredients and mix well
4. Serve when ready

Black bean burger

Servings: 4 | Preparation: 10 min | Cooking: 30 min

Ingredients
- 2 cans black beans
- 2 eggs
- ¼ cup green pepper
- 2 tablespoons cilantro
- 1 tsp cumin
- ¼ tsp coriander
- ½ cup tortilla chips

Directions
1. In a bowl combine beans, eggs, tortilla chips and seasoning
2. Mix well and form 4 5 patties
3. In a skillet heat oil and cook each burger for 4 5 min per side
4. When ready remove from heat and serve

Crockpot chicken

Servings: 4 6 | Preparation: 10 min | Cooking: 6 H

Ingredients
- 2 chicken breasts
- 1 cup barley
- 2 cups chicken broth
- 1 bag mixed vegetables
- ¼ tsp onion
- ¼ tsp garlic powder
- 2 bay leaves
- 1 cup spinach

Directions
1. Place all ingredients in a crock pot
2. Cover with a lid and cook on low until the vegetables are tender

3. When ready remove from the crockpot and serve

Chicken cutlets

Servings: 4 6 | Preparation: 10 min | Cooking: 20 min

Ingredients
- 2 lb. chicken breast
- ½ cup wheat flour
- 2 tablespoons butter
- 2 cups mushrooms
- ¼ cup red wine
- ¼ red onion

Directions
1. Season the chicken and place the chicken in the bowl with the flour
2. In a skillet heat oil and fry the chicken for 4 5 min per side
3. When ready, remove from the skillet and set aside
4. In a pan add butter, mushrooms, onion and sauté until vegetables are soft
5. Add wine and simmer until the liquid has evaporated
6. Add the chicken back to the pan and cook until has thickened
7. Serve when ready

Mushroom sandwich

Servings: 2 | Preparation: 10 min | Cooking: 20 min

Ingredients
- 1 lb. mushrooms
- 1 red onion
- ½ cup BBQ sauce
- 2 buns
- ¼ tsp pepper
- ¼ tsp salt
- 1 cup cabbage slaw

Directions
1. In a bowl toss the mushrooms, onions, pepper, salt and spread the veggies on a baking sheet
2. Bake at 375 F for 12 15 min
3. Spread BBQ sauce on each bun
4. Place the roasted mushroom mixture on a bun
5. Top with the other bun and serve

Coleslaw

Servings: 2 | Preparation: 5 min | Cooking: 5 min

Ingredients

- 2 carrots
- 2 purple carrots
- 1 cabbage
- ¼ red onion
- 1 bunch leaves
- 2 kale leaves
- 1 cup salad dressing

Directions

1. In a bowl combine all ingredients together and mix well
2. Serve with dressing

Cabbage salad

Servings: 2 | Preparation: 5 min | Cooking: 5 min

Ingredients

- ½ cup bulgur
- 1 cabbage
- 1 red onion
- 1 cup parsley
- 1 tsp seasoning
- ¼ cup lemon juice

Directions

1. In a bowl combine all ingredients together and mix well
2. Serve with dressing

Cantaloupe salad

Servings: 2 | Preparation: 5 min | Cooking: 5 min

Ingredients

- 1 cantaloupe
- 1 cup olive oil
- ¼ cup tarragon leaves

Directions

1. In a bowl combine all ingredients together and mix well
2. Serve with dressing

Steakhouse salad

Servings: 2 | Preparation: 5 min | Cooking: 5 min

Ingredients

- 2 garlic cloves
- 2 tablespoons mirin
- 2 tablespoons soy sauce

- 1 tablespoon olive oil
- 1 lb. steak
- 4 oz. snap peas
- 1 head lettuce
- 1 cucumber

Directions

1. In a bowl combine all ingredients together and mix well
2. Serve with dressing

Buttermilk & jalapenos salad

Servings: 2 | Preparation: 5 min | Cooking: 5 min

Ingredients

- 1 cabbage
- 1 tablespoon olive oil
- 1 cup buttermilk
- 1 cup Greek yogurt
- ¼ cup mayonnaise
- 1 tablespoon lemon juice
- 1 tablespoon chives

Directions

1. In a bowl combine all ingredients together and mix well
2. Serve with dressing

Watermelon & jicama salad

Servings: 2 | Preparation: 5 min | Cooking: 5 min

Ingredients

- 2 lb. watermelon
- ½ jicama
- 1 jalapeno
- 1 scallion
- ¼ cup cilantro

Directions

1. In a bowl combine all ingredients together and mix well
2. Serve with dressing

Snap pea salad

Servings: 2 | Preparation: 5 min | Cooking: 5 min

Ingredients

- 2 cups buttermilk
- 2 tablespoons lemon juice
- 1 garlic clove
- 6 oz. snap peas

- 2 tablespoon olive oil
- 1 tsp lemon zest

Directions
1. In a bowl combine all ingredients together and mix well
2. Serve with dressing

Chickpeas salad

Servings: 2 | Preparation: 5 min | Cooking: 5 min

Ingredients
- 1 can chickpeas
- 2 tablespoon olive oil
- 1 cooked chicken breast
- 1 cup tomatoes
- 1 cucumber
- 1 cup feta cheese
- 1 tsp oregano

Directions
1. In a bowl combine all ingredients together and mix well
2. Serve with dressing

Rhubarb salad

Servings: 2 | Preparation: 5 min | Cooking: 5 min

Ingredients
- 2 rhubarb stalks
- 1 tsp salt
- 2 fennel bulbs
- 2 celery stalks
- ½ cup olive oil

Directions
1. In a bowl combine all ingredients together and mix well
2. Serve with dressing

Ricotta salad

Servings: 2 | Preparation: 5 min | Cooking: 5 min

Ingredients
- 1 cantaloupe
- 4 oz. snap peas
- 4 oz. ricotta cheese
- 2 tablespoons tarragon leaves
- 2 tablespoons olive oil

Directions
1. In a bowl combine all ingredients together and mix well
2. Serve with dressing

Easy Grilled Veggie Turkey Sliders

Preparation: 15 min| Cooking: 20 min| Servings: 7

Ingredients
- ½ lbs. ground turkey
- 1/3 cup shredded carrots
- 1/3 cup shredded beets
- 1/3 cup zucchini
- ½ teaspoon garlic, minced
- 1 teaspoon onion, minced
- 1 teaspoon ginger, minced
- ½ teaspoon brown sugar
- ½ teaspoon black pepper
- ½ teaspoon paprika

Directions
1. Mix together ground turkey, shredded carrots, shredded beets, shredded zucchini, minced garlic, minced onion, minced ginger, brown sugar, black pepper, paprika.
2. Using hands form into 3 oz. patties, grill over medium-high heat 4-5 min per side.

Nutrition: Calories 85; Total Fat 4.2g; Saturated Fat 0.7g; Cholesterol 39mg; Sodium 53mg

Pegan Quinoa Salad and Baked Tuna

Preparation: 10 min| Cooking: 10 min| Servings: 2

Ingredients
- 2/3 cup quinoa, prepared ad directed
- ½ tablespoon red pepper infused olive oil
- ½ can organic whole kernel corn drained
- 3 pickled beets, quartered
- 1 teaspoon toasted coriander seeds
- 6 pickled jalapenos
- 1 ripe avocado peeled and sliced
- Juice of ½ lemon
- 2 filets tuna
- Salt and pepper
- ¼ cup coconut oil

Directions

1. Preheat broiler to hi and prepare 9x11 dish.
2. In Dutch oven combine olive oil, corn, pickled beets, toasted coriander seeds, pickled jalapenos. Toss with prepared quinoa and warm through.
3. Sprinkle Tunas with salt and pepper then brush both sides with coconut oil. Place under broiler 4-5 min per-side.

Nutrition: Calories 787; Total Fat 51.3g; Saturated Fat 28.5g; Cholesterol 38mg 13%; Sodium 284mg

Sweet Potato Gnocchi in an Herbed Dairy-Free Sauce

Preparation: 10 min| Cooking: 15 min| Servings: 2

Ingredients

- 1 cup sweet potato mash
- ½ cup cassava or almond flour
- Olive oil
- 1 sprig parsley diced

Sauce:

- 3 tablespoons unsalted butter or ghee
- 1 onion julienned
- 1 teaspoon garlic, minced
- ¾ can coconut milk
- 2 teaspoons tapioca flour
- 2 teaspoons rosemary, diced
- 2 teaspoons Italian oregano, diced
- 1/3 teaspoon red pepper flakes
- 1 cup spinach or kale

Directions

1. Mix sweet potato mash and flour together until smooth. Roll into 1-inch thick tube and cut into 4 pieces. Stick three in the refrigerator.
2. Cut each segment into 1-inch pieces and stick on baking tray. Drizzle with olive oil and bits of parsley.
3. Boil pieces until they rise to the top.
4. Transfer gnocchi pieces to skillet and cook over medium heat 1 minute or until each side is a golden brown.
5. In skillet let butter melt them add julienned onions. Turn heat to medium-low and let onions sweat 10 min.
6. Whisk in garlic and coconut milk, stirring constantly for 30 seconds. Whisk in tapioca flour, diced rosemary, diced oregano, red pepper flakes. Bring to a low boil for 1-2 min constantly stirring.
7. Remove from heat and stir in spinach/kale

Nutrition: Calories 511; Total Fat 35g; Saturated Fat 23.9g; Cholesterol 15mg; Sodium 71mg

Rosemary Watermelon & Cucumber Salad

Preparation: 15 min| Cooking: 0 min| Servings: 6

Ingredients

- 1 can of garbanzo beans drained and washed (chickpeas)
- 4 cups chunked watermelon
- 1 seedless cucumber, sliced
- 1 cup olive oil
- ½ teaspoon of red or white wine vinegar
- ½ tablespoon rosemary, diced
- ½ tablespoon Italian oregano, diced
- ½ tablespoon parsley, diced
- 2 diced scallions

Directions

1. Mix together olive oil, wine vinegar, diced rosemary, diced oregano, minced parsley, diced scallions. Cover and chill.
2. In a large bowl mix together drained and washed garbanzo beans, watermelon chunks, cucumber slices.
3. Pour vinaigrette over salad, toss, serve!

Nutrition: Calories 687; Total Fat 45.5g; Saturated Fat 6.4g; Cholesterol 0mg; Sodium 23mg

Pegan Cauliflower Gnocchi in a Creamy Sauce

Preparation: 10 min| Cooking: 55 min| Servings: 4

Ingredients

- 5 cups cauliflower, minced
- 1 cup cassava flour
- ½ teaspoon smoked paprika
- Sauce
- 1 can coconut milk
- 5 cups spinach or kale
- 1 teaspoon garlic, minced
- ½ teaspoon lemon peel
- 1/3 teaspoon pepper
- 2 ½ tablespoons tapioca flour

Directions

1. Steam cauliflower 5-7 min, ring out water, put in blender along with cassava flour and smoked paprika. Blend until mix is smooth.
2. Roll dough into 1-inch thick tube then cut into four segments, place three in the refrigerator.
3. Cut each segment into 1-inch pieces, drop them into boiling water and let rise to surface.
4. Once they have risen, transfer them to baking tray 20 min, turn over, cook another 30 min.
5. In skillet over medium-high heat whisk together coconut milk, spinach or kale, minced garlic, lemon peel, pepper, tapioca flour. Stirring continuously until smooth and thickens.
6. Remove from heat and add in spinach or kale and gnocchi.

Nutrition: Calories 641; Total Fat 29.3g; Saturated Fat 25.4g; Cholesterol 0mg; Sodium 196mg

Jalapeno Mango Salad

Preparation: 10 min| Cooking: 5 min| Servings: 4

Ingredients

* 1 medium Sweet Potato, chunked 2x2 pieces
* ¾ tablespoon Coconut Oil
* 1 cubed mango
* 1 cubed avocado
* 2/3 cup Cucumber, diced
* ½ tablespoon mint, thinly sliced
* ½ tablespoon cilantro, diced
* ½ tablespoon basil, diced
* Sauce
* 2 tablespoons lime juice
* 2/3 cup extra virgin olive oil
* ¼ tsp pepper
* 1 cup red peppers, julienned
* 1 sliced jalapeno
* 1 banana pepper sliced

Directions

1. Mix together lime juice, pepper, red peppers, jalapeno slices, banana pepper slices. Cover and chill.
2. Coat sweet potato chunks with coconut oil and cook 2-3 min per side to soften. Transfer to plate to cool then put in a bowl along with mango, avocado, cucumber slices, mint, cilantro, basil and stir.
3. Divide between four bowls and top each with vinaigrette.

Nutrition: Calories 513; Total Fat 46.6g; Saturated Fat 9.2g; Cholesterol 0mg; Sodium 78mg

Toasted Coconut and Walnut Zoodle Salad with Baked Chicken Tenders

Preparation: 10 min| Cooking: 15 min| Servings: 2

Ingredients

* 2/3 cup olive oil
* ½ teaspoon red or white wine
* 1/3 teaspoon lemon juice
* ½ teaspoon lemon peel
* 2 cups zucchini noodles
* 8 grape organic tomatoes
* ½ cup toasted coconut flakes
* ¼ cup toasted walnuts
* 8 lemon basil leaves, coarsely chopped OR 2 teaspoons organic Italian seasoning
* 6-8 organic chicken tenders
* 1 teaspoon Mexican seasoning like Tajin
* Olive oil for drizzling

Directions

1. Preheat oven to 350 and prepare 9x11 dish.
2. Coat both sides of tenders with seasoning, lay on tray and drizzle with olive oil, bake 15 min, flip and repeat.
3. Mix together olive oil, wine, lemon juice, lemon peel; cover and chill.
4. In bowl combine zoodles, toasted coconut, toasted walnuts, chopped lemon basil leaves then top with vinaigrette and toss.
5. Divide amongst two plates and serve.

Nutrition: Calories 945; Total Fat 85.8g; Saturated Fat 16.8g; Cholesterol 31mg; Sodium 118mg

Cauli-Bites

Preparation: 10 min| Cooking: 30 min| Servings: 12

Ingredients

* 4 cups cauliflower rice
* 2 tablespoon extra-virgin olive oil
* ½ teaspoon garlic, minced
* ½ teaspoon onion, minced
* 1 ½ teaspoon Italian seasoning
* 1 hamburger crumble or 1 ½ cup ground beef, browned and drained (optional)

Directions

1. Preheat oven to 350 and prepare muffin tin.
2. Mix together cauliflower rice, minced garlic, diced onion, Italian seasoning, ground beef or crumble.
3. Press into muffin tins and bake 30 min.
4. Store in airtight container in refrigerator and will keep 3-5 days.

Nutrition: Calories 53; Total Fat 3.6g; Saturated Fat 0.8g; Cholesterol 6mg; Sodium 45mg;

Crispy Baked Chicken with Sweet Potato & Broccoli Tots

Preparation: 10 min| Cooking: 45 min| Servings: 2

Ingredients

- 2 3 oz. chicken patties
- 1 cup organic breadcrumbs or crushed cornflakes
- 2 cups sweet potato mash
- 2 cups broccoli mash
- 1 tablespoon paprika
- ½ tablespoon garlic powder and parsley

Directions

1. Preheat oven to 425 and prepare medium sized baking dish.
2. Coat chicken patties with breadcrumbs, spray with olive oil, bake 35-40 min.
3. Blend together sweet potato, broccoli, paprika, garlic powder and parsley.
4. Using hands form into tater tots and fry in coconut oil 2-3 min per side.

Nutrition: Calories 727; Total Fat 24g; Saturated Fat 4.7g; Cholesterol 45mg; Sodium 1016mg

Mexican Sweet Tater Tots with Coconut-Cinnamon Pork Chops

Preparation: 10 min| Cooking: 10 min| Servings: 2

Ingredients

- 1 tablespoon coconut oil
- 2 thin pork chops
- Cinnamon for sprinkling
- 4 cup sweet potato mash
- 1 tablespoon chili powder
- 1 tablespoon paprika
- 1 tablespoon cayenne pepper
- ½ tablespoon cumin
- ½ tablespoon garlic powder and parsley

- Coconut oil for frying OR olive oil infused with red pepper

Directions

1. In skillet cook pork chops in coconut oil transfer to paper towel lined plates.
2. Mix together sweet potato, chili powder, paprika, cayenne powder, cumin, garlic powder & parsley.
3. With hands form into tater tots and fry in oil 2-3 min per side.
4. Before plating dust both sides of pork chops with cinnamon.

Nutrition: Calories 230; Total Fat 11.7g; Saturated Fat 7.2g; Cholesterol 60mg; Sodium 275mg

Creamy Dairy-Free Veggie Soup

Preparation: 5 min| Cooking: 10 min| Servings: 4

Ingredients

- 1 head of cauliflower, chopped
- 1/3 cup walnuts
- ½ cup carrots chopped
- 1/3 cup cremini mushrooms, sliced
- ¼ cup onion, minced
- 1 tsp garlic, minced
- 4 tablespoons olive oil infused with basil
- 2 tablespoon cracked black pepper
- ½ tablespoon parsley, diced

Directions

1. In Dutch oven add infused oil and sauté carrots, cremini mushrooms, minced onions, minced garlic.
2. In blender chop cauliflower and walnuts, then add to Dutch oven. Stir in pepper and parsley. Simmer 7-10 min.

Nutrition: Calories 220; Total Fat 20.3g; Saturated Fat 2.4g; Cholesterol 0mg; Sodium 32mg

Roasted Veggies with Easy Homemade Tahini Sauce

Preparation: 5 min| Cooking: 20 min| Servings: 2

Ingredients

- 2 cups broccoli trees
- 2 cups baby carrots
- 1 cup plum tomatoes, halved
- 2 cups string beans
- Olive oil spray

- 1 bunch parsley, approx. 1 cup
- 2 teaspoons lemon juice
- 2 teaspoons extra virgin olive oil
- 1 teaspoon garlic, minced
- 2 tablespoons tahini

Directions

1. Preheat oven to 400 and line baking sheet with parchment paper.
2. Layout broccoli trees, baby carrots, halved plum tomatoes and mist with olive oil. Bake 20 min.
3. Blend parsley, lemon juice, extra virgin olive oil, minced garlic, tahini together.
4. Pour sauce over roasted veggie's and enjoy

Nutrition: Calories 220; Total Fat 13.4g; Saturated Fat 1.9g; Cholesterol 0mg; Sodium 70mg

Belgian Endive Frittata

Preparation: 10 min| Cooking: 20 min| Servings: 2

Ingredients

- ½ lb. Belgian endive
- 1 tablespoon olive oil
- ½ red onion
- ¼ tsp salt
- 2 oz. cheddar cheese
- 1 garlic clove
- ¼ tsp dill

Directions

1. In a bowl whisk eggs with salt and cheese
2. In a frying pan heat olive oil and pour egg mixture
3. Add remaining ingredients and mix well
4. Serve when ready

Nutrition: Calories 83 Total fat: 5gTotal carbs: 3g Fiber: 1g Protein: 7g; Sodium: 385mg

Carrot Frittata

Preparation: 10 min| Cooking: 20 min| Servings: 2

Ingredients

- ½ lb. carrot
- 1 tablespoon olive oil
- ½ red onion
- ¼ tsp salt
- 2 oz. cheddar cheese
- 1 garlic clove
- ¼ tsp dill

Directions

1. In a bowl whisk eggs with salt and cheese
2. In a frying pan heat olive oil and pour egg mixture
3. Add remaining ingredients and mix well
4. Serve when ready

Nutrition: Calories 83 Total fat: 5g Total carbs: 3g Fiber: 1g Protein: 7g; Sodium: 385mg

Kale Frittata

Preparation: 10 min| Cooking: 20 min| Servings: 2

Ingredients

- 1 cup kale
- 1 tablespoon olive oil
- ½ red onion
- ¼ tsp salt
- 2 oz. cheddar cheese
- 1 garlic clove
- ¼ tsp dill

Directions

1. In a skillet sauté kale until tender
2. In a bowl whisk eggs with salt and cheese
3. In a frying pan heat olive oil and pour egg mixture
4. Add remaining ingredients and mix well
5. When ready serve with sautéed kale

Nutrition: Calories 83Total fat: 5g Total carbs: 3g Fiber: 1g Protein: 7g; Sodium: 385mg

Ham Frittata

Preparation: 10 min| Cooking: 20 min| Servings: 2

Ingredients

- 8-10 slices ham
- 1 tablespoon olive oil
- ½ red onion
- ¼ tsp salt
- 2 oz. parmesan cheese
- 1 garlic clove
- ¼ tsp dill

Directions

1. In a bowl whisk eggs with salt and parmesan cheese
2. In a frying pan heat olive oil and pour egg mixture
3. Add remaining ingredients and mix well

4. When the ham and eggs are cooked remove from heat and serve

Nutrition: Calories 83 Total fat: 5g Total carbs: 3g Fiber: 1g Protein: 7g; Sodium: 385mg

Broccoli Frittata

Preparation: 10 min| Cooking: 20 min| Servings: 2

Ingredients
- 1 cup broccoli
- 1 tablespoon olive oil
- ½ red onion
- ¼ tsp salt
- 2 oz. cheddar cheese
- 1 garlic clove
- ¼ tsp dill

Directions
1. In a skillet sauté broccoli until tender
2. In a bowl whisk eggs with salt and cheese
3. In a frying pan heat olive oil and pour egg mixture
4. Add remaining ingredients and mix well
5. When ready serve with sautéed broccoli

Nutrition: Calories 83 Total fat: 5g Total carbs: 3g Fiber: 1g Protein: 7g; Sodium: 385mg

Spicy Curry

Preparation: 10 min| Cooking: 10 min| Servings: 4

Ingredients
- Ginger
- 200 ml cream
- 5 garlic cloves
- 5 tbs tomato puree
- 2 chilis
- 2 cans red kidney beans
- 2 cups rice

Directions
1. Dice the garlic, ginger and chili finely
2. Fry them all together
3. After a few min, add the tomato puree
4. Pour the cream in mixing slowly
5. Add the kidney beans and season
6. Serve when ready

Nutrition: Calories: 321Total Fat: 7.4gSaturated Fat: 1.4gProtein: 38.3gCarbs: 23.7g Fiber: 7g

Mackerel Pasta

Preparation: 10 min| Cooking: 10 min| Servings: 4

Ingredients
- 250 g chard
- 4 mackerel fillets
- 2 garlic cloves
- 350 g pasta
- 3 tbs capers
- 1 lemon
- 30 g breadcrumbs
- 2 tsp chili flakes
- olive oil

Directions
1. Cook the pasta
2. Cook the chard with the pasta for about 5 min
3. Drain
4. Squeeze the lemon over and add the zest also
5. Add the capers, a drizzle of oil and chilli flakes
6. Flake the fish over, and mix everything together
7. Serve when ready

Nutrition: Calories: 247 Total Fat: 12.1g Saturated Fat: 6g Protein: 21.1g Carbs: 14.5gFiber: 3.1g Sugar: 8.9g

Tofu Noodles

Preparation: 10 min| Cooking: 20 min| Servings: 4

Ingredients
- 120 g asparagus
- 1 spring onion
- 1 lime
- 200 g noodles
- 250 g tofu
- 2 tbs oil
- 5 tbs soy sauce
- 30 g maple syrup
- 3 tbs sriracha

Directions
1. Mix the maple syrup, 3 tbs soy sauce and the sriracha together
2. Cook the noodles
3. Cut the tofu in cubes, then coat in the sriracha mixture
4. Bake at 200C for at least 20 min
5. Cut the asparagus and cook with the noodles for about 3 min
6. Drain and add ½ lime juice, 2 tbs soy sauce and oil

7. Mix everything together
8. Serve

Nutrition: Calories 83 Total fat: 5g Total carbs: 3g Fiber: 1gSugar: 1g Protein: 7g; Sodium: 385mg

Salmon with Vegetables

Preparation: 10 min| Cooking: 50 min| Servings: 2

Ingredients

- 3 cups tomatoes
- 500 g potatoes
- 2 salmon fillets
- 1 ½ cups shallots
- 2 tbs oil
- 2 tbs vinegar
- 250 g asparagus
- Salt
- Pepper

Directions

1. Dice the potatoes and cut the asparagus
2. Parboil the potatoes, then drain
3. Place the potatoes and shallots on a lined baking tray, season and add vinegar
4. Roast for at least 15 min
5. Add the asparagus and return to oven for another 15 min
6. Serve drizzled with oil and basil

Nutrition: Calories: 367 Total Fat: 24.9g Saturated Fat: 15.1g Protein: 26.6g Carbs: 13.7g Fiber: 3.6gSugar: 7g

Apple slaw

Servings: 2 | Preparation: 5 min | Cooking: 5 min

Ingredients

- 4 cups cabbage
- 2 cups apples
- ¼ cup Greek Yogurt
- 2 tablespoons honey
- ¼ tsp salt

Directions

1. In a bowl mix all ingredients and mix well
2. Serve with dressing

Broccoli salad

Servings: 2 | Preparation: 5 min | Cooking: 5 min

Ingredients

- 2 3 cups cooked macaroni
- ¼ cup celery
- ¼ cup broccoli
- ¼ cup red peppers
- ¼ cup carrots
- salad dressing

Directions

1. In a bowl mix all ingredients and mix well
2. Serve with dressing

Summer salad

Servings: 2 | Preparation: 5 min | Cooking: 5 min

Ingredients

- 4 tomatoes
- 1 red onion
- 4 5 basil leaves
- 1 tablespoon olive oil
- 1 clove garlic
- 1 cucumber

Directions

1. In a bowl mix all ingredients and mix well
2. Serve with dressing

Prosciutto salad

Servings: 2 | Preparation: 5 min | Cooking: 5 min

Ingredients

- 4 figs
- ½ cup blue cheese
- 5 6 thin strips prosciutto
- 4 cups arugula
- 1 tablespoon olive oil
- 1 tablespoon balsamic vinegar

Directions

1. In a bowl mix all ingredients and mix well
2. Serve with dressing

Caprese salad

Servings: 2 | Preparation: 5 min | Cooking: 5 min

Ingredients

- 1 tomato
- 6 oz. mozzarella
- 6 7 basil leaves

- 2 tsp olive oil
- 1 tsp balsamic vinegar

Directions
1. In a bowl mix all ingredients and mix well
2. Serve with dressing

Black bean salad

Servings: 2 | Preparation: 5 min | Cooking: 5 min

Ingredients
- 1 can black beans
- 1 cup cooked quinoa
- 1 cup corn
- 1 red bell pepper
- 1 mango
- 2 garlic cloves
- 1 tsp chili powder
- 2 tablespoons lime juice

Directions
1. In a bowl mix all ingredients and mix well
2. Serve with dressing

Pasta salad

Servings: 2 | Preparation: 5 min | Cooking: 5 min

Ingredients
- 2 tablespoons red wine vinegar
- ¼ cup olive oil
- ¼ tsp garlic powder
- 1 tsp oregano
- 4 oz. pasta
- 1 cup olives
- ½ red onion
- 1 cucumber
- 1 cup tomatoes
- ¼ cup feta cheese

Directions
1. In a bowl mix all ingredients and mix well
2. Serve with dressing

Salmon salad

Servings: 2 | Preparation: 5 min | Cooking: 5 min

Ingredients
- 2 cooked salmon fillets
- 1 tsp mustard
- 1 tsp parsley

- 1 red onion
- 2 tablespoons olive oil
- ¼ tsp garlic powder
- ½ avocado
- 1 cup red cabbage

Directions
1. In a bowl mix all ingredients and mix well
2. Serve with dressing

Chickpea salad

Servings: 2 | Preparation: 5 min | Cooking: 5 min

Ingredients
- 1 cucumber
- 1 tomato
- 1 can chickpeas
- 1 tablespoon parsley
- 1 tablespoon lemon juice
- 1 cup salad dressing

Directions
1. In a bowl mix all ingredients and mix well
2. Serve with dressing

Ranch chicken salad

Servings: 2 | Preparation: 5 min | Cooking: 5 min

Ingredients
- 1 cup buttermilk
- 1 tablespoon mayonnaise
- 1 tsp salt
- 1 tablespoon chives
- 1 tsp garlic powder
- 1 tsp parsley
- 1 tsp basil
- 1 cup cooked chicken breast

Directions
1. In a bowl mix all ingredients and mix well
2. Serve with dressing

Stuffed pasta

Servings: 4 | Preparation: 20 min | Cooking: 30 min

Ingredients
- 2 tins chopped tomatoes
- 450 g pasta
- 1 red onion
- 1 garlic clove

- 2 red peppers
- 3 mushrooms
- 275 g lentils

Directions

1. Cook the lentils and the pasta separately
2. Chop the mushrooms, peppers and onion
3. Fry the garlic and onion, then add mushrooms and pepper
4. Add the tinned tomatoes
5. Add the lentils and mix well until combined
6. Stuff the pasta shells with the mixture and pour the remaining sauce over
7. Bake in the preheated oven at 350F for at least 15 min
8. Serve warm

Mediterranean tuna salad

Servings: 4 | Preparation: 10 min | Cooking: 30 min

Ingredients

- 2 cans tuna
- 2 celery stalks
- 1 cucumber
- 4 radishes
- 2 onions
- 1 red onion
- ¼ Kalamata olives
- 1 bunch parsley
- 10 mint leaves
- 1 tomato
- 1 serving mustard vinaigrette

Directions

- In a bowl combine all ingredients together
- Add salad dressing and serve

Mexican tuna salad

Servings: 2 | Preparation: 5 min | Cooking: 5 min

Ingredients

- 2 cans tuna
- 1 red bell pepper
- 1 can black beans
- 1 can black olives
- 1 can yellow corn
- 2 tomatoes
- 2 avocados

Dressing:

- ½ cup Greek yogurt

- ¼ cup mayonnaise
- 1 tsp garlic powder
- ¼ tsp cumin

Directions

1. In a bowl combine all ingredients together
2. In another bowl combine all ingredients for the dressing
3. Add dressing, mix well and serve

Prawn noodle salad

Servings: 4 | Preparation: 10 min | Cooking: 10 min

Ingredients

- ¼ lbs. noodle
- ¼ lbs. baby spinach
- 3 oz. cooked prawn
- ¼ lbs. snap pea
- 1 carrot

Dressing:

- 1 red chili
- 1 tsp fish sauce
- 1 tablespoon mint
- 2 tablespoons rice vinegar
- 1 tsp sugar

Directions

1. In a bowl add all dressing ingredients and mix well
2. In another bowl add salad ingredients and mix well, pour dressing over salad and serve

Arugula and sweet potato salad

Servings: 2 | Preparation: 10 min | Cooking: 15 min

Ingredients

- 1 lb. sweet potatoes
- 1 cup walnuts
- 1 tablespoon olive oil
- 1 cup water
- 1 tablespoon soy sauce
- 3 cups arugula

Directions

1. Bake potatoes at 400 F until tender, remove and set aside
2. In a bowl drizzle, walnuts with olive oil and microwave for 2 3 min or until toasted
3. In a bowl combine all salad ingredients and mix well
4. Pour over soy sauce and serve

Mango tango salad

Servings: 4 | Preparation: 10 min | Cooking: 30 min

Ingredients

- 2 mangoes
- Juice of 1 lemon
- ¼ onion
- 1 tablespoon cilantro laves

Directions

1. In a bowl combine all salad ingredients and mix well
2. Add salad dressing and serve when ready

Couscous salad

Servings: 1 | Preparation: 10 min | Cooking: 10 min

Ingredients

- 3 cup water
- ¼ tsp cumin
- 1 tablespoon honey
- 1 tsp lemon juice
- 1 green onion
- 1 carrot
- ¼ red pepper
- cilantro
- ½ tsp cinnamon
- 2 cups couscous
- 1 tsp olive oil

Directions

1. Bring water boil add cumin, honey, cinnamon, add couscous and lemon juice
2. Cover and remove from heat
3. Add hers, olive oil, vegetables and serve

Nicoise salad

Servings: 4 | Preparation: 10 min | Cooking: 30 min

Ingredients

- 1 oz. red potatoes
- 1 package green beans
- 2 eggs
- ½ cup tomatoes
- 2 tablespoons wine vinegar
- ¼ tsp salt
- ½ tsp pepper
- ½ tsp thyme
- ¼ cup olive oil
- 6 oz. tuna
- ¼ cup Kalamata olives

Directions

1. In a bowl combine all ingredients together
2. Add salad dressing and serve

Crab salad

Servings: 2 | Preparation: 10 min | Cooking: 30 min

Ingredients

- ¼ cup lemon juice
- ¼ cup rice wine vinegar
- 1 tsp sugar
- 1 cucumber
- ¼ cup mint
- 10 oz. cooked crab
- 2 cups mixed salad greens
- 2 lime wedges

Directions

1. In a bowl combine all salad ingredients and mix well
2. Add salad dressing and serve when ready

Simple spaghetti

Servings: 2 | Preparation: 5 min | Cooking: 15 min

Ingredients

- 10 oz. spaghetti
- 2 eggs
- ½ cup parmesan cheese
- 1 tsp black pepper
- Olive oil
- 1 tsp parsley
- 2 cloves garlic

Directions

1. In a pot boil spaghetti (or any other type of pasta), drain and set aside
2. In a bowl whish eggs with parmesan cheese
3. In a skillet heat olive oil, add garlic and cook for 1 2 min
4. Pour egg mixture and mix well
5. Add pasta and stir well
6. When ready garnish with parsley and serve

Artichoke pasta

Servings: 2 | Preparation: 5 min | Cooking: 15 min

Ingredients

- ¼ cup olive oil
- 1 jar artichokes

- 2 cloves garlic
- 1 tablespoon thyme leaves
- 1 lb. pasta
- 2 tablespoons butter
- Cup basil
- ½ cup parmesan cheese

Directions

1. In a pot boil spaghetti (or any other type of pasta), drain and set aside
2. Place all the ingredients for the sauce in a pot and bring to a simmer
3. Add pasta and mix well
4. When ready garnish with parmesan cheese and serve

Chicken pasta

Servings: 2 | Preparation: 5 min | Cooking: 15 min

Ingredients

- 1 lb. cooked chicken breast
- 8 oz. pasta
- 2 tablespoons butter
- 1 tablespoon garlic
- 1 tablespoon flour
- ½ cup milk
- ½ cup heavy cream
- 1 jar red bell peppers
- 2 tablespoons basil

Directions

1. In a pot boil spaghetti (or any other type of pasta), drain and set aside
2. Place all the ingredients for the sauce in a pot and bring to a simmer
3. Add pasta and mix well
4. When ready garnish with parmesan cheese and serve

Tomato Red Onion Olive Spinach Pesto Pizza

Preparation: 25 min | Chill Time: 2 h | 2 h 25 min | Servings: 8

Ingredients

For the zucchini pizza crust:

- 2 medium zucchini, shredded
- ¼ teaspoon sea salt
- ½ teaspoon dried basil
- 2 garlic cloves, minced

- 1/2 teaspoon black pepper
- ½ cup coconut flour
- 2 large eggs

For the spinach pesto:

- 1 packed cup basil leaves
- 2 packed cup spinach leaves
- 2 garlic cloves
- 2 tablespoons freshly squeezed lemon juice
- 1/2 cup cashew pieces
- 1/2 cup olive oil
- 1 teaspoon coarse salt
- 1/2 teaspoon black pepper

For the toppings:

- 3 Roma tomatoes, sliced
- 1 red onion, thinly sliced
- 1/2 cup sliced olives

Directions

1. Program your oven to 450F, then place the shredded zucchini in a large microwave-safe bowl and microwave for 1 minute. Let the zucchini cool slightly, then place the zucchini onto a clean kitchen towel and squeeze as much of the water out of the zucchini as you can.
2. Place the zucchini back into a medium bowl and add the sea salt, basil, garlic, black pepper, coconut flour, and eggs.
3. Place a sheet of parchment paper cookie sheet and lightly spray it with non-stick cooking spray. Divide the zucchini dough into two 7-inch pizza crusts and place them on the cookie sheet. Bake for 16-20 until the edges become golden brown.
4. While the zucchini pizza crust is baking, make the spinach pesto. Add all of the spinach pesto Ingredients: to a food processor and blend until it becomes a smooth pesto.
5. Take the zucchini pizza crust out of the oven and slather it with the spinach pesto. Add the tomatoes, onions, and olives.
6. Serve and enjoy!

Nutrition; Carbohydrates: 19.1g; Protein: 6.5g; Fat: 20.5g; Saturated Fat: 4.2g; Cholesterol: 47mg; ; Sodium: 406mg; Potassium: 338mg; Sugar: 3.3g;

Watermelon Cucumber Salad

Preparation: 10 min | Cooking: 0 min | Servings: 4

Ingredients

- 8 cups seedless watermelon, cubed

- 2 English cucumbers, thinly sliced
- 1/4 cup minced fresh mint, minced
- 1/4 cup balsamic vinegar
- 1/4 cup olive oil
- 1 tablespoon lime juice
- 1/2 teaspoon red pepper flakes
- 1/2 teaspoon salt
- 1/2 teaspoon pepper
- 1/4 cup chopped almonds

Directions

1. Place the watermelon, cucumbers, and mint in a large bowl.
2. Place the balsamic vinegar, olive oil, lime juice, red pepper flakes, salt, and pepper into a small bowl and whisk to combine.
3. Pour the lime and balsamic dressing over the watermelon and cucumber salad toss to coat. Garnish the salad with the chopped pecans 4. Serve and enjoy!

Nutrition; Carbohydrates: 31.4g; Protein: 4.3g; Fat: 16.2g; Saturated Fat: 2.3g; Cholesterol: 0mg; ; Sodium: 301mg; Potassium: 661mg; Sugar: 21.7g;

Roasted Sweet Potato Kale Salad

Preparation: 10 min | Cooking: 0 min | Servings: 4

Ingredients

For the salad:

- 2 medium sweet potatoes, diced into cubes
- 1 tablespoon olive oil
- 2 cloves garlic, minced
- 1 teaspoon fresh rosemary
- 1/4 teaspoon salt
- 1 cup cherry tomatoes, halved
- 1/2 cup red onion, thinly sliced
- 6 cups Tuscan kale, stemmed removed and roughly chopped

For the dressing:

- 2 tablespoons extra virgin olive oil
- 1 tablespoon fresh lime juice
- 1 tablespoon apple cider vinegar
- 1 tablespoon fresh grapefruit juice
- 1 teaspoon salt
- 1/2 teaspoon black pepper

Directions

1. Program your oven to 375F, then arrange the cubed sweet potatoes on a parchment-lined cookie sheet, drizzle 1 tablespoon olive oil and

add the minced garlic, rosemary salt. Give it a toss to coat the sweet potatoes with oil and seasonings evenly.
2. Spread sweet potato cubes into an even layer and roast them for 25
3. min. Remove them from the oven and bake for another 25 min until the sweet potatoes are tender.
4. Place the Tuscan kale into a large bowl and set it aside. In another small Next prepare your dressing: In a small bowl, add the olive oil, lime juice, grapefruit juice, apple cider vinegar, and whisk to combine.
5. Pour citrus dressing on top of the chopped kale and gently massage the kale with your hands until it begins to wilt.
6. Place the herb-roasted sweet potato on top of the kale, then add the cherry tomatoes and the chopped red onion. Serve and enjoy!

Nutrition: Carbohydrates: 22.5g; Protein: 3.6g; Fat: 10.6g; Saturated Fat: 1.5g; Cholesterol: 0mg; ; Sodium: 788mg; Potassium: 386mg; Sugar: 4.9g;

Warm Pumpkin Lentil Salad With Sun-Dried Tomatoes

Preparation: 10 min | Cooking: 0 min | Servings: 4

Ingredients

For the salad:

- 1 whole pumpkin, peeled and cubed
- 1 cup lentils
- 1 tablespoon olive oil
- 1 garlic clove, minced
- 2 teaspoons freshly chopped thyme leaves
- 1 teaspoon sea salt
- 1/2 teaspoon black pepper
- 1/2 cup sundried tomatoes, sliced
- 2 cups of spinach

For the dressing:

- 1 tablespoon balsamic vinegar
- 2 tablespoons olive oil
- 1 tablespoon lemon juice

Directions

1. Program your oven to 400°F, then place the pumpkin on a parchment-lined sheet pan. Drizzle the pumpkin with olive oil, garlic, thyme, salt, and pepper, then roast it for 25-30 min until they are fork-tender.

2. Use the directions on the back of the package to cook the lentils, drain them and place them in a large bowl.
3. Place lentils in a bowl, then add the pumpkin, sundried tomatoes, and spinach.
4. To make the dressing, add the balsamic vinegar, olive oil, and lemon juice to a small bowl and whisk to combine. Pour the sauce over the pumpkin and lentil salad. Serve and enjoy!

Nutrition: Carbohydrates: 37.7g; Protein: 14.5g; Fat: 11.4g; Saturated Fat: 1.7g; Cholesterol: 0mg; ; Sodium: 625mg; Potassium: 984mg; Sugar: 4.4g

Spicy Balsamic Vinegar Roasted Cauliflower Steaks

Preparation: 30 min | Cooking: 26 min | Servings: 4

Ingredients
- 1 teaspoon crushed red pepper flakes
- 2 tablespoons olive oil
- 2 tablespoons balsamic vinegar
- 2 cloves garlic, minced
- 1 teaspoon sea salt
- 1/2 teaspoon freshly ground black pepper
- 2 medium heads cauliflower

Directions
1. Program your oven to 450°F, then combine the crushed red pepper flakes, olive oil, balsamic vinegar, minced garlic, salt, and black pepper in a small bowl.
2. Brush 1/3 of the balsamic olive oil and red pepper marinade onto the bottom of a 3-quart square baking pan.
3. To make the cauliflower steaks, remove the cauliflower leaves, then careful y trim the stemmed end. Lay the head of the cauliflower core side down on a cutting board, then slice two 1-inch-thick slices from the middle of each cauliflower and place the cauliflower steaks in the prepared baking pan.
4. Give the steaks another coating of the balsamic and red pepper oil, then roast them for 15 min. Remove the spicy balsamic cauliflower steaks from the oven and gently flip each steak over. Brush with the remaining balsamic and red pepper oil and roast for an additional 12-15 min until the cauliflower is crispy and tender.
5. Serve and enjoy!

Nutrition: Calories: 78kcal| Carbohydrates: 3.5g; Protein: 1.2g; Fat: 7.1g; Saturated Fat: 1g; Cholesterol: 0mg; ; Sodium: 133mg; Potassium: 24mg; Sugar: 1.1g; Vitamin D: 0mcg; Calcium: 15mg; Iron: 0mg

Thai Coconut Chicken Curry

Preparation: 10 min | Cooking: 15 min | Servings: 4

Ingredients
- 2 tablespoons olive oil
- 1 1/2 lb. boneless skinless thighs thinly sliced into 1/2-inch pieces
- 2 cloves garlic, minced
- 1 orange bell pepper, sliced
- 1 green bell pepper, sliced
- 1 white onion, sliced
- 1 cup of broccoli florets
- 1 cup cauliflower florets
- 2 teaspoons yellow curry powder
- 2 tablespoons red curry paste
- 2 cups unsweetened coconut milk
- 1 teaspoon kosher salt
- 1/2 teaspoon black pepper
- 1 tablespoon freshly chopped lemongrass
- 1/4 cup cold water
- 2 tablespoons tapioca flour

Directions
1. Drizzle the olive oil over a large skillet on medium-high heat, then add the chicken thighs, garlic, onions, and peppers, and sauté for 7-8 min, stirring every so often until the chicken is almost cooked through.
2. Add the broccoli, cauliflower florets, and yellow curry powder, and stir the mixture for 1 minute.
3. Next, stir in the unsweetened coconut milk, red curry paste, salt, black pepper, and lemongrass, decrease the heat to medium-low and bring the curry to a low.
4. Whisk tapioca flour into the water until it is smooth and free of lumps.
5. Pour the tapioca slurry over the curry, stir to combine, and cook for 2-3
6. min until the curry thickens. Serve and enjoy!

Nutrition: Carbohydrates: 6.1g; Protein: 61.3g; Fat: 18.4g; Saturated Fat: 6g; Cholesterol: 225mg; ; Sodium: 1154mg; Potassium: 129mg; Sugar: 2.8g;

Asian Chicken Lettuce Wraps

Preparation: 10 min | Cooking: 15 min | Servings: 4

Ingredients
- 1 tablespoon olive oil

- 1 small onion, diced
- 1 cup thinly sliced carrots
- 1 teaspoon sea salt
- 3 teaspoons ginger, minced
- 2 cloves garlic, minced
- 1 lb chicken thighs, cut into chunks
- ¼ cup coconut aminos
- 2 teaspoons rice wine vinegar
- 1 teaspoon maple syrup
- 1 teaspoon fish sauce
- 1 head butter lettuce
- 2 freshly chopped scallions

Directions

1. Place the olive oil in a skillet on medium-high heat, then add the onions and carrots. Sprinkle over the sea salt and cook for 4-5 min until the onions have softened. Add the ginger and garlic, and cook for 1 more minute until it becomes aromatic.
2. Add the chopped chicken thighs, and cook for 8-10 min until the chicken is browned and thoroughly cooked.
3. Meantime, combine the coconut aminos, rice wine vinegar, maple syrup, and fish sauce in a small bowl and add it to the pan once the chicken is thoroughly cooked. Cook the chicken until the sauce reduces by half.
4. Top each lettuce wrap with the chicken filling, and top with the freshly chopped scallions. Serve and enjoy!

Nutrition; Carbohydrates: 11.5g; Protein: 34.2g; Fat: 12g; Saturated Fat: 2.8g; Cholesterol: 101mg; ; Sodium: 722mg; Potassium: 547mg; Sugar: 3.9g;

Roasted Butternut Squash Pumpkin Soup

Preparation: 15 min | Cooking: 40 min | Servings: 4

Ingredients

- 2 lbs. butternut squash, peeled chopped into 1-inch pieces
- 1 pumpkin, peeled and chopped
- 1 onion, roughly chopped
- 3 cloves of garlic, minced
- 3 tablespoon olive oil
- 3 sprigs fresh thyme, chopped
- 3 sprigs fresh rosemary chopped
- 1 teaspoon kosher salt

- 1 teaspoon black pepper
- 2 cup low-sodium vegetable broth
- 1/4 cup roasted pumpkin seeds

Directions

1. Program your oven to 400F, then place the butternut squash, pumpkin, onions, and garlic on a parchment-lined baking sheet. Add the olive oil thyme, rosemary, salt, and pepper and toss to coat the Ingredients: in the seasonings.
2. Roast the pumpkin and butternut squash for 25-35 min until it is slightly browned and tender. Remove the pumpkin mixture from the oven and allow it to cool slightly.
3. Add a third of the butternut squash mixture to a blender and add about 1/2 cup of the vegetable broth and blend until the soup is smooth. Pour the soup into a pot and repeat the process until all of the pumpkin and butternut squash mixture is gone.
4. Heat the roasted butternut squash and pumpkin soup for 4-5 min over medium-low heat until the soup is ful y heated. Serve and enjoy!

Nutrition: Carbohydrates: 25.4g; Protein: 3.9g; Fat: 10g; Saturated Fat: 1.6g; Cholesterol: 0mg; ; Sodium: 397mg; Potassium: 822mg; Sugar: 5g; Vitamin D: 0mcg; Calcium: 105mg; Iron: 3mg

Summer Gazpacho

Preparation: 25 min | Servings: 6

Ingredients

- 3 lbs. ripe red tomatoes, cored and roughly chopped
- 2 cups tomato juice
- 1 sweet yellow onion, roughly chopped into 1-inch pieces
- 1 large cucumber, peeled and seeded
- 1 medium red bell pepper
- ¼ cup fresh basil leaves
- 2 cloves garlic, minced
- 1 tablespoon fresh lemon juice
- ¼ cup extra-virgin olive oil
- 2 tablespoons red wine vinegar
- 1 teaspoon sea salt
- 1/2 teaspoon black pepper

Directions

1. Add the tomato juice, tomatoes, red pepper, cucumber, onion, basil, garlic, lemon juice, and olive oil to a blender and blend the vegetables into a smooth puree.

2. Add in the seasonings red wine vinegar, sea salt, black pepper, and blend for an additional 30 seconds.
3. Pour the gazpacho into an airtight container and chill it for 2 h.
4. Before serving, stir the gazpacho to combine the Ingredients:. Pour the gazpacho into six bowls or glasses and garnish with fresh basil, chopped cucumber, and tomatoes, or your preferred toppings.
5. Serve and enjoy!

Nutrition: Carbohydrates: 20g; Protein: 3.9g; Fat: 9.2g; Saturated Fat: 1.3g; Cholesterol: 0mg; ; Sodium: 547mg; Potassium: 960mg; Sugar: 13.5g;

Basil Garlic Zucchini Noodles

Preparation: 15 min | Cooking: 2 min | Servings: 4

Ingredients

- 1 tablespoon olive oil
- 4 spiralized zucchini
- 1 tablespoon freshly chopped basil leaves
- 2 cloves garlic, minced
- 2 tablespoon spinach basil pesto (from the Tomato Red Onion Olive Spinach Pesto Pizza)
- 1 teaspoon kosher salt
- 1/2 teaspoon black pepper
- 1/2 teaspoon red pepper flakes

Directions

1. Place the olive oil into a large skillet over medium-low heat; once it is hot, add the garlic and basil and cook for 1 minute until it is aromatic.
2. Add in the pesto and the zucchini noodles and sauté for 1-2 min until the zucchini noodles are tender.
3. Serve and enjoy!

Nutrition: Calories: 87kcal| Carbohydrates: 8.6g; Protein: 3.6g; Fat: 5.9g; Saturated Fat: 1.1g; Cholesterol: 1mg; ; Sodium: 624mg; Potassium: 530mg; Sugar: 3.4g;

Maple Glazed Salmon

Preparation: 5 min | Cooking: 25 min | Servings: 4

Ingredients

- 1/3 cup maple syrup
- 1/4 coconut aminos
- 2 tablespoon lemon juice
- 1 tablespoon orange juice
- 1 teaspoon red pepper flakes
- 3 tablespoon extra-virgin avocado oil, divided
- 4 6-oz. salmon fillets
- 1 teaspoon sea salt
- 1/2 teaspoon black pepper
- 3 cloves garlic, minced
- 1 teaspoon ginger, minced

Directions

1. Whisk the maple syrup, coconut aminos, lemon juice, orange juice and red pepper flakes in a medium bowl.
2. Pat your salmon filets dry using a paper towel. Place two tablespoons of avocado oil into a large skillet set over medium-high heat. Once the avocado oil is hot, place the salmon skin-side up into the pan and season with the sea salt and black pepper. Sear the salmon for 5-6 min until it is a rich golden brown color Cook salmon until deeply golden.
3. Turn the maple glazed salmon over and add the remaining tablespoon of avocado oil. Add minced garlic and ginger to the salmon and cook for 1
4. minute until aromatic. Add the maple syrup mixture, decrease the heat to medium-low and cook the salmon until sauce is reduced by 1/3. Brush the salmon with the maple sauce. Serve and enjoy!

Nutrition; Carbohydrates: 17.6g; Protein: 41.3g; Fat: 22.6g; Saturated Fat: 4.4g; Cholesterol: 36mg; ; Sodium: 583mg; Potassium: 72mg; Sugar: 12g;

Herb Roasted Vegetable Medley

Preparation: 5 min | Cooking: 25 min | Servings: 6

Ingredients

- 3 tablespoons olive oil
- 1 teaspoon freshly chopped basil leaves
- 1 teaspoon dried thyme
- 1 teaspoon fresh rosemary
- 2 cloves garlic, minced
- 1 teaspoon salt
- 1/2 teaspoon black pepper
- 1 red onion, sliced
- 1 red bell pepper, sliced
- 1 yellow bell pepper
- 1 green bell pepper
- 2 eggplant, sliced lengthwise and cut into 1/2-inch slices

- 4 medium zucchini, cut into 1/2-inch slices
- 1 large carrot, cut into 1/2-inch slices

Directions

1. Program the oven to 450F, then line a baking sheet with parchment paper. Add the olive oil, basil, thyme, rosemary, garlic, salt, and pepper to a large bowl and stir to combine.
2. Add the onion, bell peppers, eggplant, zucchini, and carrot and toss to coat the vegetables in the herbs and oil.
3. Arrange the seasoned vegetables on the prepared baking sheet and roast them in the oven for 30 min.
4. Serve and enjoy!

Nutrition; Carbohydrates: 20.4g; Protein: 4g; Fat: 7.7g; Saturated Fat: 1.1g; Cholesterol: 0mg; Sodium: 421mg; Potassium: 964mg; Sugar: 10.4g;

Quinoa Tabbouleh

Preparation: 15 min | Cooking: 15 min | Servings: 4

Ingredients

- 1 cup quinoa, rinsed wel
- 1/2 cup water
- 3/4 cup low-sodium vegetable broth
- 2 teaspoon kosher salt
- 4 tablespoon fresh lemon juice
- 2 garlic clove, minced
- 1/2 cup extra-virgin olive oil
- 1/2 teaspoon black pepper
- 1 large English cucumber cut into 1/4» pieces
- 1 cup cherry tomatoes halved
- 1/2 cup chopped flat-leaf parsley
- 1/4 cup chopped fresh mint
- 3 scallions, thinly sliced

Directions

1. Add the quinoa, 1 teaspoon salt, water, and vegetable broth to a medium saucepan over medium-high heat. Bring the quinoa to a boil, decrease the heat to medium-low, cover the pot with the lid, and cook the quinoa for 10 min until it is tender. Take the quinoa off of the stove and let it rest for 5 min covered before fluffing with a fork.
2. Meantime, place the lemon juice and garlic into a small bowl, whisk to combine, then slowly whisk in olive oil. Season the dressing with the remaining kosher salt and pepper.
3. Pour the quinoa onto a large sheet pan and spread it into an even layer to cool. Once the

quinoa is thoroughly cooled, place it into a large bowl and add about 1/3 cup of the tabouleh dressing and mix to combine.
4. Stir in the cucumber, tomatoes, parsley, mint, and scallions, stir to combine, and pour over the remaining dressing. Serve and enjoy!

Nutrition; Carbohydrates: 36.7g; Protein: 8.5g; Fat: 30.9g; Saturated Fat: 4.5g; Cholesterol: 0mg; ; Sodium: 179mg; Potassium: 477mg; Sugar: 4.2g; Vitamin D: 0mcg; Calcium: 79mg; Iron: 4mg

Stir - fry Bulgogi Eggplant

Preparation: 15 min | Cooking: 15 min | Servings: 4

Ingredients

- 1 small onion, minced
- 3 garlic cloves, minced
- 1 scallion, finely chopped
- 2 tablespoon agave nectar
- 1 tablespoon coconut aminos
- 2 teaspoon red pepper flakes
- 1 teaspoon toasted sesame oil
- 1 tablespoon kosher salt
- 1 lb. eggplants
- 1 tablespoon olive oil

Directions

1. Add the onion, garlic, scallion, agave nectar, coconut aminos, red pepper flakes, and sesame oil to a medium bowl and whisk to combine.
2. Slice the eggplants in half crosswise, then cut the eggplant into 1/4-inch strips. Cut the 1/2 inch strips into 1/2 inch wide strips, then place the eggplant in a large bowl with the kosher salt. Stir until every piece of eggplant is coated with salt crystals and let it sit for 15-20 min, stirring at 5-minute intervals.
3. Drain the liquid from the eggplant, then use your hands to squeeze the las much of the liquid from the eggplant as you can. Place the eggplant into a clean bowl, pour the marinade over the eggplant, and toss to combine. Cover the bulgogi eggplant with plastic wrap and place it in the refrigerator for 30
4. min.
5. Place the olive oil into a large skillet over high heat and add the eggplant in an even layer once it is hot. Sear the eggplant fr 2-3 min until the bottom is slightly brown. Flip the eggplant and let the other side cook for 2-3 min until it is browned. Lower the flame to medium-low and

cook the eggplant for 5-6 min, flipping every so often until the eggplant is thoroughly cooked.

6. Serve and enjoy!

Nutrition; Carbohydrates: 18.6g; Protein: 1.6g; Fat: 5g; Saturated Fat: 0.7g; Cholesterol: 0mg; ; Sodium: 1753mg; Potassium: 323mg; Sugar: 11.8g; Vitamin D: 0mcg; Calcium: 23mg; Iron: 0mg

Creamy Chickpea Curry

Preparation: 5 min | Cooking: 30 min | Servings: 4

Ingredients
- 2 tablespoon avocado oil
- 1 red onion, chopped
- 2 cloves garlic, crushed
- 1 large tomato, diced
- 1 small carrot thinly sliced into strips
- 1 tablespoon garam masala
- 2 tablespoon red curry paste
- 1/2 teaspoon ground cumin
- 1/2 teaspoon, ground coriander
- 1/4 teaspoon cayenne pepper
- 2 15oz. cans chickpeas, drained
- 1 14oz. can unsweetened coconut milk
- 1 teaspoon kosher salt
- 1/2 teaspoon black pepper

Directions
1. Place the olive oil into a heavy bottom saucepot. Once it is hot, add the red onions, garlic, garam masala, cumin, coriander powder, and cayenne pepper and sauté until the onions soften.
2. Add the chopped tomatoes and sauté for 3-4 min until the tomatoes have cooked down. Stir in the chickpeas, chopped carrots, and coconut milk, then bring the chickpea curry to a simmer. Let the curry simmer for 8-10
3. min, then add the salt and black pepper. Serve and enjoy!

Nutrition; Carbohydrates: 25.1g; Protein: 6.4g; Fat: 5.3g; Saturated Fat: 2.2g; Cholesterol: 0mg; ; Sodium: 1010mg; Potassium: 404mg; Sugar: 3.4g; Vitamin D: 0mcg; Calcium: 99mg; Iron: 2mg

Chicken Mushroom Stew

Preparation: 15 min | Cooking: 30 min | Servings: 4
Ingredients
- 1 lb. boneless skinless chicken thighs, cut into bite-sized pieces

- 2 tablespoons olive oil
- 1 medium onion, finely diced
- 4 cloves garlic, minced
- 1 tablespoon tapioca flour
- 1 tablespoon tomato paste
- 1 medium tomato, finely diced
- 1 teaspoon dried sage
- 1 tablespoon fresh rosemary, chopped
- 8 oz. cremini mushrooms
- 8 oz. button mushrooms
- 2 teaspoon coconut aminos
- 1 1/2 cup low-sodium vegetable broth
- 1 teaspoon salt
- 1/2 teaspoon black pepper
- 2 tablespoon freshly chopped parsley

Directions
1. Place the one tablespoon of olive oil into a large saucepan over medium-high heat, then add the chicken once it is hot. Liberal y sprinkle the chicken thighs with 1/2 teaspoon salt and 1/4 teaspoon pepper and cook for 5 min until the chicken's exterior is no longer pink. Remove the sauteed chicken from the saucepan and set it aside.
2. Place the remaining olive oil into the saucepan and add the onions and garlic along with the remaining salt and black pepper and cook for 3-4 min until the onions soften.
3. Stir in the tapioca flour and stir for a few min to remove the raw taste. Next, add the tomato paste, stir to combine, then add chopped tomatoes and cook for 2-3 min.
4. Add the dried sage and fresh rosemary and cook for a minute until it becomes fragrant. Add the cremini and button mushrooms, then cook for 3-4
5. min until the mushrooms have started to release moisture, then add the chicken, coconut aminos, and vegetable stock.
6. Let the chicken mushroom stew come to a boil and cook for 8-10
7. min. Garnish the chicken mushroom stew with the freshly chopped parsley.
8. Serve and enjoy!

Nutrition; Carbohydrates: 13.1g; Protein: 24g; Fat: 13.5g; Saturated Fat: 2.6g; Cholesterol: 80mg; ; Sodium: 976mg; Potassium: 624mg; Sugar: 4.5g; Vitamin D: 204mcg; Calcium: 44mg; Iron: 4mg

Ricotta pizza

Servings: 6 8 | Preparation: 10 min | Cooking: 15 min

Ingredients
- 1 pizza crust
- 8 oz. ricotta cheese
- 1 clove garlic
- 2 oz. parmesan cheese
- ½ lb. baby leaf greens
- 1 tablespoon olive oil

Directions
1. Spread tomato sauce on the pizza crust
2. Place all the toppings on the pizza crust
3. Bake the pizza at 425 F for 12 15 min
4. When ready remove pizza from the oven and serve

Salmon pizza

Servings: 6 8 | Preparation: 10 min | Cooking: 15 min

Ingredients
- 1 pizza crust
- 1 shallot
- 1 parmesan cheese
- ½ red onion
- 2 tablespoons olive oil
- ½ lb. smoked salmon
- ½ lemon

Directions
1. Spread tomato sauce on the pizza crust
2. Place all the toppings on the pizza crust
3. Bake the pizza at 425 F for 12 15 min
4. When ready remove pizza from the oven and serve

Green olive pizza

Servings: 6 8 | Preparation: 10 min | Cooking: 15 min

Ingredients
- 1 onion
- 1 pizza crust
- 1 cup green olives
- 1 clove garlic
- ½ lb. potatoes
- ½ lb. taleggio

Directions
1. Spread tomato sauce on the pizza crust
2. Place all the toppings on the pizza crust
3. Bake the pizza at 425 F for 12 15 min
4. When ready remove pizza from the oven and serve

Cauliflower pizza

Servings: 6-8 | Preparation: 10 min | Cooking: 15 min

Ingredients
- 1 pizza crust
- 2 oz. parmesan cheese
- 1 tablespoon olive oil
- 4 5 basil leaves
- 1 cup mozzarella cheese
- 1 cup cauliflower

Directions
1. Spread tomato sauce on the pizza crust
2. Place all the toppings on the pizza crust
3. Bake the pizza at 425 F for 12 15 min
4. When ready remove pizza from the oven and serve

Artichoke and spinach pizza

Servings: 6-8 | Preparation: 10 min | Cooking: 15 min

Ingredients
- 1 pizza crust
- 1 garlic clove
- ½ lb. spinach
- ½ lb. soft cheese
- 2 oz. artichoke hearts
- 1 cup mozzarella cheese
- 1 tablespoon olive oil

Directions
1. Spread tomato sauce on the pizza crust
2. Place all the toppings on the pizza crust
3. Bake the pizza at 425 F for 12 15 min
4. When ready remove pizza from the oven and serve

Mint pizza

Servings: 6-8 | Preparation: 10 min | Cooking: 15 min

Ingredients
- 1 pizza crust
- 1 olive oil
- 1 garlic clove
- 1 cup mozzarella cheese
- 2 oz. mint
- 2 courgettes

Directions
1. Spread tomato sauce on the pizza crust
2. Place all the toppings on the pizza crust
3. Bake the pizza at 425 F for 12 15 min

4. When ready remove pizza from the oven and serve

Sausage pizza

Servings: 6-8 | Preparation: 10 min | Cooking: 15 min

Ingredients

- 2 pork sausages
- 1 tablespoon olive oil
- 2 garlic cloves
- 1 tsp fennel seeds
- ½ lb. ricotta
- 1 cup mozzarella cheese
- 1 oz. parmesan cheese
- 1 pizza crust

Directions

1. Spread tomato sauce on the pizza crust
2. Place all the toppings on the pizza crust
3. Bake the pizza at 425 F for 12 15 min
4. When ready remove pizza from the oven and serve

Healty pizza

Servings: 6-8 | Preparation: 10 min | Cooking: 15 min

Ingredients

- 1 pizza crust
- 1 tablespoon olive oil
- 1 garlic clove
- 1 cup tomatoes
- 1 cup mozzarella cheese
- 1 carrot
- 1 cucumber

Directions

1. Spread tomato sauce on the pizza crust
2. Place all the toppings on the pizza crust
3. Bake the pizza at 425 F for 12 15 min
4. When ready remove pizza from the oven and serve

Casserole pizza

Servings: 6-8 | Preparation: 10 min | Cooking: 15 min

Ingredients

- 1 pizza crust
- ½ cup tomato sauce
- ¼ black pepper
- 1 cup zucchini slices

- 1 cup mozzarella cheese
- 1 cup olives

Directions

1. Spread tomato sauce on the pizza crust
2. Place all the toppings on the pizza crust
3. Bake the pizza at 425 F for 12 15 min
4. When ready remove pizza from the oven and serve

Whole 30 Veggie-Packed Breakfast Frittata

Ingredients

- 2 Tbsp extra-virgin olive oil
- 1 small green bell pepper, diced
- 1 small red bell pepper, diced
- ½ red onion, thinly sliced
- 2 cups packed baby spinach
- ¼ cup sun-dried tomatoes (not packed in oil), chopped
- 1 clove garlic, sliced
- 10 large eggs, beaten
- Kosher salt and freshly ground black pepper
- Hot sauce, for serving

Directions

1. Preheat the oven to 375°F.
2. Heat the oil in a medium oven-safe nonstick skillet over medium-high heat. Add the bell peppers and onion and cook, stirring occasionally, until softened, 6 to 7 min. Add the spinach, sun-dried tomatoes and garlic and cook, stirring frequently, until the spinach is just wilted and still vibrant green, about 1 minute.
3. Reduce the heat to low and add the eggs, 1 teaspoon salt and a few grinds of black pepper. Stir gently to distribute the vegetables. Bake until the eggs are set, 13 to 15 min.
4. Let stand for 5 min, then slice into 6 pieces. Serve with hot sauce. Refrigerate in an airtight container for up to 1 week.

Paleo Granola

Preparation: 5 min | Cooking: 7 min | Servings: 4

Ingredients

- 1/2 cup hazelnuts, roughly chopped
- 1/2 cup walnuts, roughly chopped
- 1/2 cup unsalted sunflower seeds
- 3 Tbsp coconut oil, very soft or melted

- 1 to 2 Tbsp maple syrup, less or more for desired sweetness level
- 2 tsp ground cinnamon
- 1 cup unsweetened toasted coconut chips or pieces (not shredded)
- 1/2 cup raisins
- 1/4 cup cacao nibs

Directions

1. Preheat the oven to 350°F. Line a large rimmed baking sheet with parchment paper.
2. Scatter hazelnuts, walnuts and sunflower seeds on prepared baking sheet. Toss nut and seed mixture with coconut oil, maple syrup and cinnamon. Bake for 5 to 7 min, or until lightly browned (watch closely to be careful not to burn the mixture).
3. Remove nut and seed mixture from oven. Mix in coconut chips, raisins and cacao nibs. Cool before serving, if desired.
4. Serve granola in a bowl with dairy-free milk of choice and fresh fruit.
5. For storing, cool granola completely and keep in airtight jar at room temperature for up to one month.

Egg Baked In Acorn Squash

Ingredients

- 1 acorn squash
- ½ tsp kosher salt
- ½ tsp chili powder
- ¼ tsp freshly ground black pepper
- 2 Tbsp olive oil
- 4 large eggs
- ¼ cup crumbled queso fresco
- 2 Tbsp minced fresh cilantro
- Hot sauce, if desired

Directions

1. Preheat the oven to 425°F. Line a baking sheet with parchment paper.
2. Thoroughly wash and dry the acorn squash. Use a sharp knife to make a few slits in the squash. Microwave for 2 min, then let stand until cool to the touch. Slice off the stem and bottom of the squash. Cut the squash into 4 slices, each about 1/2 to 3/4 inch thick. Remove the seeds with a spoon, creating a hole in each slice (you may need to scoop out a bit of the squash to create the hole). Put the squash slices on the prepared baking sheet.
3. In a small dish, mix the salt, chili powder and pepper. Use a pastry brush to brush both sides of the squash slices with oil, then sprinkle with the salt mixture (reserve a small amount of seasoning for the eggs). Bake for 25 min.
4. Remove the squash from the oven and crack an egg into the hole of each slice. Sprinkle with the reserved salt mixture. Return to the oven and bake until the whites are set and the yolks are the desired doneness, about 10 min. Serve sprinkled with queso fresco, cilantro and hot sauce if desired.

Sautéed collard green omelet

Ingredients

- 3 Tbsp unsalted butter, cut into tablespoons
- 1/2-inch piece American pancetta, cut into small dice, or 4 oz double smoked bacon, cut into small dice
- 1 lb(s) baby hearty greens (collard greens, mustard greens, dandelion greens, beet greens), large stems removed if needed
- ¼ cup vegetable stock, chicken stock or water, more if needed
- Few dashes chipotle hot sauce
- Splash of chardonnay vinegar
- Kosher salt and freshly ground black pepper
- 4 large eggs
- Chopped fresh flat-leaf parsley

Directions

1. Melt 1 tablespoon butter in a 10-inch nonstick pan over medium heat. Add the pancetta and cook until golden brown and crispy and the fat has rendered, about 10 min. Add the greens, stock, hot sauce vinegar. Cook until the greens are just wilted, about 5 min. Season with salt and pepper and add another tablespoon of stock if the greens dry out before they are soft.
2. In a small nonstick pan over medium heat, add the remaining 2 tablespoons butter and cook until the butter begins to shimmer.
3. Whisk the eggs in a bowl until light and fluffy and sprinkle with salt and pepper. Pour the eggs into the pan and let the eggs cook until the bottom starts to set, up to a minute.
4. With a heat-resistant rubber spatula, gently push one edge of the egg into the center of the pan while tilting the pan to allow the liquid egg to flow in underneath. Repeat with the other edges, until there's no liquid left.
5. Place the greens down the center of the omelet and roll into a cylinder. Remove to a platter, season the top with salt and pepper and top with the parsley.

Sweet Potato Toast

Ingredients

Fried Egg & Avocado Sweet Potato Toast:

- 2 sweet potato slices
- 1/2 avocado
- Pinch of sea salt and pepper
- 1 tsp extra virgin olive oil
- 1/4 cup sunflower sprouts or pea shoots
- 2 eggs
- 1 Tbsp butter

Almond Butter, Apple & Banana Sweet Potato Toast:

- 2 sweet potato slices
- 2 Tbsp crunchy almond butter
- 1/4 granny smith apple, thinly sliced
- 1/3 banana, sliced
- 1 tsp honey
- 1/2 tsp ground cinnamon
- 1 tsp hemp seeds

Directions

Fried Egg & Avocado Sweet Potato Toast:

1. Cut a sweet potato lengthwise into slices that are 1/4-inch thick.
2. Place 2 of these sweet potato slices in the toaster and toast for 10 min, flipping them after 5 min.
3. Meanwhile, cook 2 over-easy eggs. Heat 1 Tbsp of butter over medium-high and swirl around to coat the pan. Crack each egg into a small dish, like a ramekin, and pour into the pan. Flip the eggs after about 15-20 sec and then cook for another 15-20 sec. Remove the eggs and place on a separate plate.
4. Once the sweet potato slices are toasted, fan the avocado slices over them and place the over easy eggs on top.
5. Sprinkle sea salt and pepper over. Finish with a drizzle of extra virgin olive oil and pea shoot sprouts.

Almond Butter, Apple & Banana Sweet Potato Toast:

6. Cut a sweet potato lengthwise into slices that are 1/4-inch thick.
7. Place 2 of these sweet potato slices in the toaster and toast for 10 min, flipping them after 5 min.
8. Smear crunchy almond butter over the toast.
9. Fan a granny smith apple over one slice and bananas over the other.
10. Drizzle honey on top and sprinkle with cinnamon and hemp seeds.

Toasted coconut chia pudding

Ingredients

For the Chia Pudding:

- 1 cup unsweetened plain almond milk
- 1 cup full-fat coconut milk (thick, canned)
- 2 Tbsp maple syrup
- 1 tsp lime juice
- 1 tsp vanilla extract
- 1 pinch sea salt
- ⅓ cup chia seeds

For Serving

- ⅓ cup unsweetened coconut flakes or shredded coconut
- 2 cups cubed tropical fruit (dragonfruit, mango, pineapple, etc.)

Directions

For the Chia Pudding:

- In a large bowl, whisk together all pudding ingredients except chia seeds. Whisk in chia seeds; continue to whisk for 1 minute. Rest at room temperature for 20 min, whisking every so often. Cover and chill for at least 3 h (overnight best).
- To a large non-stick skillet, add coconut, toasting over medium for 1 to 2 min until light brown; immediately transfer to a plate.

For Serving:

- Stir pudding vigorously. To bowls, add chilled pudding; top with fruit and toasted coconut. Serve.

Immune-Boosting Bone Broth, Chicken and Vegetable Soup

Ingredients

- 1 whole chicken (2-3 lbs) or 2-3 lbs of chicken bones
- 1 yellow onion, sliced
- 1 bulb garlic (about 6 cloves)
- 3 carrots, chopped
- 2 celery stalks, chopped
- 1 ½ cups shiitake mushrooms, sliced (about 12 mushrooms)
- 1 inch fresh ginger, peeled and roughly chopped
- 1 inch fresh turmeric, peeled and roughly chopped (or 2 tsp dried turmeric)
- 1 bunch of parsley

- 1 tsp sea salt
- ½ tsp peppercorns
- 10 cups water
- Few handfuls baby spinach (optional)

Directions

1. Place all the ingredients, except for the water, in a large pot.
2. Then, pour the water in the pot until almost everything is submerged, but do not overflow. You will likely use around 10 cups of water.
3. Bring to a boil, then cover the pot and simmer.
4. After about half an hour, skim the top of the soup with a wide slotted spoon to discard the scum that's risen to the top.
5. Allow to simmer on low heat for minimum 2 hours and up to 6 hours.
6. Place the soup through a sieve to catch the veggies and chicken (you can use some of the extra chicken meat to make other delicious dishes). Place the sieve over top of another large pot for the broth to go into.
7. You can serve the soup as this nutrient-rich broth. Or, you can add the carrots, mushrooms and chicken meat back into the broth. You can also stir in some baby spinach if you'd like.
8. Store the soup in airtight jars, containers or sealed bags. Freeze them in individual portion sizes.

Roasted Cauliflower Steaks with Golden Raisins and Pine Nuts

Ingredients

- 2 heads cauliflower, cut vertically into 1/2 inch - thick steaks (4 to 6 steaks total)
- Extra-virgin olive oil, for drizzling
- Kosher salt and freshly ground black pepper
- 2 Tbsp pine nuts
- ¼ cup golden raisins
- 1 Tbsp butter
- ¼ cup fresh parsley leaves

Directions

1. Preheat the oven to 425°F.
2. Place the cauliflower steaks on a baking sheet. Drizzle with olive oil and sprinkle with salt and pepper on both sides. Transfer to the oven and bake until golden brown, 20 to 25 min, flipping after the first 10 min.
3. Meanwhile, add the pine nuts to a dry medium saute pan and toast over medium heat until brown, about 3 min. Add the raisins and the butter, and season with salt. Cook until the butter

has melted and coats the pine nuts and raisins. Off the heat, stir in the parsley.
4. Transfer the roasted cauliflower to a serving platter. Pour the pine nut-raisin mixture over the top.

Pan-seared salmon with kale and apple salad

Ingredients

- 4 5-oz center-cut salmon fillets (about 1" thick)
- 3 Tbsp fresh lemon juice
- 3 Tbsp olive oil
- Kosher salt
- 1 bunch kale, ribs removed, leaves very thinly sliced (about 6 cups)
- ¼ cup dates
- 1 Honeycrisp apple
- ¼ cup finely grated pecorino
- 3 Tbsp toasted slivered almonds
- Freshly ground black pepper
- 4 whole wheat dinner rolls

Directions

1. Bring the salmon to room temperature 10 min before cooking.
2. Meanwhile, whisk together the lemon juice, 2 tablespoons of the olive oil and 1/4 teaspoon salt in a large bowl. Add the kale, toss to coat and let stand 10 min.
3. While the kale stands, cut the dates into thin slivers and the apple into matchsticks. Add the dates, apples, cheese and almonds to the kale. Season with pepper, toss well and set aside.
4. Sprinkle the salmon all over with 1/2 teaspoon salt and some pepper. Heat the remaining 1 tablespoon oil in a large nonstick skillet over medium-low heat. Raise the heat to medium-high. Place the salmon, skin-side up in the pan. Cook until golden brown on one side, about 4 min. Turn the fish over with a spatula, and cook until it feels firm to the touch, about 3 min more.
5. Divide the salmon, salad and rolls evenly among four plates.

Pegan "Tuna" Salad Sandwich

Ingredients

- 1 cup walnuts (soaked for minimum 15 min up to overnight)
- 1/2 cup sunflower seeds (soaked for minimum 15 min up to overnight)

- 1/2 cup pumpkin seeds (soaked for minimum 15 min up to overnight)
- ⅓ cup vegan mayo
- 1 cup cucumber, diced
- 1 cup celery, diced
- ¼ cup green onions, chopped finely
- 2 tsp dulse or kelp flakes
- 2 tsp fresh dill, chopped finely
- 1/2 lemon, juiced
- ½ tsp sea salt
- 4 slices or 1 cup vegan shredded cheese (like Daiya, Chao or Earth Island)
- 8 slices of your favourite bread or sweet potato "toast"

Directions

1. Soak walnuts, sunflower seeds and pumpkin seeds in water, then drain and rinse.
2. Pulse the walnuts, sunflower seeds and pumpkin seeds in a food processor until smooth but partially crumbled (don't over-blend into a paste).
3. Place the nut mixture into a bowl, stir in the mayo and, once combined, add in the rest of the ingredients.
4. Scoop the tuna onto the bread, layer with vegan cheese, then add the second slice of bread on top.
5. If you have a sandwich maker, oil it, then pop the sammie in there, close the lid and let it heat for about 5-7 min until the cheese melts.
6. Alternatively, place a skillet on medium-low heat, oil it, then add your sandwich and place a small lid over the sandwich to press it down. Let the sandwich heat for about 4 min, then flip it over for another few min until the cheese melts.
7. The paleo bread and sweet potato "toast" will be more delicate than the vegan one, so you may want to use the skillet method instead.

Garden Egg Salad

Ingredients

- 6 large eggs
- ½ cup low-fat mayonnaise
- 2 Tbsp whole-grain mustard
- Kosher salt and freshly ground black pepper
- 2 scallions (white and green), thinly sliced
- 1 rib celery, minced, scant 1/2 cup
- 2 radishes, grated on the large holes of a box grater
- 8 Romaine lettuce leaves
- 1 cup pea or other sprouts

Directions

1. Put the eggs in a saucepan with enough cold water to cover. Bring to a boil, cover, and remove from the heat. Set aside for 12 min. Drain the eggs and roll them between your palm and the counter to crack the shell, then peel under cool running water.
2. Dice the eggs. Combine the eggs with mayonnaise, mustard and season with the salt and pepper. Stir in the scallions, celery, and radish.
3. Divide the egg salad among the lettuce leaves, top with the sprouts and roll up. Serve 2 rolls per serving.

Chicken Fennel Bake

Ingredients

- 2 fennel bulbs, trimmed
- Kosher salt and freshly ground black pepper
- 5 lemons
- ¼ cup extra-virgin olive oil
- 1 lb(s) baby potatoes
- 1 cup baby carrots
- 6 chicken thighs

Directions

1. Preheat the oven to 375°F. Line a baking sheet with foil.
2. Cut the fennel into thick slices. Shingle them onto the center of the baking sheet and season with salt and pepper.
3. Zest 2 of the lemons and set aside, then juice these lemons into a medium bowl. Whisk the olive oil into the lemon juice and season with salt and pepper. Halve the remaining 3 lemons and add them to the bowl along with the potatoes and carrots. Toss to coat.
4. Spread the vegetables and lemon halves around the outside of the baking sheet. Put the chicken thighs in the same bowl along with the reserved lemon zest and more salt and pepper. Toss to coat.
5. Put the chicken on top of the fennel skin-side up, leaving a little space between pieces.
6. Bake, stirring the potatoes and carrots halfway through, until the chicken is cooked through and the vegetables are tender, 50 min to 1 h. Serve the chicken with the vegetables and roasted lemon halves.

Zucchini "Hash Browns" And Eggs

Ingredients

- 1 ½ Tbsp extra-virgin olive oil
- 1 medium onion, diced
- 2 tsp finely chopped sage
- 1 clove garlic, minced
- 1 small jalapeno pepper, minced with some seeds
- 3 large zucchini or yellow summer squash, cut into 1/2-inch pieces
- 2 tsp white wine vinegar
- Kosher salt and freshly ground black pepper
- ¼ cup chopped roasted red pepper
- ¼ cup chopped fresh parsley or cilantro
- 8 large eggs

Directions

1. Heat the oil in a large nonstick skillet over medium-high heat. Add the onions and cook, stirring, until soft and lightly browned, about 6 min. Add the sage, garlic and jalapenos and cook, stirring, until fragrant, about 30 seconds.
2. Add the squash, vinegar, 3/4 teaspoon salt and a few grinds of pepper and stir to combine. Cover and cook, stirring occasionally, until the squash begins to soften, 6 to 8 min. Uncover and add the red pepper and half of the parsley.
3. Cook until the squash is completely soft and lightly brown, 6 to 8 min more. Remove from the heat.
4. Make 8 small indentations in the squash with a measuring cup or the back of a ladle. Crack the eggs into the indentations and sprinkle with salt and pepper. Return the pan to medium heat, cover and cook until the egg whites are set and the yolks are still runny, about 4 min. Sprinkle with the remaining parsley and serve.

Vegetarian Spinach-Walnut Pate

Ingredients

- 1 ½ lb(s) fresh spinach (not baby), large stems removed
- ¾ cup walnuts, plus more, chopped, for garnish
- ½ cup loosely packed fresh cilantro leaves
- ¼ cup loosely packed fresh tarragon leaves
- ¼ cup loosely packed fresh dill fronds
- 2 Tbsp white wine vinegar
- 3 scallions, roughly chopped
- 2 small cloves garlic, smashed
- Kosher salt
- ¼ tsp ground coriander
- Pinch cayenne pepper
- 2 Tbsp pomegranate seeds
- Crackers or crudites, for serving

Directions

1. Bring a large pot of water to a boil. Line a 5-inch ramekin with plastic wrap, leaving at least a 2-inch overhang; smooth out the plastic in the ramekin as much as possible.
2. Add the spinach to the pot of water, stir to submerge and cook until wilted and tender, about 2 min. Drain and let cool completely. Squeeze every last drop of water out of the spinach, then finely chop. Transfer to a medium bowl.
3. Process the walnuts, 1/3 cup warm water, cilantro, tarragon, dill, vinegar, scallions, garlic, 1 1/4 teaspoons salt, coriander and cayenne in a food processor until the mixture is the consistency of mayonnaise.
4. Add the walnut-herb mixture to the bowl with the spinach, and stir to combine thoroughly. Spoon into the prepared ramekin, and pat down with the back of the spoon to compact. Cover with the plastic overhang, and refrigerate at least 4 hours up to overnight.
5. To serve, unwrap and invert onto a serving platter. Garnish with pomegranate seeds and chopped walnuts. Serve with crackers or crudites.

Grilled Chicken Breasts With Shiitake Mushroom Vinaigrette

Ingredients

- 5 large shiitake mushrooms, stems removed
- 6 Tbsp canola oil
- Salt and freshly ground black pepper
- 1 tsp whole-grain mustard
- 3 Tbsp balsamic vinegar
- 3 Tbsp extra-virgin olive oil
- 4 Tbsp finely chopped flat-leaf parsley, plus torn leaves for garnish
- 4 bone-in, skin on chicken breasts (about 8 oz each)

Directions

1. Heat the grill to high.
2. Brush both sides of the mushroom caps with 4 tablespoons of the canola oil and season with salt and pepper. Place on the grill, cap side down and grill until golden brown and slightly charred, 4 to 5 min. Turn the mushrooms over and continue cooking until just cooked through, 3 to 4 min longer. Remove from the grill and coarsely chop.

3. Whisk together the shallots, vinegar, extra virgin olive oil and parsley in a medium bowl until combined and season with salt and pepper. Add the mushrooms and stir to coat. Let sit at room temperature for at least 15 min before serving.
4. Brush both sides of the chicken with the remaining canola oil and season with salt and pepper. Place on the grill, skin side down and grill until golden brown, 4 to 5 min. Flip over, reduce the heat of the grill to medium, close the cover and continue grilling until just cooked through, about 7 min longer. Remove chicken from the grill and let rest 5 min before serving. Serve 1 breast per person topped with some of the shiitake vinaigrette. Garnish with parsley leaves.

Salad Nicoise With Seared Tuna

Ingredients

Vinaigrette:

- 2 cloves garlic, minced
- 1 tsp Dijon mustard
- 3 Tbsp red wine vinegar
- ½ lemon, juiced
- 2 Tbsp chopped flat-leaf parsley
- 2 Tbsp minced tarragon
- Sea salt and freshly ground black pepper
- ½ cup extra-virgin olive oil

Salad:

- 1 lb(s) red new potatoes, scrubbed and halved
- 8 large eggs
- ½ lb(s) haricots verts or French green beans, stems trimmed
- 2 lb(s) sushi-quality tuna
- 2 Tbsp extra-virgin olive oil
- Sea salt and freshly ground black pepper
- 1 pt teardrop or cherry tomatoes, halved
- 1 cup nicoise olives
- 16 anchovy fillets
- 16 caper berries with stems
- ½ bunch fresh chives, snipped in 1/2

Directions

Vinaigrette:

1. Combine all of the vinaigrette ingredients in a mason jar. Screw the cap on the jar and shake the vinaigrette vigorously to emulsify. Set the dressing aside while preparing the salad so the flavors can marry.

Salad:

2. Cooking the potatoes, eggs, and green beans in the same pot cuts down on prep time and clean up. To do this, put the potatoes in a large saucepan, add water to cover and a nice pinch of salt; bring to a boil over medium heat.
3. Simmer the potatoes for 12 min to give them a head start, and then add the eggs. Place a steamer basket or colander on top of the simmering water. Put the green beans in the steamer and cover with a lid.
4. Steam the beans for 5 min until crisp-tender while continuing to cook the potatoes until fork tender. Drain out the water and put the potatoes, eggs, and green beans in a colander; rinse briefly under cold water.
5. Peel the shells off the eggs and cut them in 1/2 lengthwise.
6. Place a large skillet over medium-high heat. Rub the tuna on all sides with olive oil, and a bit of the vinaigrette; season with a fair amount of salt and pepper.
7. Lay the tuna in the hot pan and sear for approximately 2 min on each side; as the tuna cooks, the red meat will become whiter. Transfer the tuna to a cutting board and slice.

To assemble the salad:

8. Combine the potatoes, green beans, tomatoes, olives, anchovies, capers, and chives in a large mixing bowl.
9. Take the vinaigrette and give it another good shake to recombine. Drizzle the salad with enough vinaigrette to fully moisten and toss gently to coat; season with salt and pepper. Take care not to mush up the ingredients - the important thing about salad nicoise is that it is arranged nicely on a platter with all the elements keeping their individual integrity.
10. Put the tossed salad down the center of a serving platter and lay the seared tuna attractively across the top and the eggs around the rim. Drizzle with the remaining vinaigrette and serve.

Paleo Turkey Stuffed Peppers

Ingredients

- 1 Tbsp (15 mL) olive oil
- 1 lb(s) (450 g) ground turkey
- 3 cups (700 mL) spinach
- 2 cups (500 mL) crushed tomatoes
- 2 cloves garlic, minced
- 1 Tbsp (15 mL) chopped fresh parsley

- 1 Tbsp (15 mL) chopped fresh basil
- 1 tsp (5 mL) dried oregano
- 1 tsp (5 mL) sea salt
- 3 red bell peppers, stems removed, halved and seeded

Directions

1. In large skillet over medium heat, heat oil. Add turkey; sauté no longer pink inside. Add spinach, stirring until wilted
2. Stir in tomatoes, garlic, parsley, basil, oregano and salt. Simmer for 20 min.
3. Place on rimmed baking sheet. Divide turkey mixture evenly among pepper halves. Cook in 425°F (220ºC) oven for 25 min, or until meat mixture has browned and peppers are tender.

Pork Chops Alla Pizzaiola

Ingredients

- 2 Tbsp olive oil
- 2 (1-inch thick) bone-in pork loin center-cut chops (about 12 oz each)
- Salt and freshly ground black pepper
- 1 small onion, thinly sliced
- 1 (15-oz) can diced tomatoes, in juice
- 1 tsp herbes de provence
- ¼ tsp dried red pepper flakes, or more to taste
- 1 Tbsp chopped fresh Italian parsley leaves

Directions

1. Heat the oil in a heavy large skillet over medium heat. Sprinkle the pork chops with salt and pepper. Add the pork chops to the skillet and cook until they are brown and an instant-read meat thermometer inserted horizontally into the pork registers 160ºF, about 3 min per side. Transfer the pork chops to a plate and tent with foil to keep them warm.
2. Add the onion to the same skillet and saute over medium heat until crisp-tender, about 4 min. Add the tomatoes with their juices, herbes de Provence, and 1/4 teaspoon red pepper flakes. Cover and simmer until the flavors blend and the juices thicken slightly, stirring occasionally, about 15 min. Season the sauce, to taste, with salt and more red pepper flakes. Return the pork chops and any accumulated juices from the plate to the skillet and turn the pork chops to coat with the sauce.
3. Place 1 pork chop on each plate. Spoon the sauce over the pork chops. Sprinkle with the parsley and serve.

Zucchini Noodles With Everything Pesto And Fried Eggs

Ingredients

Everything Pesto:

- ¼ cup + 2 Tbsp pine nuts, toasted
- 1 cup lightly packed fresh herbs of choice (I used basil)
- 2 scallions, trimmed and roughly chopped
- 1 clove garlic, crushed
- ¼ tsp flaky sea salt, or more to taste
- 3 Tbsp extra-virgin olive oil
- 1 tsp fresh lime or lemon juice

Squash Noodles and Fried Eggs:

- 2 - 3 lb(s) zucchini, summer squash or cousa squash, julienned or spiralized (I used zucchini)
- ½ tsp flaky sea salt, or more to taste
- 3 tsp ghee or extra-virgin olive oil
- Freshly ground black pepper
- 2 large eggs

Directions

Everything Pesto:

1. Pulse 1/4 cup of the pine nuts, the herbs, scallion, garlic and salt in a food processor until coarsely chopped. Add in the olive oil and lime juice and pulse again, scraping down the sides of the bowl as needed. Taste the pesto and add more salt if desired.

Squash Noodles and Fried Eggs:

2. Put the squash in colander lined with paper towels. Toss with 1/2 tsp of salt and set aside for a few min so the salt can draw some of the moisture out of the squash.
3. Heat 1 tsp of the ghee in a large skillet with a lid over over medium-high heat . Add the squash noodles and cook, tossing frequently, until cooked to your liking. Take it off the heat and add the pesto. Toss to combine, and season with salt and pepper to taste. Cover the skillet to leave the noodles hot while you make the eggs.
4. Heat the remaining 2 tsps of ghee in a medium-sized skillet over medium heat, and fry the eggs until cooked to your liking.
5. Divide the noodles between 2 plates. Top each pile of noodles with a fried egg and 1 Tablespoon of pine nuts. Serve immediately.

Cucumber Avocado Watermelon Salad

Ingredients

- 2 1/2 cups uniformly cubed watermelon
- 1 small english cucumber, thinly sliced with a mandoline (I used this type of cucumber because it has fewer seeds and is less watery)
- 1 ripe avocado, scooped into small balls with a melon baller
- 3 tablespoons extra virgin olive oil
- juice from one lime (or lemon, but I prefer lime)
- 2 tablespoons freshly chopped basil
- salt to taste
- freshly ground black pepper

Directions

1. Prepare watermelon, cucumber, and avocado and place in a large bowl. Squeeze lime over the top and gently stir.
2. Then add olive oil, basil, salt and pepper. Gently stir and pour onto on a large plate.
3. Finish with a few cracks of black pepper and torn pieces of basil to garnish.

Roasted vegetable & lentil salad with coriander yoghurt dressing

Ingredients

- 2 small sweet potatoes peeled & cut into 1 inch cubes
- 100 g (1/2 pack) chestnut mushrooms quartered
- 10 cherry / plum tomatoes
- 1 yellow pepper sliced into 1/2 inch strips
- 1/2 head broccoli cut into florets
- 1/2 tbsp olive oil
- 1 tsp chilli flakes
- Sea salt & freshly ground black pepper
- 100 g (1/2 cup) dry puy lentils / lentilles vertes

FOR THE DRESSING:

- 15 g (1/2 bunch) fresh coriander
- 2 tbsp natural yoghurt
- 1 clove garlic peeled
- Juice of 1/2 a lemon
- Pinch of sea salt

TO SERVE:

- 60 g (1 bag) wild rocket
- 15 g (1/2 bunch) corriander leaves only
- 1 red chilli thinly sliced

Directions

1. Preheat the oven to 170°c fan/190°c/375°f.
2. Line a baking tray with parchment paper and spread over the sweet potato. Roast for 10 min.
3. Remove the tray from the oven and add the mushrooms, tomatoes, pepper and broccoli to the sweet potato. Drizzle over the oil, chilli flakes and a generous pinch of salt and pepper before giving everything a mix. Return to the oven for another 30-35 min until the vegetables are soft and cooked through.
4. Meanwhile place the lentils in a medium sauce pan and cover with cold water. Bring the pan to boil before reducing the heat and simmering gently for 18-20 min until tender. Drain and set aside.
5. To make the dressing place the coriander, yoghurt, garlic, lemon juice and salt into a blender / food processor. Blend until smooth. Taste and adjust the seasoning if needed.
6. To assemble, mix the rocket, lentils and 2/3rds of the roasted vegetables together in a large bowl. Transfer onto a serving platter and top with the remaining roasted veg, coriander and chilli slices. Liberally drizzle over the dressing and serve!

Vegan/Paleo Cauliflower Walnut Taco Meat

Ingredients

TACO MEAT:

- 1 cup raw walnuts (sub 2/3 C sunflower or pumpkin seeds)
- 12 ounces 1" cauliflower florets (I buy bagged from Trader Joe's; equals 4 1/2 cups)
- 8-10 ounces sliced baby bella or button mushrooms
- 2 teaspoons olive oil or avocado oil
- 2 tablespoons nutritional yeast
- For Serving: tortillas or shells, guac, salsa, avocado, clantro, shredded lettuce

TACO SPICE MIXTURE:

- 2 1/2 teaspoons smoked paprika
- 2 teaspoons chili powder
- 1 teaspoon garlic powder
- 1 1/2 teaspoons onion powder
- 3/4 teaspoon cumin
- 1 teaspoon dried oregano
- 1 teaspoon sea salt, plus more to taste
- 1/4 teaspoon black pepper

- 1 tablespoon coconut sugar

Directions:

1. Preheat oven to 350 degrees F and add walnuts to a baking sheet (can be unlined). Roast walnuts until slightly darkened in color and fragrant, approximately 10 min (start checking at 8).
2. Remove walnuts and place in a heatproof bowl and set aside. Turn oven up to 400 degrees. Now line baking sheet with parchment paper. Add cauliflower and mushrooms to the baking sheet. Drizzle oil over vegetables and toss gently to coat.
3. Roast veggies for 20 min, until the cauliflower florets have golden brown edges. While roasting, make Taco Spice Mixture. Add 1/4 cup of spice mixture, walnuts and nutritional yeast to a food processor. Pulse just 1-2x to incorporate.
4. When veggies have finished roasting, allow to cool until they are easy to handle with your fingers but still warm to touch. Add to food processor and pulse another few times, until mixture is incorporated but still has a chunky texture. Taste and stir in extra spice mixture and salt as you like—I personally use all the spice mixture and add an extra 1/2 teaspoon salt.
5. Serve immediately and enjoy! Leftover "meat" will keep tightly sealed in the refrigerator up to 5 days or frozen for 1 month.

Vegetable Ratatouille

Ingredients

- 2 tbs olive oil
- 1 large onion, diced
- 1 tsp red pepper flakes, optional
- 1 large eggplant, about 2-1/2 lbs
- 3 bell peppers, assorted colors
- 2 zucchini, about 1 lb
- 1 yellow squash, about 1/2 lb
- 8 oz mushrooms
- 1 tbs garlic, minced
- 1 tbs tomato paste
- 2 cans diced no-salt added tomatoes
- 2 tbs fresh thyme
- 1/4 c fresh basil
- 1/4 c fresh parsley
- 1/2 tbs balsamic vinegar
- salt and pepper, to taste

Directions

1. Toss the cubed eggplant with 1 tbs salt and set aside in a strainer while you prep the rest of the ingredients. This will draw out any bitter juices.

2. Roast peppers in a broiler or over a gas burner until skin is charred. Put in a plastic bag and let sit 10 min before removing skin and seeds. Dice.
3. Meanwhile, heat 2 tbs olive oil in a Dutch oven over medium heat. Add onion and red pepper and cook until just translucent, about 5 min. Thoroughly rinse the eggplant to remove salt and add it to the pot. Continue to cook, stirring regularly, until eggplant is partially cooked, about 5 min.
4. Add zucchini, squash, and mushrooms. Season with salt and pepper to taste and cook until mushrooms release their juices, about 10 min.
5. Add tomato paste and garlic, cook for another 1-2 min until fragrant. Add tomatoes, stir in roasted peppers, and simmer 5 more min.
6. Stir in fresh herbs, reserving some for garnish, and adjust seasoning. Brighten with a splash of vinegar and serve either warm or at room temperature.

Pico de Gallo Stuffed Avocado

Ingredients

- 2 Roma tomatoes
- 3 tbsp diced onions
- 1 1/2 - 2 tbsp minced cilantro packed
- 1 tbsp minced jalapeno optional
- 1 tbsp freshly squeezed lime juice
- 1/2 tsp salt
- 3 medium/large avocados

Directions

1. Dice tomatos and onions. Drain juice from tomatoes (optional). Mince cilantro and jalapeno.
2. In a bowl, mix diced tomatoes, diced onions, minced cilantro, and minced jalapeño. Sprinkle with lime juice and salt, and combine.
3. Cut avocados in half and remove seeds. Using a spoon, gently carve the sides of the oval hole (where the seeds resided) to make the hole larger (wider, not deeper).

Roasted Butternut Squash Cauliflower Salad

Ingredients

FOR THE SALAD:

- 1 medium cauliflower head — cut into florets
- 1 small butternut squash — peeled and cut in cubes
- 1 tbsp olive oil

- salt and black pepper
- ¼ cup red onion — chopped
- 1 tablespoon green onions — chopped

FOR DRESSING:

- 1/2 cup vegenaise or traditional mayonnaise
- 2 tablespoon Dijon mustard
- 1 teaspoon garlic — minced
- Salt and pepper

Directions

1. First, steam the head of cauliflower. In a large pot add about 2 cups of water and place a steamer basket in the bottom.
2. Bring the water to a boil. Add the cauliflower florets into the steamer basket.
3. Cover the pot and steam until the cauliflower florets are tender 6-8 min. The time will depend on how tender you prefer your cauliflower florets to be.
4. Remove from the heat and also remove the lid from the pot. Let the cauliflower cool down for 5 min.
5. While the cauliflower florets are been steamed, roast the butternut squash. Preheat oven to 400 degrees. On a baking sheet lined with parchment paper or silicone mat, place butternut squash and toss in olive oil and season with salt and black pepper. Mix well to combine.
6. Roast in the oven for 15-20 min (It'll depend on the size of the butternut squash diced).
7. Place the steamed cauliflower, the roasted butternut squash and the red onions in a bowl.
8. In a small glass bowl, add all the ingredients for the dressing and whisk everything together to combine.
9. Taste to check the seasoning and pour over the salad.
10. Mix all the ingredients together until well combined and garnish it with green onions.

Coconut and Ginger Pumpkin Soup

Preparation:10 min | Cook Time: 45 min | Servings: 4 400mL

Ingredients

- 1 kilogram pumpkin – any variety will do
- 500 mL chicken broth or stock – substitute vegetable stock for a vegan/vegetarian soup
- 250 mL coconut milk
- 60 grams fresh ginger (about 3-4 thumb sized pieces)
- 1 tsp ground cumin
- 1/2 tsp ground cinnamon
- 2 tbsp extra virgin olive oil for roasting the pumpkin – can also use coconut oil
- salt and pepper to taste

Directions

1. Preheat oven to 180 C and line a large tray with baking paper (or use a non-stick tray).
2. Peel pumpkin and cut into even-sized chunks. Place on tray, drizzle over olive oil and toss around with your hands to coat. Roast pumpkin in the oven for approximately 45 min or until super soft and starting to caramelize at the edges.
3. While the pumpkin is roasting, peel the ginger and gather the rest of the ingredients.
4. Place cooked pumpkin, chicken broth/stock, coconut milk, ginger, cumin and cinnamon into blender jug. Blend until super smooth. Season with salt and pepper to taste.
5. To serve, heat a portion of the soup in a saucepan over the stove (or microwave the soup if that's more convenient for you). Enjoy!

Notes:

As noted above, to make this recipe vegan just swap the chicken stock base for a vegetable stock.

Nutrition: Calories: 271kcal | Carbohydrates: 22g; Protein: 5g; Fat: 21g; Saturated Fat: 13g; Sodium: 471mg; Potassium: 1159mg; Fiber: 2g; Sugar: 7g; Vitamin A: 21283IU | Vitamin C: 33mg; Calcium: 76mg; Iron: 5mg

Zucchini Pasta Salad

Ingredients

For the Salad:

- 2 medium zucchini spiralized, #2 blade
- 1 cup grape tomatoes sliced in half
- 1/2 cup red onion diced
- 1/2 cup artichoke hearts water drained & roughly chopped
- 1 green bell pepper diced

For the Dressing:

- 2 tbsp extra virgin olive oil
- 1 tbsp balsamic vinegar
- 1 tbsp lemon juice
- 1 tbsp minced garlic
- 1 1/2 tbsp basil

Directions

1. In a bowl, whisk together the ingredients for the dressing. Set aside.
2. In a separate large bowl, toss together the vegetables for the salad. Drizzle with the dressing and serve.
3. If not serving immediately, store the dressing separate from the salad until ready to eat.

Lemon Coconut Zoodles with Asparagus & Tomatoes

Ingredients

- 2 large zucchini
- 1 lb. asparagus
- 1 cup cherry or grape tomatoes (halved)
- 1 can coconut milk
- 1 lemon (zest and juice)
- 1 clove garlic
- 1 tbsp. arrowroot starch
- 1/2 tsp. sea salt
- pinch pepper
- 1/2 tbsp. olive oil

Directions

1. Snap the ends of the asparagus off and cut into 1-1/2 inch pieces. Heat the olive oil in a large pan on medium heat.
2. While the oil is heating, chop your tomatoes in half and spiralize your zucchini.
3. Once oil is heated, add your asparagus and saute a few min.
4. While asparagus is sauteing, prepare the sauce. Simply combine coconut milk, lemon juice, lemon zest, garlic, arrowroot starch, salt, and pepper into vitamix or other high speed blender. Blend until nice and creamy.
5. After cooking asparagus 3-4 min add the tomatoes and zoodles to the pan. Pour sauce over pan and cover with lid.
6. Allow veggies to cook a few more min, stirring here and there to prevent the veggies on the bottom from overcooking.
7. Once veggies are tender to your liking, remove pan from heat, serve in bowls and enjoy!

Spring Sauté with New Potatoes, Peas, Leeks & Artichokes

Ingredients

- 1 tablespoon butter or coconut oil
- 1 leek, roots and dark green pieces removed, and washed well
- 1 clove garlic, minced
- 1 cup diced young potatoes
- 1 cup fresh or frozen english peas
- 1 cup canned artichoke hearts, halved or quartered, drained
- Salt & ground black pepper to taste

Directions

1. Heat butter/oil in a medium sized skillet over medium heat.
2. Slice leek into thin rounds, and add to pan. Sauté until leeks are softened.
3. Add minced garlic, diced potatoes, and peas to the pan, and cover. Cook, stirring every 3-4 min, until potatoes are softened through.
4. Add artichoke hearts and cook for 2 min more, until artichokes are warmed through. Season to taste with salt & pepper and serve hot.

Mexican toasted corn quinoa salad

Ingredients

- 100 g (2/3 cup) quinoa rinsed
- 1/4 vegetable stock cube
- 1 tsp rapeseed / olive oil
- 200 g tin of sweetcorn drained
- 100 g (large handful) cherry / plum tomatoes quatered
- 1 large handful corriander roughly chopped
- 4 spring onions finely sliced
- Juice and zest of 1 lime
- 1/2 tsp chilli flakes
- 1 ripe avocado peeled and sliced
- Generous pinch sea salt and freshly ground black pepper

Directions

1. Fill a medium saucepan with water and add the stock cube and quinoa, stir and bring to the boil. Reduce the heat and simmer for 15-18 min until the quinoa is tender. Drain and set aside.
2. Meanwhile, heat the oil in a frying pan over a medium heat. Add the corn and pinch of salt and pepper and fry for 5 min or so until the sweetcorn is golden brown and slightly crisp. Remove from the heat
3. In a large bowl add the cooked quinoa, 3/4 of the sweetcorn, 3/4 of the avocado and all the remaining ingredients. Stir well to combine.

4. To serve, divide the salad between two plates before garnishing with the remaining sweetcorn and avocado.

Creamy Cauliflower Vegetable Whole30 Soup

Ingredients
- 1 medium cauliflower head chopped
- 2 large carrots chopped
- 8 oz brown cirmini mushrooms sliced
- 1/2 large white onion minced
- 4 large garlic cloves minced
- 6 tablespoons olive oil
- 1-2 teaspoons sea salt to taste
- fresh cracked black pepper to taste
- 1 cup spinach optional

Directions
1. In a soup pot saute minced garlic, onion, chopped carrots, and mushrooms with 2 tablespoons olive oil until golden and soft (add water if needed- to keep from sticking to pan).
2. Steam cauliflower in a saucepan with water until soft, then puree in a high speed blender with olive oil, salt, and pepper until smooth (add more or less olive oil, based on the size of your cauliflower head to get the right thick and creamy consistency). Stir pureed cauliflower into sautéed vegetables, add spinach and wilt, then serve!

Spicy Beef Curry Stew for the Slow Cooker

Ingredients
- 1 teaspoon ground cinnamon
- 1 teaspoon ground cumin
- ½ teaspoon ground ginger
- ¼ teaspoon ground cloves
- ¼ teaspoon ground nutmeg
- ¼ teaspoon ground turmeric
- ⅛ teaspoon curry powder
- 1 teaspoon kosher salt
- 1 pound ground lamb
- 1 tablespoon butter
- 1 sweet onion, chopped
- 1 (14.5 ounce) can organic beef broth
- 1 (14.5 ounce) can organic chicken broth
- 2 (14.5 ounce) cans beef consomme
- 1 (14.5 ounce) can diced tomatoes, undrained
- 1 tablespoon honey
- 3 large carrots, chopped
- 2 small sweetpotato, (5")s sweet potatoes, peeled and diced
- 1 (15 ounce) can garbanzo beans, drained and rinsed
- ½ cup chopped dried apricots
- 1 cup dried lentils, rinsed
- 1 teaspoon ground black pepper, to taste

Directions
1. Combine cinnamon, cumin, ginger, cloves, nutmeg, turmeric, curry powder, and salt in a large bowl. Mix in the ground lamb. For most flavorful results, allow mixture to rest, refrigerated, overnight.
2. Melt butter in a large pot over medium heat. Cook the onion in the butter until soft and just beginning to brown, 5 to 10 min. Mix the spiced lamb mixture to the onions. Cook and stir until meat is browned, about 5 min.
3. Pour the beef broth, chicken broth, and consomme into the pot. Stir in the tomatoes, honey, carrots, sweet potatoes, garbanzo beans, dried apricots and lentils. Bring to boil; reduce heat to low.
4. Simmer stew for 30 min or until the vegetables and lentils are cooked and tender. Season with black pepper to taste.

Fish stew

Servings: 4 | Preparation: 15 min | Cooking: 45 min

Ingredients
- 1 fennel bulb
- 1 red onion
- 2 garlic cloves
- 2 tablespoons olive oil
- 1 cup white wine
- 1 tablespoon fennel seeds
- 4 bay leaves
- 2 cups chicken stock
- 8 oz. halibut
- 12 oz. haddock

Directions
1. Chop all ingredients in big chunks
2. In a large pot heat olive oil and add ingredients one by one
3. Cook for 5 6 or until slightly brown
4. Add remaining ingredients and cook until tender, 35 45 min
5. Season while stirring on low heat
6. When ready remove from heat and serve

Butternut squash stew

Servings: 4 | Preparation: 15 min | Cooking: 45 min

Ingredients

- 2 tablespoons olive oil
- 2 red onions
- 2 cloves garlic
- Tablespoon rosemary
- 1 tablespoon thyme
- 2 lb. beef
- 1 cup white wine
- 1 cup butternut squash
- 2 cups beef broth
- ½ cup tomatoes

Directions

1. Chop all ingredients in big chunks
2. In a large pot heat olive oil and add ingredients one by one
3. Cook for 5 6 or until slightly brown
4. Add remaining ingredients and cook until tender, 35 45 min
5. Season while stirring on low heat
6. When ready remove from heat and serve

Chapter 3: Dinner Recipes

Chicken Salad

Servings: 8 | Preparation: 15 min

Ingredients

For Dressing:

- ½ teaspoon fresh ginger, minced
- ¼ cup fresh lemon juice
- 2 tablespoons Dijon mustard
- 2 tablespoons olive oil
- Salt and ground black pepper, as required

For Salad:

- 3 cups grass-fed cooked chicken, shredded
- ½ of small pineapple, peeled, cored and sliced thinly
- 4 plum tomatoes, thinly sliced lengthwise
- 1½ pounds Napa cabbage, shredded
- ½ cup scallions, sliced thinly

Directions

For dressing:

- in a bowl, add all the ingredients and beat until well combined.

For salad:

- in a large serving bowl, add all the ingredients and mix.
- Place the vinaigrette over salad and gently toss to coat well.
- Serve immediately.

Nutrition: Calories: 153; Total Fat: 5.7g; Saturated Fat: 1.1g; Protein: 17.5g; Carbs: 9.2g; Fiber: 2.4g; Sugar: 6g

Beef & Plum Salad

Servings: 4 | Preparation: 15 min | Cooking time: 10 min

Ingredients

- 4 teaspoons fresh lemon juice, divided
- 1½ tablespoons extra-virgin olive oil, divided
- Salt and ground black pepper, as required
- 1 pound grass-fed flank steak, trimmed
- Cooking spray, as required
- 1 teaspoon raw honey
- 8 cups fresh baby arugula
- 3 plums, pitted and sliced thinly

Directions

1. In a large bowl, place 1 teaspoon of lemon juice, 1½ teaspoons of oil, salt and black pepper and mix well.
2. Add the steak and coat with mixture generously.
3. Grease a nonstick skillet with a bit of cooking spray and heat over medium-high heat.
4. Add the beef steak and cook for about 5-6 min per side.
5. Transfer the steak onto a cutting board and set aside for about 10 min before slicing.
6. With a sharp knife, cut the beef steak diagonally across grain in desired size slices.
7. In a large bowl, add the remaining lemon juice, oil, honey, sea salt and black pepper and beat well.
8. Add the arugula and toss well.
9. Divide arugula onto 4 serving plates.
10. Top with beef slices and plum slices evenly and serve.

Nutrition: Calories: 304; Total Fat: 15.1g; Saturated Fat: 4.7g; Protein: 33g; Carbs: 9g; Fiber: 1.3g; Sugar: 7.6g

Salmon & Veggie Salad

Servings: 2 | Preparation: 15 min

Ingredients

- 6 ounces grilled salmon, cut into bite-sized pieces
- 1 medium zucchini, spiralized with Blade C
- 1 medium cucumber, peeled and spiralized with Blade C
- ½ cup celery stalk, chopped
- ½ cup unsweetened coconut milk
- 1 small garlic clove, minced
- Salt and ground black pepper, as required
- 2 organic hard-boiled large eggs, peeled and chopped

Directions

1. In a large serving bowl, mix together salmon, zucchini, cucumber and celery.
2. In another bowl, add the coconut milk, garlic and seasoning and mix until well combined.
3. Pour the coconut milk mixture over vegetables and gently, toss to coat.
4. Top with chopped eggs and serve.

Nutrition: Calories: 367; Total Fat: 24.9g; Saturated Fat: 15.1g; Protein: 26.6g; Carbs: 13.7g; Fiber: 3.6g; Sugar: 7g

Chicken & Zucchini Soup

Servings: 4 | Preparation: 15 min | Cooking time: 20 min

Ingredients

- 1 tablespoon olive oil
- ½ cup onion, chopped
- 1 cup carrot, peeled and chopped
- 2 garlic cloves, minced
- 2 tablespoons fresh rosemary, chopped
- 4½ cups homemade chicken broth
- 1¼ cups fresh spinach, torn
- 1¼ cups grass-fed cooked chicken, shredded
- 1¼ cups zucchini, spiralized with Blade C
- Salt and ground black pepper, as required
- 2 tablespoons fresh lemon juice

Directions

1. In a large soup pan, heat the oil over medium heat and sauté the onion and carrots for about 8-9 min.
2. Add the garlic and rosemary and sauté for about 1 minute.
3. Add the broth and spinach and bring to a boil over high heat.
4. Reduce the heat to medium-low and simmer for about 5 min.
5. Add the cooked chicken and zucchini and simmer for about 5 min.
6. Stir in the salt, black pepper and lemon juice and remove from heat.
7. Serve hot.

Nutrition: Calories: 174; Total Fat: 6.8g; Saturated Fat: 1.5g; Protein: 19.5g; Carbs: 8.3g; Fiber: 2.4g; Sugar: 3.6g

Quinoa Soup

Servings: 6 | Preparation: 15 min | Cooking time: 35 min

Ingredients

- 1 tablespoon coconut oil
- 3 carrots, peeled and chopped
- 3 celery stalks, chopped
- 1 onion, chopped
- 4 garlic cloves, minced
- 4 cups tomatoes, chopped
- 1 cup red lentils, rinsed and drained
- ½ cup dried quinoa, rinsed and drained
- 1½ teaspoons ground cumin
- 1 teaspoon red chili powder
- 5 cups homemade vegetable broth
- 2 cups fresh spinach, chopped

Directions

1. In a large pan, heat the oil over medium heat and sauté the celery, onion and carrot for about 8 min.
2. Add the garlic and sauté for about 1 minute.
3. Add the remaining ingredients except spinach and bring to a boil.
4. Reduce the heat to low and simmer, covered for about 20 min.
5. Stir in spinach and simmer for about 3-4 min.
6. Serve hot.

Nutrition: Calories: 268; Total Fat: 5.1g; Saturated Fat: 2.5g; Protein: 16.4g; Carbs: 40.2g; Fiber: 13.9g; Sugar: 6.9g

Beef & Veggie Stew

Servings: 5 | Preparation: 15 min | Cooking time: 2 h 5 min

Ingredients

- 1 pound grass-fed beef stew meat, trimmed and cubed
- Salt and ground black pepper, as required
- 2 tablespoons olive oil, divided
- 2 medium carrots, peeled and chopped
- 2 celery stalks, chopped
- 1 medium onion, chopped
- 1 cup pumpkin, peeled and cube
- 3 cups fresh tomatoes, chopped finely
- 4 cups homemade beef broth
- 1 cup frozen peas, thawed
- ¼ cup fresh cilantro, chopped

Directions

1. Season the beef with a bit of salt and black pepper evenly.
2. In a large heavy-bottomed pan, heat 1 tablespoon of oil over medium heat and sear beef for about 4-5 min.
3. Transfer the beef into a large bowl and keep aside.
4. In the same pan, heat remaining oil over medium heat and sauté carrot, celery and onion for about 5 min.
5. Add the pumpkin and tomatoes and sauté for about 5 min.
6. Add the broth and beef and bring to a boil over high heat.

7. Reduce the heat to low and simmer, covered for about 1 h.
8. Uncover and simmer for about 35 min.
9. Stir in the peas, salt and black pepper and simmer for 15 min more.
10. Serve hot with the garnishing of cilantro.

Nutrition: Calories: 328; Total Fat: 12.8g; Saturated Fat: 3.4g; Protein: 35.1g; Carbs: 18.1g; Fiber: 5.7g; Sugar: 8.7g

Chicken Chili

Servings: 6 | Preparation: 15 min | Cooking time: 40 min

Ingredients
- 4 cups homemade chicken broth, divided
- 3 cups cooked black beans, divided
- 1 tablespoon extra-virgin olive oil
- 1 large onion, chopped
- 2 medium poblano peppers, seeded and chopped
- 1 jalapeño pepper, seeded and chopped
- 4 garlic cloves, minced
- 1 teaspoon dried thyme, crushed
- 1½ tablespoons ground coriander
- 1 tablespoon ground cumin
- ½ tablespoon ancho chili powder
- 4 cups grass-fed cooked chicken, shredded
- 1 tablespoon fresh lime juice
- ¼ cup fresh cilantro, chopped

Directions
1. In a food processor, add 1 cup of broth and 1½ cups of black beans and pulse until smooth.
2. Transfer the beans puree into a bowl and set aside.
3. In a large pan, heat the oil over medium heat and sauté the onion, poblano and jalapeño for about 4-5 min.
4. Add the garlic, spices and sea salt and sauté for about 1 minute.
5. Add the beans puree and remaining broth and bring to a boil.
6. Reduce the heat to low and simmer for about 20 min.
7. Stir in the remaining beans, chicken and lime juice and bring to a boil.
8. Reduce the heat to low and simmer for about 5-10 min.
9. Serve hot with the topping of cilantro.

Nutrition: Calories: 321; Total Fat: 7.4g; Saturated Fat: 1.4g; Protein: 38.3g; Carbs: 23.7g; Fiber: 7g; Sugar: 2.4g

Beef Chili

Servings: 8 | Preparation: 15 min | Cooking time: 2¼ h

Ingredients
- 2 tablespoons extra-virgin olive oil
- 1 large onion, chopped
- 1 large green bell pepper, seeded and chopped
- 4 garlic cloves, minced
- 1 jalapeño pepper, chopped
- 1 teaspoon dried thyme, crushed
- 1 teaspoon dried basil, crushed
- 2 tablespoons red chili powder
- 1 tablespoon ground cumin
- 1 teaspoon ground allspice
- 2 pounds grass-fed lean ground beef
- 3 cups fresh tomatoes, chopped finely
- 2 cups homemade chicken broth
- 1 cup water

Directions
1. In a large pan, heat the oil over medium heat and sauté the onion and bell pepper for about 5-7 min.
2. Add garlic, jalapeño pepper, herbs, spices and black pepper and sauté for about 1 minute.
3. Add the beef and cook for about 4-5 min.
4. Stir in the tomatoes and cook for about 2 min.
5. Add the broth and water and bring to a boil.
6. Reduce the heat to low and simmer, covered for about 2 h.
7. Serve hot.

Nutrition: Calories: 277; Total Fat: 14.6g; Saturated Fat: 5.2g; Protein: 25.7g; Carbs: 8g; Fiber: 2.3g; Sugar: 3.7g

Lamb Chili

Servings: 6 | Preparation: 15 min | Cooking time: 2 h

Ingredients
- 1½ tablespoons extra-virgin olive oil, divided
- 1 cup onion, chopped
- 6 large garlic cloves, minced
- 2 dried New Mexico chiles, stemmed, seeded and torn

- 3 dried ancho chiles, stemmed, seeded and torn
- 2 teaspoons dried oregano, crushed
- 1½ teaspoons ground cumin
- 2 large plum tomatoes, chopped
- 2 cups homemade chicken broth
- 1 pound grass-fed lamb stew meat, trimmed and cubed
- Salt and ground black pepper, as required
- 15 ounces cooked kidney beans

Directions

1. In an oven-proof pan, heat 1 tablespoon of oil over medium heat and sauté the onion for about 4-5 min.
2. Add the garlic, both chiles and spices and sauté for about 1 minute.
3. Add the tomatoes and broth and bring to a boil.
4. Reduce the heat to medium-low and simmer, covered for about 30 min.
5. Preheat the oven to 325 degrees F. Arrange a rack in the center of the oven.
6. Remove the pan from heat and set aside to cool slightly.
7. Transfer the chile mixture into a blender and pulse until pureed.
8. Return the puree in the same pan.
9. Meanwhile, in another pan, heat the remaining oil over medium-high heat and cook the lamb with salt and black pepper k for about 3-4 min.
10. Transfer the cooked lamb in the pan with puree and stir to combine.
11. Cover the pan and bake for about 50 min.
12. Remove pan from the oven and place over medium-low heat.
13. Simmer, uncovered for about 25 min.
14. Stir in kidney beans and simmer for about 5 min.
15. Serve hot.

Nutrition: Calories: 430; Total Fat: 8.3g; Saturated Fat: 2.4g; Protein: 40g; Carbs: 49.7g; Fiber: 12.4g; Sugar: 4.4g

Glazed Chicken Thighs

Servings: 6 | Preparation: 10 min | Cooking time: 20 min

Ingredients

- 3 garlic cloves, minced
- ½ cup fresh orange juice
- 1 tablespoon apple cider vinegar
- 2 tablespoons coconut aminos
- ½ teaspoon orange blossom water
- ¼ teaspoon ground ginger
- ¼ teaspoon ground cinnamon
- Salt, as required
- 2 pounds grass-fed skinless, bone-in chicken thighs

Directions

1. For marinade: in a large bowl, place all ingredients except chicken and mix well.
2. Add the chicken and coat with marinade generously.
3. Cover the bowl of chicken and refrigerate for about 2 h.
4. Remove the chicken from bowl, reserving marinade.
5. Heat a large nonstick wok, over medium-high heat and cook the chicken for about 5-6 min or until golden brown.
6. Flip the side and cook for about 4 min.
7. Add the reserved marinade and bring to a boil.
8. Now, reduce the heat to medium-low heat and cook, covered for about 6-8 min or until sauce becomes thick.
9. Serve hot.

Nutrition: Calories: 305; Total Fat: 11.3g; Saturated Fat: 3.1g; Protein: 44g; Carbs: 8.3g; Fiber: 0.1g; Sugar: 1.8g

Grilled Chicken Breast

Servings: 4 | Preparation: 15 min | Cooking time: 20 min

Ingredients

- 1 (1-inch) piece fresh ginger, minced
- 2 garlic cloves, minced
- 1 cup fresh pineapple juice
- ¼ cup coconut aminos
- ¼ cup extra-virgin olive oil
- 1 teaspoon ground cinnamon
- 1 teaspoon ground cumin
- Salt, as required
- 4 grass-fed skinless, boneless chicken breasts

Directions

1. In a large Ziploc bag add all ingredients and seal it.
2. Shake the bag to coat the chicken with marinade well.
3. Refrigerate to marinade for about 1 h.
4. Preheat the grill to medium-high heat. Grease the grill grate.

5. Place the chicken breasts onto the grill and cook for about 10 min per side.
6. Serve hot.

Nutrition: Calories: 341; Total Fat: 17.9g; Saturated Fat: 3.7g; Protein: 32.1g; Carbs: 12.6g; Fiber: 0.6g; Sugar: 6.3g

Chicken with Pineapple & Bell Peppers

Servings: 5 | Preparation: 20 min | Cooking time: 25 min

Ingredients
- 1 tablespoon extra-virgin olive oil
- 1 large onion, chopped
- 1 garlic clove, minced
- 1 teaspoon fresh ginger, minced
- 2 grass-fed skinless, boneless chicken breasts, cubed
- 2 cups fresh pineapple, cubed
- 2 tomatoes, seeded and chopped
- 1 medium red bell pepper, seeded and chopped
- 1 medium green bell pepper, seeded and chopped
- 1 medium orange bell pepper, seeded and chopped
- 2 tablespoons coconut aminos
- 1 tablespoon apple cider vinegar
- Ground black pepper, as required

Directions
1. In a large skillet, heat oil over medium heat.
2. Add onion and sauté for about 4-5 min.
3. Add garlic and ginger and sauté for about 1 minute.
4. Add chicken and cook for about 10 min or until browned from all sides.
5. Add pineapple, tomatoes, and bell peppers and cook for about 5-6 min or until vegetables become tender.
6. Add the coconut aminos, vinegar, and pepper and cook for about 2-3 min.
7. Serve hot.

Nutrition: Calories: 194; Total Fat: 5.6g; Saturated Fat: 1.3g; Protein: 17.1g; Carbs: 20.5g; Fiber: 3.2g; Sugar: 12.2g

Chicken with Fruit & Veggies

Servings: 3 | Preparation: 15 min | Cooking time: 15 min

Ingredients
- 2 zucchinis, spiralized with Blade C
- Salt, as required
- 1½ teaspoons olive oil
- ½ teaspoon fresh ginger, minced
- ¾ cup rhubarb, chopped
- 10 ounces grass-fed skinless, boneless chicken breasts, cubed
- 4 teaspoons raw honey
- 1 teaspoon fresh lime zest, grated finely
- ¼ cup plus 2 teaspoons fresh orange juice, divided
- 1 tablespoon fresh lime juice
- 2 teaspoons fresh mint leaves, minced
- ½ cup fresh strawberries, hulled and sliced
- 2 tablespoons almonds, toasted and slivered

Directions
1. Arrange a large strainer over the sink.
2. Place the zucchini noodles in a strainer and sprinkle with a pinch of salt.
3. Set aside to release the excess moisture.
4. In a large skillet, heat the oil over medium heat and cook the ginger and rhubarb for about 2-3 min.
5. Stir in the chicken cubes and cook for about 4-5 min.
6. Add the honey, lime zest, ¼ cup of orange juice, lime juice and a pinch of salt and stir to combine.
7. Now, increase the heat to high and bring to a boil.
8. Now, reduce the heat to medium and simmer for about 4-5 min, stirring occasionally.
9. Remove from the heat.
10. Meanwhile, squeeze the moisture from zucchini and pat dry with paper towels.
11. In a small bowl, place the remaining orange juice and mint and mix.
12. Divide the zucchini noodles in serving plates and drizzle with mint mixture.
13. Place the chicken mixture, strawberries and almonds over zucchini noodles and gently stir to combine.
14. Serve immediately.

Nutrition: Calories: 236; Total Fat: 8.1g; Saturated Fat: 1.8g; Protein: 24.2g; Carbs: 18.8g; Fiber: 3.2g; Sugar: 13.4g

Chicken & Broccoli Casserole

Servings: 6 | Preparation: 15 min | Cooking time: 45 min

Ingredients

- 6 (6-ounce) grass-fed skinless, boneless chicken thighs
- 3 broccoli heads, cut into florets
- 4 garlic cloves, minced
- ¼ cup extra-virgin olive oil
- 1 teaspoon dried oregano, crushed
- 1 teaspoon dried rosemary, crushed
- Salt and ground black pepper, as required

Directions

1. Preheat the oven to 375 degrees F. Grease a large baking dish.
2. In a large bowl, add all ingredients and toss to coat well.
3. In the bottom of prepared baking dish, arrange the broccoli florets and top with chicken breasts in a single layer.
4. Bake for about 45 min.
5. Serve hot.

Nutrition: Calories: 329; Total Fat: 14.9g; Saturated Fat: 3.5g; Protein: 41.5g; Carbs: 8.8g; Fiber: 3.3g; Sugar: 2g

Stuffed Turkey Breast

Servings: 12 | Preparation: 20 min | Cooking time: 2 h

Ingredients

For Turkey Rub:

- 1 (5-pound) whole, bone-in turkey breast
- 2 tablespoons fresh thyme leaves, chopped
- 2 tablespoons fresh rosemary, chopped
- 2 tablespoons olive oil

For Stuffing:

- 1 small onion, thinly sliced
- 1 apple, peeled and thinly sliced
- 1 pear, peeled and thinly sliced
- ¼ cup dried cranberries

For Glaze:

- 2 cups fresh apple juice, divided
- 1 tablespoon olive oil
- 1 tablespoon brown mustard
- ½ tablespoon coconut sugar

Directions

1. Preheat the oven to 325 degrees F. Arrange a rack in a roasting pan.
2. Arrange turkey breast into the prepared roasting pan, skin-side up.

3. With your fingers, gently loosen the skin from the meat, making deep pockets between the skin and flesh.
4. For rub: in a small bowl, mix together fresh herbs and oil.
5. Rub half of herb mixture on the meat and then, spread the remaining paste evenly over the top of the skin.
6. For stuffing: in a bowl, mix together all ingredients.
7. Stuff each pocket with the stuffing mixture.
8. In the bottom of roasting pan, pour 1 cup of apple juice.
9. Roast for about 1¾-2 h. (If skin becomes brown during roasting, then cover the pan with a piece of foil).
10. Meanwhile, for glaze: in a pan, add remaining apple juice, oil, mustard and brown sugar and bring to a boil.
11. Reduce the heat and simmer until thick glaze is formed.
12. In the last 30 min of cooking, coat turkey breast with glaze evenly.
13. Remove from oven and cut turkey into desired slices before serving.

Nutrition: Calories: 290; Total Fat: 9.2g; Saturated Fat: 1.5g; Protein: 32.5g; Carbs: 19.1g; Fiber: 2.4g; Sugar: 14.5g

Glazed Flank Steak

Servings: 4 | Preparation: 15 min | Cooking time: 12 min

Ingredients

- 2 tablespoons arrowroot flour
- Salt and ground black pepper, as required
- 1 pound grass-fed flank steak, cut into ¼-inch thick slices
- ½ cup plus 1 tablespoon coconut oil, divided
- 2 garlic cloves, minced
- 1 teaspoon ground ginger
- Pinch of red pepper flakes, crushed
- 1|3 cup raw honey
- ½ cup homemade beef broth
- ½ cup coconut aminos
- 3 scallions, chopped

Directions

1. In a bowl, add the arrowroot flour, salt and black pepper and mix well.
2. Coat the beef slices with arrowroot flour mixture evenly.

3. Shake off the excess arrowroot flour mixture and set aside for about 10-15 min.
4. For sauce: in a pan, melt 1 tablespoon of coconut oil over medium heat and sauté the garlic, ginger powder and red pepper flakes for about 1 minute.
5. Add the honey, broth and coconut aminos and stir to combine well.
6. Now, increase the heat to high and cook for about 3 min, stirring continuously.
7. Remove from the heat and set aside.
8. In a large skillet, melt the remaining coconut oil over medium heat and stir fry the beef for about 2-3 min.
9. Remove the oil from skillet and stir fry for about 1 minute.
10. Stir in the honey sauce and cook for about 3 min.
11. Stir in the scallion and cook for about 1 minute more.
12. Serve hot.

Nutrition: Calories: 586; Total Fat: 36.9g; Saturated Fat: 27.5g; Protein: 32.8g; Carbs: 31.6g; Fiber: 0.5g; Sugar: 23.6g

Beef with Cauliflower

Servings: 4 | Preparation: 15 min | Cooking time: 12 min

Ingredients

- 1 tablespoon coconut oil
- 4 garlic cloves, minced
- 1 pound grass-fed beef sirloin steak, cut into bite-sized pieces
- 3½ cups cauliflower florets
- 3 tablespoons coconut aminos
- ¼ cup fresh cilantro leaves, chopped

Directions

1. In a large skillet, heat the oil over medium heat and sauté the garlic for about 1 minute.
2. Add beef and stir to combine.
3. Increase the heat to medium-high and cook for about 6-8 min or until browned from all sides.
4. Meanwhile, in a pan of boiling filtered water, add cauliflower and cook for about 5-6 min.
5. Drain the cauliflower thoroughly.
6. Add the cauliflower and coconut aminos in skillet with beef and cook for about 2-3 min.
7. Serve with the garnishing of cilantro.

Nutrition: Calories: 278; Total Fat: 10.6g; Saturated Fat: 5.6g; Protein: 36.3g; Carbs: 7.9g; Fiber: 2.3g; Sugar: 2.1g

Beef with Lentils

Servings: 6 | Preparation: 15 min | Cooking time: 50 min

Ingredients

- 3 tablespoons extra-virgin olive oil, divided
- 1 onion, chopped
- 1 tablespoon fresh ginger, minced
- 4 garlic cloves, minced
- 3 plum tomatoes, chopped finely
- 2 cups dried red lentils, soaked for 30 min and drained
- 2 cups homemade chicken broth
- 2 teaspoons cumin seeds
- ½ teaspoon cayenne pepper
- 1 pound grass-fed lean ground beef
- 1 jalapeño pepper, seeded and chopped
- 2 scallions, chopped

Directions

1. In a Dutch oven, heat 1 tablespoon of oil over medium heat and sauté the onion, ginger and garlic for about 5 min.
2. Stir in the tomatoes, lentils and broth and bring to a boil
3. Reduce the heat to medium-low and simmer, covered for about 30 min.
4. Meanwhile, in a skillet, heat remaining oil over medium heat.
5. Add the cumin seeds and sauté for about 30 seconds.
6. Add the paprika and sauté for about 30 seconds.
7. Transfer the mixture into a small bowl and set aside.
8. In the same skillet, add the beef and cook for about 4-5 min.
9. Add jalapeño and scallion and cook for about 4-5 min.
10. Add the spiced oil mixture and stir to combine well.
11. Transfer the beef mixture into the simmering lentils and simmer for about 10-15 min or until desired doneness.
12. Serve hot.

Nutrition: Calories: 469; Total Fat: 13.3g; Saturated Fat: 3.1g; Protein: 42.3g; Carbs: 45.1g; Fiber: 21.1g; Sugar: 4.2g

Ground Beef with Peas

Servings: 6 | Preparation: 15 min | Cooking time: 40 min

Ingredients

- 2 tablespoons olive oil
- 1 pound grass-fed lean ground beef
- 1 large onion, chopped finely
- 2 garlic cloves, minced
- ½ tablespoon fresh ginger, minced
- 1 teaspoon ground coriander
- 1 teaspoon ground cumin
- ¼ teaspoon chili powder
- 2 medium tomatoes, seeded and chopped
- ½ cup homemade chicken broth
- Salt and ground black pepper, as required
- 2¼ cups fresh peas, shelled
- 2 tablespoons fresh cilantro, chopped

Directions

1. In a large skillet, heat the oil over medium heat and cook the beef for about 4-5 min or until browned completely.
2. With a slotted spoon, transfer the beef into a large bowl.
3. In the same skillet, add onion and sauté for about 4-6 min.
4. Add the garlic, ginger, coriander, cumin and chili powder and sauté for about 1 minute.
5. Add the tomatoes and cook for about 2-3 min, crushing entirely with the back of spoon.
6. Stir in the beef and broth and bring to a boil.
7. Reduce the heat to medium-low and simmer, covered for about 8-10 min, stirring occasionally.
8. Stir in peas and cook for 10-15 min.
9. Remove from heat and serve hot with the garnishing of almonds and cilantro leaves.

Nutrition: Calories: 243; Total Fat: 11.9g; Saturated Fat: 3.8g; Protein: 19.5g; Carbs: 12.7g; Fiber: 4g; Sugar: 5.3g

Stuffed Bell Peppers

Servings: 5 | Preparation: 20 min | Cooking time: 40 min

Ingredients

- 5 large bell peppers, tops and seeds removed
- 1 tablespoon coconut oil
- ½ large onion, chopped
- ½ teaspoon dried oregano
- ½ teaspoon dried thyme
- Salt and ground black pepper, as required
- 1 pound grass-fed ground beef
- 1 large zucchini, chopped

- 3 tablespoons homemade tomato paste

Directions

1. Preheat the oven to 350 degrees F. Grease a small baking dish.
2. In a large pan of the boiling water, place the bell peppers and cook for about 4-5 min.
3. Remove from the water and place onto a paper towel, cut side down.
4. Meanwhile, in a large nonstick skillet, melt coconut oil over medium heat and sauté onion for about 3-4 min.
5. Add the ground beef, oregano, salt, and pepper and cook for about 8-10 min.
6. Add zucchini and cook for about 2-3 min.
7. Remove from the heat and drain any juices from the beef mixture.
8. Add the tomato paste and stir to combine.
9. Arrange the bell peppers into the prepared baking dish, cut side upward.
10. Stuff the bell peppers with the beef mixture evenly and bake for 15 min.
11. Serve warm.

Nutrition: Calories: 247; Total Fat: 12.1g; Saturated Fat: 6g; Protein: 21.1g; Carbs: 14.5g; Fiber: 3.1g; Sugar: 8.9g

Broiled Lamb Shoulder

Servings: 6 | Preparation: 10 min | Cooking time: 10 min

Ingredients

- 2 tablespoons fresh ginger, minced
- 2 tablespoons garlic, minced
- ¼ cup fresh lemongrass stalk, minced
- ¼ cup fresh orange juice
- ¼ cup coconut aminos
- Ground black pepper, as required
- 2 pounds grass-fed lamb shoulder, trimmed

Directions

1. In a bowl, add all ingredients except lamb shoulder and mix well.
2. In a baking dish, place the lamb shoulder and coat the lamb with half of the marinade mixture generously.
3. Reserve remaining mixture.
4. Refrigerate to marinate overnight.
5. Preheat the broiler of oven. Place a rack in a broiler pan and arrange about 4-5-inches from the heating element.
6. Remove lamb shoulder from refrigerator and shake off excess marinade.

7. Broil for about 4-5 min per side.
8. Serve alongside the reserved marinade as a sauce.

Nutrition: Calories: 306; Total Fat: 11.2g; Saturated Fat: 4g; Protein: 42.9g; Carbs: 5.3g; Fiber: 0.3g; Sugar: 1g

Pan Seared Lamb Chops

Servings: 4 | Preparation: 15 min | Cooking time: 6 min

Ingredients

- 4 garlic cloves, peeled
- Salt, as required
- 1 teaspoon black mustard seeds, crushed finely
- 2 teaspoons ground cumin
- 1 teaspoon ground ginger
- 1 teaspoon ground coriander
- ½ teaspoon ground cinnamon
- Ground black pepper, as required
- 1 tablespoon coconut oil
- 8 grass-fed medium lamb chops, trimmed

Directions

1. Place the garlic cloves onto a cutting board and sprinkle with some salt.
2. With a knife, crush the garlic until a paste forms.
3. In a bowl, mix together garlic paste and spices.
4. With a sharp knife, make 3-4 cuts on both side of the chops.
5. Rub the chops with garlic mixture generously.
6. In a large skillet, melt the coconut oil over medium heat and cook the chops for about 2-3 min per side or until desired doneness.
7. Serve hot.

Nutrition: Calories: 571; Total Fat: 24.7g; Saturated Fat: 10.4g; Protein: 80.3g; Carbs: 2.3g; Fiber: 0.5g; Sugar: 0.1g

Poached Salmon

Servings: 3 | Preparation: 15 min | Cooking time: 12 min

Ingredients

- 3 garlic cloves, crushed
- 1½ teaspoons fresh ginger, grated finely
- 1|3 cup fresh orange juice
- 3 tablespoons coconut aminos
- 3 (6-ounce) salmon fillets

Directions

1. In a bowl, add all the ingredients except salmon and mix well.
2. In the bottom of a large pan, place the salmon fillet.
3. Place the ginger mixture over the salmon and set aside for about 15 min.
4. Place the pan over high heat and bring to a boil.
5. Reduce the heat to low and simmer, covered for about 10-12 min or until desired doneness.
6. Serve hot.

Nutrition: Calories: 260; Total Fat: 10.6g; Saturated Fat: 1.5g; Protein: 33.5g; Carbs: 7.5g; Fiber: 0.2g; Sugar: 2.4g

Shrimp with Zoodles

Servings: 4 | Preparation: 15 min | Cooking time: 8 min

Ingredients

- 2 tablespoons coconut oil
- 3 garlic cloves, minced
- 1 pound shrimp, peeled and deveined
- 4 large zucchinis, spiralized with blade C
- Salt and ground black pepper, as required
- 4-6 fresh basil leaves, chopped

Directions

1. In a large skillet, melt the coconut oil over medium heat and sauté garlic for about 1 minute.
2. Add the shrimp and cook for about 2-3 min.
3. Add the zucchini and cook for about 2-3 min, tossing occasionally.
4. Stir in the salt and black pepper and remove from heat.
5. Serve with the garnishing of basil leaves.

Nutrition: Calories: 249; Total Fat: 9.3g; Saturated Fat: 6.6g; Protein: 29.9g; Carbs: 13.3g; Fiber: 3.6g; Sugar: 5.6g

Shrimp & Veggies Curry

Servings: 6 | Preparation: 15 min | Cooking time: 15 min

Ingredients

- 2 teaspoons coconut oil
- 1½ medium white onions, sliced
- 2 medium green bell peppers, seeded and sliced
- 3 medium carrots, peeled and sliced thinly

- 3 garlic cloves, chopped finely
- 1 tablespoon fresh ginger, chopped finely
- 2½ teaspoons curry powder
- 1½ pounds shrimp, peeled and deveined
- 1 cup unsweetened coconut milk
- 2 tablespoons water
- 2 tablespoons fresh lime juice
- Salt and ground black pepper, as required
- 2 tablespoons fresh cilantro, chopped

Directions
1. In a large skillet, heat oil over medium-high heat and sauté the onion for about 4-5 min.
2. Add the bell peppers and carrot and sauté for about 3-4 min.
3. Add the garlic, ginger and curry powder and sauté for about 1 minute.
4. Add the shrimp and sauté for about 1 minute.
5. Stir in the coconut milk and water and cook for about 3-4 min, stirring occasionally.
6. Stir in lime juice and remove from heat.
7. Serve hot with the garnishing of cilantro.

Nutrition: Calories: 285; Total Fat: 13.3g; Saturated Fat: 10.4g; Protein: 28g; Carbs: 14.2g; Fiber: 3.2g; Sugar: 6.1g

Shrimp & Fruit Curry

Servings: 6 | Preparation: 15 min | Cooking time: 12 min

Ingredients
- 1 tablespoon coconut oil
- ½ cup onion, sliced thinly
- 1½ pounds shrimp, peeled and deveined
- ½ of red bell pepper, seeded and sliced thinly
- 1 mango, peeled, pitted and sliced
- 8 ounces can of pineapple tidbits with unsweetened juice
- 1 cup unsweetened coconut milk
- 1 tablespoon red curry paste
- 2 tablespoons red boat fish sauce
- 2 tablespoons fresh cilantro, chopped

Directions
1. In a skillet, melt the coconut oil over medium-high heat and sauté the onion for about 3-4 min.
2. With a spoon, push the onion to sides of the pan.
3. Add the shrimp and cook for about 2 min per side.
4. Stir in the bell peppers and cook for about 3-4 min.

5. Add the remaining ingredients except cilantro and simmer for about 5 min.
6. Serve hot with the garnishing of cilantro.

Nutrition: Calories: 325; Total Fat: 14.8g; Saturated Fat: 11.3g; Protein: 28.9g; Carbs: 20.4g; Fiber: 2.4g; Sugar: 15.4g

Squid with Veggies

Servings: 4 | Preparation: 15 min | Cooking time: 10 min

Ingredients
- 1 teaspoon olive oil
- 2 carrots, peeled and chopped
- 2 red bell peppers, seeded and cut into strips
- ½ of eggplant, chopped
- ¾ pound squids, cleaned
- 2 tablespoons red boat fish sauce
- 1 teaspoon fresh ginger, minced
- ½ teaspoon paprika
- Salt and ground black pepper, as required
- 1 cup fresh spinach, chopped

Directions
1. In a skillet, heat the oil over medium heat and stir fry the carrots, bell pepper and eggplant for about 3-4 min.
2. Add the remaining ingredients except spinach and cook for about 1-2 min.
3. Stir in the spinach and cook for about 3-4 min.
4. Remove from the heat and serve immediately.

Nutrition: Calories: 138; Total Fat: 2.7g; Saturated Fat: 0.5g; Protein: 17g; Carbs: 14.2g; Fiber: 3.9g; Sugar: 6.3g

Lentils in Tomato Sauce

Servings: 4 | Preparation: 10 min | Cooking time: 20 min

Ingredients

For Tomato Puree:

- 1 cup tomatoes, chopped
- 1 garlic clove, chopped
- 1 (1-inch) piece fresh ginger, chopped
- 1 green chili, chopped
- ¼ cup water

For Lentils:

- 1 cup red lentils

- 3 cups water
- 1 tablespoon olive oil
- ½ of medium onion, chopped finely
- ½ teaspoon ground cumin
- ½ teaspoon cayenne pepper
- ¼ teaspoon ground turmeric
- ¼ cup fresh parsley leaves, chopped

Directions

1. For tomato paste: in a blender, add all ingredients and pulse until a smooth puree forms. Set aside.
2. In a large pan, place 3 cups of the water and lentils over high heat and bring to a boil.
3. Now, reduce the heat to medium-low and simmer, covered for about 15 min or until tender enough.
4. Drain the lentils thoroughly.
5. Meanwhile, in a large skillet, heat the oil over medium heat and sauté the onion for about 2-3 min.
6. Add the spices and sauté for about 1 minute.
7. Add the tomato puree and cook for about 4-5 min, stirring continuously.
8. Stir in the lentils and cook for about 4-5 min or until desired doneness.
9. Serve hot with the garnishing of parsley.

Nutrition: Calories: 219; Total Fat: 4.3g; Saturated Fat: 0.6g; Protein: 13.2g; Carbs: 32.9g; Fiber: 15.8g; Sugar: 2.9g

Kidney Beans Chili

Servings: 3 | Preparation: 10 min | Cooking time: 21 min

Ingredients

- 1 tablespoon olive oil
- 1 onion, chopped
- 8 ounces fresh button mushrooms, sliced
- 1|3 cup sun-dried tomatoes, chopped roughly
- 1 (15-ounce) can kidney beans
- 3 tablespoons homemade tomato paste
- 2 tablespoons red chili powder
- 1 tablespoon ground cumin
- Salt and ground black pepper, as required
- 1 tablespoon fresh parsley, chopped

Directions

1. In a large pan, heat the oil over medium heat and sauté the onion for about 4-5 min.
2. Add the mushrooms and sundried tomatoes and sauté for about 5-6 min.

3. Add the kidney beans with liquid, tomato paste, chili powder and cumin and bring to a boil.
4. Reduce the heat to low and simmer for about 10 min.
5. Stir in the salt and black pepper and remove from the heat.
6. Serve hot with the garnishing of parsley.

Nutrition: Calories: 228; Total Fat: 6.4g; Saturated Fat: 0.9g; Protein: 14g; Carbs: 34.4g; Fiber: 16g; Sugar: 5.8g

Chickpeas Curry

Servings: 3 | Preparation: 10 min | Cooking time: 5 min

Ingredients

- 2 tablespoons olive oil
- 2 medium onions, chopped
- 3 garlic cloves, chopped
- 1-2 teaspoons curry paste
- 1 (14-ounce) can unsweetened coconut milk
- 1 (15-ounce) can low-sodium chickpeas, rinsed and drained
- 1 tablespoon coconut aminos
- 2-3 medium tomatoes, chopped
- 1 cup fresh basil, chopped
- 1 teaspoon raw honey
- 1 tablespoon fresh lime juice

Directions

1. In a large pan, heat the oil over medium heat and sauté the onions for about 2-3 min.
2. Add the garlic and curry paste and sauté for about 1 minute.
3. Stir in the coconut milk and cook for about 1 minute, stirring continuously.
4. Stir in the chickpeas and coconut aminos and bring to a boil.
5. Cook for about 1-2 min.
6. Add the tomatoes, basil, honey and lime juice and simmer for about 2 min.
7. Remove from the heat and serve hot.

Nutrition: Calories: 472; Total Fat: 30.5g; Saturated Fat: 18.1g; Protein: 10g; Carbs: 37.3g; Fiber: 6.7g; Sugar: 11.1g

Cauliflower recipe

Servings: 6 8 | Preparation: 10 min | Cooking: 15 min

Ingredients

- 1 pizza crust
- ½ cup tomato sauce
- ¼ black pepper
- 1 cup cauliflower
- 1 cup mozzarella cheese
- 1 cup olives

Directions

1. Spread tomato sauce on the pizza crust
2. Place all the toppings on the pizza crust
3. Bake the pizza at 425 F for 12 15 min
4. When ready remove pizza from the oven and serve

Broccoli recipe

Servings: 6-8 | Preparation: 10 min | Cooking: 15 min

Ingredients

- 1 pizza crust
- ½ cup tomato sauce
- ¼ black pepper
- 1 cup broccoli
- 1 cup mozzarella cheese
- 1 cup olives

Directions

1. Spread tomato sauce on the pizza crust
2. Place all the toppings on the pizza crust
3. Bake the pizza at 425 F for 12 15 min
4. When ready remove pizza from the oven and serve

Tomatoes & ham pizza

Servings: 6-8 | Preparation: 10 min | Cooking: 15 min

Ingredients

- 1 pizza crust
- ½ cup tomato sauce
- ¼ black pepper
- 1 cup pepperoni slices
- 1 cup tomatoes
- 6 8 ham slices
- 1 cup mozzarella cheese
- 1 cup olives

Directions

1. Spread tomato sauce on the pizza crust
2. Place all the toppings on the pizza crust
3. Bake the pizza at 425 F for 12 15 min
4. When ready remove pizza from the oven and serve

Mushroom soup

Servings: 4 | Preparation: 10 min | Cooking: 20 min

Ingredients

- 1 tablespoon olive oil
- 1 lb. mushrooms
- ¼ red onion
- ½ cup all purpose flour
- ¼ tsp salt
- ¼ tsp pepper
- 1 can vegetable broth
- 1 cup heavy cream

Directions

1. In a saucepan heat olive oil and sauté mushrooms until tender
2. Add remaining ingredients to the saucepan and bring to a boil
3. When all the vegetables are tender transfer to a blender and blend until smooth
4. Pour soup into bowls, garnish with parsley and serve

Artichocke soup

Servings: 4 | Preparation: 10 min | Cooking: 20 min

Ingredients

- 1 tablespoon olive oil
- 1 lb. artichoke
- ¼ red onion
- ½ cup all purpose flour
- ¼ tsp salt
- ¼ tsp pepper
- 1 can vegetable broth
- 1 cup heavy cream

Directions

1. In a saucepan heat olive oil and sauté onion until tender
2. Add remaining ingredients to the saucepan and bring to a boil
3. When all the vegetables are tender transfer to a blender and blend until smooth
4. Serve when ready

Amaranth leaves soup

Servings: 4 | Preparation: 10 min | Cooking: 20 min

Ingredients

- 1 tablespoon olive oil

- 1 lb. amaranth leaves
- ¼ red onion
- ½ cup all purpose flour
- ¼ tsp salt
- ¼ tsp pepper
- 1 can vegetable broth
- 1 cup heavy cream

Directions

1. In a saucepan heat olive oil and sauté onion until tender
2. Add remaining ingredients to the saucepan and bring to a boil
3. When all the vegetables are tender transfer to a blender and blend until smooth
4. Serve when ready

Carrot soup

Servings: 4 | Preparation: 10 min | Cooking: 20 min

Ingredients

- 1 tablespoon olive oil
- 1 lb. carrots
- ¼ red onion
- ½ cup all purpose flour
- ¼ tsp salt
- ¼ tsp pepper
- 1 can vegetable broth
- 1 cup heavy cream

Directions

1. In a saucepan heat olive oil and sauté carrots until tender
2. Add remaining ingredients to the saucepan and bring to a boil
3. When all the vegetables are tender transfer to a blender and blend until smooth
4. Pour soup into bowls, garnish with parsley and serve

Greens soup

Servings: 4 | Preparation: 10 min | Cooking: 20 min

Ingredients

- 1 tablespoon olive oil
- 1 lb. greens
- ¼ red onion
- ½ cup all purpose flour
- ¼ tsp salt
- ¼ tsp pepper
- 1 can vegetable broth
- 1 cup heavy cream

Directions

1. In a saucepan heat olive oil and sauté onion until tender
2. Add remaining ingredients to the saucepan and bring to a boil
3. When all the vegetables are tender transfer to a blender and blend until smooth
4. Serve when ready

Bacon casserole

Servings: 4 | Preparation: 10 min | Cooking: 15 min

Ingredients

- 4 5 slices bacon
- 3 4 tablespoons butter
- 5 6 tablespoons flour
- 2 cups milk
- 3 cups cheddar cheese
- 2 cups chicken breast
- 1 tsp seasoning mix

Directions

1. Sauté the veggies and set aside
2. Preheat the oven to 425 F
3. Transfer the sautéed veggies to a baking dish, add remaining ingredients to the baking dish
4. Mix well, add seasoning and place the dish in the oven
5. Bake for 12 15 min or until slightly brown
6. When ready remove from the oven and serve

Chicken casserole

Servings: 4 | Preparation: 10 min | Cooking: 40 min

Ingredients

- 1 cup Greek yogurt
- ½ cup grape juice
- 1 cup mushroom soup
- 1 cup cooked rice

Directions

1. In a bowl add mushrooms, yogurt, grape juice and combine
2. Place the chicken breast in a prepare baking dish and pour the mixture over the chicken
3. Bake for 35 40 min at 325 F
4. When ready remove from the oven and serve with rice

Enchilada casserole

Servings: 4 | Preparation: 10 min | Cooking: 25 min

Ingredients

- 1 tablespoon olive oil
- 1 red onion
- 1 bell pepper
- 2 cloves garlic
- 1 can black beans
- 1 cup chicken
- 1 can green chilis
- 1 can enchilada sauce
- 1 cup cheddar cheese
- 1 cup sour cream

Directions

1. Sauté the veggies and set aside
2. Preheat the oven to 425 F
3. Transfer the sautéed veggies to a baking dish, add remaining ingredients to the baking dish
4. Mix well, add seasoning and place the dish in the oven
5. Bake for 15 25 min or until slightly brown
6. When ready remove from the oven and serve

Mediterranean Stuffed Peppers

Preparation: 20 min | Cooking: 50 min | Servings: 4

Ingredients

- 4 bell peppers seeded and halved lengthwise
- 1 cup low-sodium vegetable broth
- 1 cup uncooked couscous
- 1/4 teaspoon kosher salt
- 1/4 teaspoon ground turmeric
- 1 tablespoon olive oil
- 1/2 medium yellow onion, chopped
- 2 cloves garlic, minced
- 1 cup sun-dried tomatoes, drained and chopped
- 1/4 cup sliced black olives
- 1 teaspoon kosher salt
- 1/2 teaspoon black pepper
- 1/4 cup pine nuts
- 1/4 cup fresh basil chopped

Directions

1. Program your oven to 400F, then grease a 9 x 13-inch baking pan with olive oil or mom-stick spray.
2. Add the vegetable broth to a heavy-bottom saucepan and bring it to a boil over medium-high heat. Remove the vegetable broth from the stove and add the couscous, 1/4 teaspoon of salt, turmeric and stir to combine. Cover the saucepan with the lid and let the couscous sit for ten min until the couscous has absorbed the broth

3. While the couscous is sitting, place one tablespoon of olive oil in a skillet over medium-high heat. Add the onion and sauté for 3-4 min until it is softened. Stir in the garlic and oregano and cook for a minute until it is aromatic.
4. Add the sundried tomatoes and olives and cook for 1-2 min. Add the couscous, pine nuts, basil, salt, and pepper and stir to combine.
5. Fill the halved bell peppers with the couscous filling and place each pepper into the prepared baking dish. Cover the Mediterranean stuffed peppers tightly with aluminum foil and bake for 35-40 min, then take the foil off and cook 10-15 min until the peppers are tender and golden brown on top.
6. Serve and enjoy!

Nutrition; Carbohydrates: 45.7g; Protein: 9.2g; Fat: 10.8g; Saturated Fat: 1.1g; Cholesterol: 0mg; ; Sodium: 831mg; Potassium: 488mg; Sugar: 4.9g; Vitamin D: 0mcg; Calcium: 51mg; Iron: 2mg

Ratatouille

Preparation: 15 min | Cooking: 60 min | Servings: 6

Ingredients

- 2 zucchini, sliced into 1/4 inch rounds
- 2 yellow squash, sliced into 1/4 inch rounds
- 2 small eggplants, sliced into 1/4 inch rounds
- 5 Roma tomatoes, sliced into 1/4 inch rounds
- 1 26 oz. jar of tomato basil pasta sauce
- 2 teaspoons fresh thyme
- 2 tablespoons fresh basil
- 2 teaspoon fresh oregano
- 1 teaspoon of minced garlic
- 1 teaspoon paprika
- 1 teaspoon kosher salt
- 1/4 teaspoon black pepper
- 4 tablespoons of olive oil

Directions

1. Program the oven to 375 F, then pour the pasta sauce into a baking dish, then layer the zucchini, eggplant, and tomato rounds in the plate in a spiral pattern until the baking dish is completely covered.
2. Add the minced garlic, thyme, basil, oregano, paprika, salt, pepper, and olive oil to a small bowl and whisk to combine. Pour the garlic herb mixture over the vegetables and cover the ratatouille with aluminum foil.
3. Bake the ratatouille for 35-40 min, remove the foil from the ratatouille and bake for an

additional 15-20 min until the vegetables are tender and soft.

Nutrition; Carbohydrates: 32.6g; Protein: 6.8g; Fat: 16.8g; Saturated Fat: 2.5g; Cholesterol: 0mg; ; Sodium: 1052mg; Potassium: 968mg; Sugar: 17.1g; Vitamin D: 0mcg; Calcium: 91mg; Iron: 3mg

Black Bean Quinoa Corn Chili

Preparation: 15 min | Cooking: 45 min | Servings: 10

Ingredients

- 1 cup uncooked quinoa, rinsed
- 2 cups water
- 1 tablespoon olive oil
- 1 red onion, chopped
- 4 cloves garlic, minced
- 1 tablespoon chili powder
- 1 tablespoon ground cumin
- 1 teaspoon paprika
- 1 28 oz. can fire-roasted crushed tomatoes
- 2 19 oz. cans black beans, rinsed and drained
- 2 red bell pepper, chopped
- 1 teaspoon dried oregano
- 1 teaspoon kosher salt
- 1/2 teaspoon black pepper
- 1 cup frozen corn

Directions

1. Place the quinoa and water into a sauce pot and bring it to a boil over medium-high heat. Decrease the flame to medium-low, cover the saucepot with the lid, and cook the quinoa for 15-20 min until it is tender, then set the cooked quinoa aside.
2. While the quinoa is cooking, place the olive oil into a large, heavy-bottom saucepot over medium-high heat. Add the red onion, and sauté for 5
3. min until the onion has softened. Stir in the garlic, chili powder, cumin, and paprika, and cook for a minute until it becomes fragrant.
4. Add the tomatoes, black beans, red bell peppers, oregano, salt, and pepper. Let the chili base gently simmer over medium-high heat, decrease the flame to medium-low, seal the saucepot with the lid, and simmer for 20 min.
5. Add the quinoa and frozen corn and stir to combine. Cook the chili for 5
6. min until it is thoroughly heated.
7. Serve and enjoy!

Nutrition; Carbohydrates: 76g; Protein: 24.5g; Fat: 3.5g; Saturated Fat: 0.7g; Cholesterol: 0mg; ; Sodium: 289mg; Potassium: 1739mg; Sugar: 5.6g;

Sesame Ginger Salmon With Vegetables

Preparation: 20 min | Cooking: 50 min | Servings: 4

Ingredients

For the salmon:

- 2 tablespoons olive oil
- 2 tablespoons coconut aminos
- 2 tablespoons rice wine vinegar
- 2 tablespoons sesame oil
- 1 tablespoon honey
- 2 cloves garlic, minced
- 1 tablespoon grated fresh ginger
- 1 tablespoon sesame seeds
- 2 green onions, thinly sliced
- 4 5.oz salmon filets

For the vegetables:

- 1 large head of broccoli, cut into florets
- 2 large carrots cut into 1/2 inch rounds
- 1 lb. button mushrooms, sliced

Directions

1. To prepare the honey ginger marinade, whisk the olive oil, coconut aminos, rice wine vinegar, sesame oil, honey, garlic, ginger, sesame seeds, and green onions in a large bowl.
2. Place the salmon fillets into the honey ginger marinade and let it sit for at least 1 h or overnight to allow the salmon to absorb the marinade's flavor.
3. Program the oven to 400F, then lightly grease a 9×13-inch baking dish with nonstick spray. Add the broccoli, carrots, and mushrooms to the prepared baking dish in an even layer, then place the honey ginger marinated salmon fillets on top of the vegetables and pour the marinade over the salmon. Bake the salmon for 15-20 min. Serve and enjoy!

Nutrition: Carbohydrates: 18g; Protein: 46.8g; Fat: 27.4g; Saturated Fat: 5.1g; Cholesterol: 36mg; ; Sodium: 151mg; Potassium: 660mg; Sugar: 9g; Vitamin D: 0mcg; Calcium: 64mg; Iron: 4mg

Lentil Stew

Preparation: 10 min | Cooking: 45 min | Servings: 6

Ingredients

- 2 tablespoons olive oil
- 1 onion, chopped
- 2 garlic cloves, minced
- 1 large carrot, diced
- 2 cups dried lentils, rinsed
- 1 14 oz, can diced fire-roasted tomatoes
- 6 cup low-sodium vegetable broth
- 1/2 teaspoon cumin
- 1 1/2 teaspoon smoked paprika
- 2 bay leaves
- 1 teaspoon kosher salt
- 1/2 teaspoon black pepper
- juice and zest of 1 lemon

Directions

1. Place the olive oil into a large saucepot over medium-low heat. Once it is hot, add the onion, cook for 2 min. Stir in the carrots and garlic, then cook for 8-10 min until the onions are caramelized.
2. Add the lentils, tomatoes, vegetable broth, cumin, smoked paprika, bay leaves, salt, and pepper and stir to combine. Turn up the heat to medium-high and bring the lentil stew to a boil. Cover the saucepot with the lid, decrease the heat to medium-low and cook the soup for 35 - 40 min until the lentils have softened and are tender. Stir in the lemon juice and lemon zest.
3. Serve and enjoy!

Nutrition: Carbohydrates: 45g; Protein: 19.3g; Fat: 5.5g; Saturated Fat: 0.8g; Cholesterol: 0mg; ; Sodium: 545mg; Potassium: 765mg; Sugar: 3.9g; Vitamin D: 0mcg; Calcium: 55mg; Iron: 6mg

Rosemary Coconut Almond Crusted Salmon

Preparation: 10 min | Cooking: 15 min | Servings: 4

Ingredients

For the crusted salmon:

- 4 salmon fillets
- 1/2 cup roasted almonds, coarsely ground in the food processor
- 1/4 cup sesame seeds
- 1/4 cup shredded unsweetened coconut
- 2 sprigs of fresh rosemary
- 2 tablespoons olive oil
- 1 teaspoon kosher salt
- 1/4 teaspoon black pepper

For the honey lime sauce:

- 3 tablespoons honey
- 1 tablespoon lime juice
- 2 tablespoons coconut aminos
- 1 clove garlic, minced

Directions

1. To make the sauce, place the honey, lime juice, coconut aminos, and minced garlic into a small bowl, whisk to combine, and set aside.
2. To make the salmon combine the almonds, sesame seeds, and shredded coconut in a bowl, then transfer the almond mixture onto a plate.
3. Brush the tops of the salmon fillets with one tablespoon of olive oil.
4. Then press the top of each salmon fillet into the almond coconut breading and season each fillet with salt and pepper.
5. Place the remaining tablespoon of olive oil in a large skillet over medium-high heat. Once it is hot, place each salmon fillet, crust side down, into the skillet and sear it for 4-5 min, checking every so often to ensure the crust does not burn. Turn the salmon over, and roast it for an additional 5-7 min until salmon reaches your preferred doneness.
6. Place the salmon on a serving dish, and drizzle with the honey lime sauce.
7. Serve and enjoy!

Nutrition: Carbohydrates: 23.5g; Protein: 40.4g; Fat: 38.5g; Saturated Fat: 11.8g; Cholesterol: 30mg; ; Sodium: 675mg; Potassium: 194mg; Sugar: 14.9g; Vitamin D: 0mcg; Calcium: 140mg; Iron: 3mg

Spicy Peanut Chicken Stir-Fry With Sweet Potato Noodles

Preparation: 10 min | Cooking: 20 min | Servings: 4

Ingredients

For the peanut sauce:

- 3 tablespoons all-natural smooth peanut butter
- 2 tablespoons coconut aminos
- 1 teaspoon ginger, minced
- 1 garlic clove, minced
- 1 tablespoon red pepper flakes

- 1/2 tablespoon agave nectar
- 1 teaspoon sesame oil
- 3/4 cup light coconut milk

For the stir fry:

- 3 medium sweet potatoes, peeled and spiralized
- 1 pound organic chicken thighs, cut into 1-inch pieces
- 1 teaspoon kosher salt
- 1/2 teaspoon black pepper
- 1 tablespoon sesame oil3 cups broccoli florets
- 2 medium red bell pepper, sliced into thin strips
- 1 large carrot, cut into thin strips

Directions

1. To make the peanut sauce whisk the peanut butter, coconut aminos, ginger, garlic, red pepper flakes, agave nectar, sesame oil, and coconut milk in a medium bowl until it is smooth. Set the peanut sauce aside.
2. Generously season the chicken thighs with salt and pepper, then place 1/2 tablespoon of sesame oil in a large skillet on medium-high heat. When the sesame oil is hot, add the chicken thighs and sauté for 4-6 min until the chicken is no longer pink. Transfer the chicken thighs to a bowl and set aside.
3. Add 1/2 tablespoon of sesame oil to the skillet, then add the broccoli florets, red pepper strips, and carrots. Sauté the vegetables for 5 min until the broccoli and carrots are semi-tender. Add the spiralized sweet potato and cook for 2-3 min.
4. Pour the peanut sauce and add the chicken to the pot, tossing to coat the vegetables in the sauce. Decrease the flame to medium-low and cook for another 2-3 min until sweet potato noodles are tender.
5. Serve and enjoy!

Nutrition: Carbohydrates: 22.51g; Protein: 17.7g; Fat: 26.4g; Saturated Fat: 10.78g; Cholesterol: 74mg; ; Sodium: 537mg; Potassium: 618mg; Sugar: 8.21g; Vitamin D: 0mcg; Calcium: 72mg; Iron: 2mg

Pomegranate Lime Quinoa Salad

Preparation: 15 min | Cooking: 15 min | Servings: 4

Ingredients

For the salad:

- 2 cups cooked quinoa, cooled
- 1 cup pomegranate seeds
- ¼ cup chopped pecans
- 2 cups arugula

For the vinaigrette:

- juice of 1 lime
- 2 tablespoon extra virgin olive oil
- 1/4 cup pomegranate juice
- 2 cloves garlic, minced
- 1 teaspoon sea salt
- ¼ teaspoon black pepper

Directions

1. For the salad, add the quinoa, pomegranate, pecans to a bowl, then place the arugula onto a serving platter.
2. For the vinaigrette, whisk the lime juice, extra virgin olive oil, pomegranate juice, garlic, black pepper, and salt in a bowl.
3. Drizzle the lime pomegranate vinaigrette over the quinoa salad, then stir to combine well and pour the salad onto the bed of arugula.
4. Serve and enjoy!

Nutrition: Carbohydrates: 43.4g; Protein: 17.3g; Fat: 10.3g; Saturated Fat: 1.1g; Cholesterol: 0mg; ; Sodium: 483mg; Potassium: 333mg; Sugar: 17.3g;

Cauliflower Fried Rice

Preparation: 15 min | Cooking: 15 min | Servings: 4

Ingredients

- 1 2 lb. head of cauliflower
- 4 tablespoon olive oil
- 2 large eggs, beaten
- 1 teaspoon kosher salt
- 1 onion, diced
- 1 red bell pepper, diced
- 3 garlic cloves, minced
- 1 tablespoon fresh ginger, minced
- 4 tablespoons low sodium gluten-free soy sauce
- 1/4 teaspoon crushed red pepper flakes
- 1 cup frozen peas and carrots
- 1 teaspoon rice wine vinegar
- 1 teaspoon toasted sesame oil
- 1/4 cup chopped cashews
- 2 tablespoon freshly chopped parsley

Directions

1. Process the cauliflower in a food processor outfitted with the grater attachment and set it aside.
2. Add two tablespoons of the olive oil into a nonstick skillet over medium-high heat. Once it is hot, add the eggs and 1/2 teaspoon of salt and

scramble the eggs until they are thoroughly cooked. Place the scrambled eggs onto a plate and set it aside.

3. Wipe the skillet clean, then add the remaining olive oil to the pan and place it over medium-high heat. Add the onion, red pepper, garlic, and ginger and cook for 3-4 min, constantly stirring until the vegetables have softened.
4. Stir in the processed cauliflower, soy sauce, red pepper flakes, and the remaining salt. Sauté for 3 min, frequently stirring, then add the peas and carrots and continue to cook for 5-7 min until the cauliflower fried rice is tender and slightly crisp and the vegetables are heated through.
5. Add the rice wine vinegar, sesame oil, cashews, and scrambled eggs.
6. Cook for another minute until everything is thoroughly heated.
7. Serve and enjoy!

Nutrition: Carbohydrates: 26.8g; Protein: 12.1g; Fat: 22.2g; Saturated Fat: 3.8g; Cholesterol: 93mg; ; Sodium: 1207mg; Potassium: 968mg; Sugar: 10.6g;

Cajun Shrimp Avocado Salad

Preparation: 10 min | Cooking: 15 min | Servings: 6

Ingredients

For the Cajun shrimp:

- 1 lb. medium shrimp peeled and deveined
- 1 teaspoon Cajun seasoning
- 2 cloves garlic, minced
- 1 teaspoon onion powder
- 1/2 teaspoon kosher salt
- 2 tablespoon olive oil

For the salad:

- 6 cups mixed greens
- 3 Roma tomatoes, sliced
- 2 avocados peeled, pitted, and sliced
- 3 hard-boiled eggs, chopped

For the cilantro-lime dressing:

- 3 tablespoon fresh lime juice
- 1/2 cup finely minced cilantro
- 3 tablespoon olive oil
- 1/2 teaspoon kosher salt
- 1/4 teaspoon black pepper

Directions

1. Remove the excess moisture from the shrimp with a paper towel, then place them into a bowl.

Add the Cajun seasoning, garlic, onion powder, and salt. Set a nonstick skillet over medium-high heat, then add the olive oil 2. Place a large nonstick pan over medium-high heat and add the olive oil.

2. Place the seasoned shrimp into the hot pan in an even layer. Cook the shrimp for 2 min, then flip the shrimp and cook for another 2 min until the shrimp are cooked through. Remove the shrimp and place it on a plate.
3. Place the mixed green on your serving platter and add the tomatoes, avocadoes, hard-boiled eggs, and shrimp.
4. For the cilantro-lime dressing, add the lime juice, cilantro, olive oil, salt, and black pepper to a small bowl and whisk to combine. Drizzle the cilantro-lime sauce on the shrimp avocado salad.
5. Serve and enjoy!

Nutrition: Carbohydrates: 34.5g; Protein: 29.6g; Fat: 24.1g; Saturated Fat: 3.7g; Cholesterol: 242mg; ; Sodium: 1135mg; Potassium: 548mg; Sugar: 3.1g;

Borscht

Preparation: 15 min | Cooking: 25 min | Servings: 4

Ingredients

- 2 tablespoons olive oil
- 3 medium beets, peeled, chopped into ½ inch pieces
- 2 medium carrots, peeled, chopped into ½ inch pieces
- 1 medium red onion, chopped
- 2 garlic cloves, minced
- 4 cups low-sodium vegetable broth
- 2 tablespoons tomato paste
- 2 cups finely shredded cabbage
- 1 tablespoon apple cider vinegar
- 1 ½ tablespoon lemon juice
- ¼ cup chopped fresh dil
- 1 teaspoon kosher salt
- 1/2 teaspoon black pepper

Directions

1. Place the olive oil into a large, heavy-bottom pot and set it over medium-high heat. Once the olive oil is hot, add the beets, carrots, and onions and cook for 8-10 min until the vegetables soften. Stir in the garlic and sauté for a minute until it is fragrant.
2. Stir in the tomato paste and cook for 1-2 min, then add the vegetable broth and cabbage, and bring the borscht to a boil. Lower the flame to

medium-low, then cook the borscht for 18-20 min until the vegetables are tender.

3. Remove the borscht from the stove and stir in the apple cider vinegar, lemon juice, dil , salt, and pepper. Serve and enjoy!

Nutrition: Carbohydrates: 18.5g; Protein: 5.1g; Fat: 7.4g; Saturated Fat: 1.1g; Cholesterol: 0mg; ; Sodium: 744mg; Potassium: 597mg; Sugar: 9.1g;

Curried Cauliflower Soup

Preparation: 15 min | Cooking: 45 min-1 h| Servings: 4

Ingredients

- 1 large head of cauliflower, stems removed and cut into small florets
- 4 tablespoons olive oil
- 1 medium yellow onion, diced
- 2 cloves garlic, minced
- 2 tablespoons ginger, minced
- 2 tablespoons Thai red curry paste
- zest of 1 lemon teaspoon
- 1 ½ cups vegetable broth
- 1 14.oz. can coconut milk
- 1 tablespoon fresh lemon juice
- 1 teaspoon kosher salt
- 1/2 teaspoon black pepper

Directions

1. Program your oven to 400F, then place the cauliflower florets into a bowl and toss with the two tablespoons of olive oil. Arrange the cauliflower onto a parchment-lined baking sheet in an even layer and roast for 28-30 min until the florets are golden brown.

2. 102

3. Place the remaining olive oil into a large, heavy-bottomed pot over medium-high heat. Once the olive oil is hot, add the onion and cook for 3-5 min, stirring every so often until the onions are translucent and has softened. Stir in the garlic and ginger and saute for a minute until it is fragrant.

4. Next, add the curry paste and lemon zest, and stir to combine. Add the roasted cauliflower florets to the soup, then stir in the vegetable broth and coconut milk. Cook the cauliflower soup for 8-10 min, stirring every so often. Remove the curried cauliflower soup from the stove and allow it to cool for 5 min.

5. Working in batches, blend the curried cauliflower soup until smooth in a high-speed blender.

Return the curried cauliflower soup to the pot and season with salt, pepper, and lemon juice.

6. Serve and enjoy!

Nutrition: Carbohydrates: 9.5g; Protein: 3.4g; Fat: 18.5g; Saturated Fat: 4.4g; Cholesterol: 0mg; ; Sodium: 1276mg; Potassium: 169mg; Sugar: 2.1g;

Green Curried Sweet Potato

Preparation: 25 min | Cooking: 25 min | Servings: 4

Ingredients

- 2 tablespoons olive oil
- 1 small onion, chopped
- 2 cloves garlic, minced
- 1 1/2 tablespoons freshly grated ginger
- 4 cups peeled sweet potatoes diced into 1/2 inch pieces
- 1/2 cup low-sodium vegetable broth
- 1 14 oz. can full-fat coconut milk
- 1/4 cup green curry paste
- 1/4 teaspoon red pepper flakes
- 1/2 teaspoon fine sea salt
- 1 tablespoon fresh lime juice
- 1 head of broccoli, cut into florets
- 1 tablespoon freshly chopped cilantro

Directions

1. Place the olive oil into a heavy bottom saucepan over medium-high heat; once it is hot, add the chopped onions and cook for 3-4 min until they have softened. Stir in the ginger and garlic and cook for 1 minute until it becomes fragrant.

2. 105

3. Add the sweet potatoes and vegetable broth and bring it to a boil. Once it is simmering, cover the pot with the lid and cook the sweet potatoes for 8

4. min until they have slightly softened.

5. In another bowl, whisk the coconut milk, green curry paste separate bowl, mix the coconut milk, curry paste, red pepper flakes, and salt until it is completely incorporated. Pour the coconut milk mixture into the sweet potatoes, then add the broccoli florets and stir to combine.

6. Bring the sweet potato curry to a gentle simmer and cook for 5-8

7. min until the sweet potatoes and broccoli florets are tender, and the sauce has slightly thickened. Add the lime juice, cook the curry for one more minute, and then remove it from the heat and garnish with the cilantro.

8. Serve and enjoy!

Nutrition: Carbohydrates: 53g; Protein: 4.8g; Fat: 15g; Saturated Fat: 5.2g; Cholesterol: 0mg; ; Sodium: 884mg; Potassium: 1468mg; Sugar: 2.9g;

Cauliflower Gnocchi Chicken And Vegetables

Preparation: 10 min | Cooking: 20 min | Servings: 4

Ingredients

- 1 lb. chicken breast, cut into 1/2-inch pieces
- 1 teaspoon black pepper
- 1 1/2 teaspoon kosher salt
- 2 tablespoon olive oil
- 1/2 cup onion, chopped
- 1 red pepper cut into strips
- 2 medium zucchini, cut into 1/2 rounds
- 2 cloves garlic, minced
- 1 tablespoon smoked paprika
- 1/2 cup chicken broth
- 1 12 oz. bag cauliflower gnocchi

Directions

1. Place a tablespoon of olive oil into a skillet, then season the chicken with 1/2 teaspoon of pepper and a teaspoon of salt. Place the chicken breast into the skillet in an even layer and cook for 3-4 min without flipping it until it is slightly browned. Flip the chicken and cook for 3-4 min, stirring every so often until it is browned and thoroughly cooked through, then transfer the cooked chicken breast to a plate.
2. Add one tablespoon of olive to the pan and add the onions and red bell pepper. Cook the onions and red bell peppers for 3-4 min until they have softened.
3. Add the zucchini, garlic, the remaining salt and pepper, and smoked paprika, and stir for 1 minute until the garlic is fragrant. Add the chicken broth and gnocchi and cook for 3-5 min until the gnocchi is tender. Stir in the cooked chicken and cook for 1-2 min until everything is heated through.

Nutrition: Carbohydrates: 31.4g; Protein: 31.4g; Fat: 12.6g; Saturated Fat: 2.3g; Cholesterol: 78mg; ; Sodium: 1241mg; Potassium: 903mg; Sugar: 6.7g;

Brussel Sprout Chicken Zucchini Noodle Soup

Preparation: 15 min | Cooking: 30 min | Servings: 4

Ingredients

- 2 tablespoons olive oil
- 2 cloves garlic, minced
- 1 small onion, diced
- 1 medium red bell pepper, diced
- 1 bay leaf
- 2 tablespoons fresh thyme
- 6 cups low-sodium vegetable broth
- 1 lb. boneless, skinless chicken breasts
- 2 medium zucchini, spiralized into thick spirals
- 1 medium carrot, cut into strips
- 2 cups Brussel sprouts
- 1 teaspoon kosher salt
- 1/2 teaspoon black pepper

Directions

1. Place the olive oil into a soup pot over medium-high heat. Once it is hot, add the onions and red peppers and cook for 3-4 min until the onions and peppers soften, then add in the garlic and cook for a minute until it is fragrant.
2. Add the bay leaf, thyme, and vegetable broth, arrange the chicken breasts in a single layer to the broth and let it come to a boil. Decrease the flame to medium low, cover the pot with the lid and cook the chicken for 8-12 min until it reaches an internal temperature of 165°F. Remove the chicken zucchini noodle soup from the stove.
3. Remove the chicken pot and place it onto your cutting board. Once the chicken has cooled slightly, use the tines of two forks to shred the chicken into smaller pieces.
4. Place the soup base onto the stove over medium-high heat and bring it up to a gentle simmer. Add the zucchini, carrot, and Brussel sprouts and simmer for 4-5 min until the vegetables are tender. Season the Brussel sprout zucchini noodle soup with salt and pepper.
5. Serve and enjoy!

Nutrition: Carbohydrates: 15.7g; Protein: 23.6g; Fat: 9.3g; Saturated Fat: 1.6g; Cholesterol: 43mg; ; Sodium: 865mg; Potassium: 578mg; Sugar: 5.7g;

Roasted Seasonal Vegetables With Hummus

Preparation: 20 min | Cooking: 35 min | Servings: 4

Ingredients

For the seasonal roasted vegetables:

- 2 medium sweet potato peeled & cut into ½-inch pieces
- 2 cups canned chickpeas, drained and rinsed
- 2 carrots peeled & cut into ½-inch strips
- 2 medium zucchini cut into 1/2 inch rounds
- 2 tablespoons olive oil
- 1 teaspoon kosher salt
- 1 teaspoon paprika
- 1 teaspoon garlic powder
- 1 teaspoon onion powder
- ½ teaspoon black pepper

For the hummus:

- 1 1/2 cups canned chickpeas, rinsed and drained
- 4 tablespoon fresh lemon juice
- 1/4 cup tahini
- 1 clove garlic, minced
- 2 tablespoons olive oil
- 1/2 teaspoon ground cumin
- 1/2 teaspoon paprika
- 1 teaspoon kosher salt
- 2-3 tablespoons water

Directions

1. To make the seasonal vegetables, preheat your oven to 425F, then lightly spray a cookie sheet or baking dish with non-stick cooking spray.
2. Add the sweet potatoes, chickpeas, carrots, zucchini, olive oil, paprika, salt, onion and garlic powder, and pepper to a large bowl. Toss the sweet potatoes vegetable mixture to coat them in the seasoning.
3. Place the seasonal vegetables onto the prepared baking sheet and roast them for 15 min. Rotate the baking sheet and cook for another 10-15 min until the vegetables are tender.
4. For the hummus, add the tahini and lemon juice to a food processor and blend for 30-seconds to a minute. Scrape the sides of the food processors bowl and process for another 30 seconds.
5. Add the olive oil, minced garlic, cumin, paprika, and salt to the food processor and blend for 30 seconds, then place half of the chickpeas in the food processor and blend for 1 minute. Scrape the sides food processor's bowl, add the rest of the chickpeas, and mix for 2-3 min until it is smooth and creamy.
6. Gradual y drizzle the water a tablespoon at a time into the food processor and blend until it is smooth and creamy.
7. Divide the seasonal vegetables and hummus between 4 plates.
8. Serve and enjoy!

Nutrition: Carbohydrates: 39.3g; Protein: 10.9g; Fat: 24.4g;
Saturated Fat: 3.3g; Cholesterol: 0mg; ; Sodium: 1525mg; Potassium: 1012mg; Sugar: 8.6g;

Chickpea Tomato Broccoli Salad

Preparation: 15 min | Cooking: 30 min | Servings: 4

Ingredients

For the chickpea tomato salad:

- 3 cups canned chickpeas, rinsed and drained
- 1 cup cherry tomatoes, quartered
- 1 cup steamed broccoli florets, cooled
- 1 small red onion
- 1/4 cup toasted pine nuts

For the honey citrus dressing:

- 3 tablespoons lemon juice
- 1/4 cup olive oil
- 1 tablespoon honey
- 1 clove pressed garlic
- 1/2 teaspoon dried oregano
- 1 teaspoon paprika
- 1/2 teaspoon kosher salt
- 1/2 teaspoon black pepper

Directions

1. Place the chickpeas, tomatoes, broccoli, florets, red onion, and pine nuts into a large salad bowl.
2. In another bowl, whisk the freshly squeezed lemon juice, olive oil, honey, garlic, paprika, oregano, kosher salt, and pepper.
3. Pour the lemon and olive oil dressing onto the chickpea tomato and broccoli salad and toss to evenly coat the chickpea salad in the dressing 4. Serve and enjoy!

Nutrition: Carbohydrates: 20.1g; Protein: 7.2g; Fat: 8.3g; Saturated Fat: 2.3g; Cholesterol: 0mg; ; Sodium: 556mg; Potassium: 400mg; Sugar: 8.3g

Roasted Brussels Sprouts with Grapes and Walnuts

Preparation: 10 min | Cooking: 35 min | Servings: 6

Ingredients

- 2 lbs. Brussels sprouts trimmed cut in half lengthwise
- 1 cup red seedless grapes
- 1/2 cup pecan halves
- 4 tablespoons olive oil
- 1 teaspoon sea salt
- 1/2 teaspoon black pepper
- 1 teaspoon garlic powder
- 1 teaspoon onion powder
- 3 tablespoons balsamic vinegar

Directions

1. Program your oven to 400°F, then place Brussel sprouts, grapes, and pecans onto a parchment-lined rimmed baking sheet. Pour the olive oil, salt, pepper, onion powder, and garlic powder onto the Brussel sprouts and toss .to coat them evenly.
2. Roast the Brussel sprouts for 32-35 min until they are golden brown, the pecans are toasted and aromatic, and the grapes have swollen and darkened in color.
3. Drizzle the balsamic vinegar over the roasted Brussel sprouts, grapes, and pecans and toss to coat.
4. Serve and enjoy!

Nutrition: Carbohydrates: 19.4g; Protein: 5.7g; Fat: 11.7g; Saturated Fat: 1.7g; Cholesterol: 0mg; ; Sodium: 351mg; Potassium: 663mg; Sugar: 7.5g

Basil Couscous with Caramelized Onions and Spinach

Preparation: 10 min | Cooking: 35 min | Servings: 4

Ingredients

- 2 tablespoons olive oil,
- 1 medium onion, thinly sliced
- 2 garlic cloves, minced
- 1 teaspoon sea salt
- 1/2 teaspoon black pepper
- 1 teaspoon crushed red pepper flakes
- 3 tablespoons freshly chopped basil
- 1 1/4 cup low-sodium vegetable broth
- 10 oz. frozen spinach
- 10 oz. couscous
- 2 tablespoons lemon juice
- ½ cup frozen green peas

Directions

1. Place the olive oil into a saucepot; once it is hot, add the onions cook for 3-5 min until the onions have caramelized. Stir in the garlic, basil, salt, pepper, and red pepper flakes and cook for 1 minute until the garlic is fragrant.
2. Pour the vegetable broth and spinach into the pot and stir until the spinach is completely thawed, bringing the mixture to a boil.
3. Add the couscous, lemon juice, and green peas and stir to combine.
4. Remove the couscous from the stove, cover the pot with the lid and let it sit for 5 min until the basil couscous has absorbed all of the vegetable broth.
5. Serve and enjoy!

Nutrition: Carbohydrates: 35.9g; Protein: 7.3g; Fat: 4.5g; Saturated Fat: 0.7g; Cholesterol: 0mg; ; Sodium: 324mg; Potassium: 342mg; Sugar: 1.2g

Pan-Seared Salmon

Preparation: 5 min | Cooking: 5 min

Ingredients

- 2 salmon fillets skin-on and descaled
- 2 tablespoon olive oil
- 1 teaspoon sea salt
- 1/2 teaspoon white pepper
- juice of 1 lemon

Directions

1. Heat a large uncoated skillet for 3-5 min on medium-high heat. Place the olive oil into the skillet and swirl it around to coat the pan's bottom.
2. Careful y score the skin of the salmon using a sharp knife. Liberal y season both sides of the salmon with the salt and pepper, then add the salmon skin side down to the scorching hot skillet.
3. Sear the salmon for 4-5 min until the skin is crispy and golden brown, then flip it over and cook for 30 seconds to 1 minute. Remove the salmon from the pan and squeeze the lemon juice over the salmon.
4. Serve and enjoy!

Nutrition: Carbohydrates: 3g; Protein: 41.4g; Fat: 26.1g; Saturated Fat: 5g; Cholesterol: 36mg; ; Sodium: 1031mg; Potassium: 47mg; Sugar: 0.7g

Cheese macaroni

Servings: 1 | Preparation: 10 min | Cooking: 20 min

Ingredients

- 1 lb. macaroni
- 1 cup cheddar cheese
- 1 cup Monterey Jack cheese
- 1 cup mozzarella cheese
- ¼ tsp salt
- ¼ tsp pepper

Directions

1. In a pot bring water to a boil
2. Add pasta and cook until al dente
3. In a bowl combine all cheese together and add it to the pasta
4. When ready transfer to a bowl, add salt, pepper and serve

Potato casserole

Servings: 2 | Preparation: 10 min | Cooking: 20 min

Ingredients

- 5 6 large potatoes
- ¼ cup sour cream
- ½ cup butter
- 5 6 bacon strips
- 1 2 cups mozzarella cheese
- ¼ cup heavy cream

Directions

1. Place the potatoes in a pot with boiling water, cook until tender
2. Place the potatoes in a bowl, add sour cream, butter, cheese and mix well
3. In a baking dish place the bacon strips and cover with potato mixture
4. Add remaining mozzarella cheese on top
5. Bake at 325 F for 15 18 min or until the mozzarella is fully melted
6. When ready remove from the oven and serve

Cheese stuffed shells

Servings: 2 | Preparation: 10 min | Cooking: 30 min

Ingredients

- 2 3 cups macaroni
- 2 cups cream cheese
- 1 cup spaghetti sauce
- 1 cup onions
- 1 cup mozzarella cheese

Directions

1. In a pot boil water and add shells
2. Cook for 12 15 min
3. In a baking dish add spaghetti sauce
4. In a bowl combine cream cheese, onion and set aside
5. Add cream cheese to the shells and place them into the baking dish
6. Bake at 325 F for 30 min or until golden brown
7. When ready remove from the oven and serve

Potato soup

Servings: 4-6 | Preparation: 10 min | Cooking: 50 min

Ingredients

- 1 onion
- 2 3 carrots
- 2 tablespoons flour
- 5 6 large potatoes
- 2 cups milk
- 2 cups bouillon
- 1 cup water
- 2 cups milk
- 1 tsp salt
- 1 tsp pepper

Directions

1. In a saucepan melt butter and sauce carrots, garlic and onion for 4 5 min
2. Add flour, milk, potatoes, bouillon and cook for another 15 20 min
3. Add pepper and remaining ingredients and cook on low heat for 20 30 min
4. When ready remove from heat and serve

Chicken alfredo

Servings: 2 | Preparation: 10 min | Cooking: 20 min

Ingredients

- 2 3 chicken breasts
- 1 lb. rotini
- 1 cup parmesan cheese
- 1 cup olive oil
- 1 tsp salt
- 1 tsp black pepper
- 1 tsp parsley

Directions

1. In a pot add the rotini and cook on low heat for 12 15 min
2. In a frying pan heat olive oil, add chicken, salt, parsley, and cook until the chicken is brown

3. Drain the rotini and place the rotini in pan with chicken
4. Cook for 2 3 min
5. When ready remove from heat and serve with parmesan cheese on top

Butternut squash pizza

Servings: 4-6 | Preparation: 10 min | Cooking: 15 min

Ingredients
- 2 cups butternut squash
- ¼ tsp salt
- 1 pizza crust
- 5 6 tablespoons alfredo sauce
- 1 tsp olive oil
- 4 5 cups baby spinach
- 2 3 oz. goat cheese

Directions
1. Place the pizza crust on a baking dish and spread the alfredo sauce
2. In a skillet sauté spinach and place it over the pizza crust
3. Add goat cheese, butternut squash, olive oil and salt
4. Bake pizza at 425 F for 8 10 min
5. When ready remove from the oven and serve

Penne with asparagus

Servings: 2 | Preparation: 10 min | Cooking: 20 min

Ingredients
- 6 7 oz. penne pasta
- 2 3 bacon slices
- ¼ cup red onion
- 2 cups asparagus
- 1 cup chicken broth
- 2 3 cups spinach leaves
- ¼ cup parmesan cheese

Directions
1. Cook pasta until al dente
2. In a skillet cook bacon until crispy and set aside
3. In a pan add onion, asparagus, broth and cook on low heat for 5 10 min
4. Add spinach, cheese, pepper, pasta and cook for another 5 6 min
5. When ready sprinkle bacon and serve

Noodle soup

Servings: 4 | Preparation: 10 min | Cooking: 20 min

Ingredients
- 2 3 cups water
- 1 can chicken broth
- 1 tablespoon olive oil
- ¼ red onion
- ¼ cup celery
- ¼ tsp salt
- ¼ tsp black pepper
- 5 6 oz. fusilli pasta
- 2 cups chicken breast
- 2 tablespoons parsley

Directions
1. In a pot boil water with broth
2. In a saucepan heat oil, add carrot, pepper, celery, onion, salt and sauté until tender
3. Add broth mixture to the mixture and pasta
4. Cook until al dente and stir in chicken breast, cook until chicken breast is tender
5. When ready remove from heat, stir in parsley and serve

Tomato wrap

Servings: 4 | Preparation: 5 min | Cooking: 15 min

Ingredients
- 1 cup corn
- 1 cup tomatoes
- 1 cup pickles
- 1 tablespoon olive oil
- 1 tablespoon mayonnaise
- 6 7 turkey slices
- 2 3 whole wheat tortillas
- 1 cup romaine lettuce

Directions
1. In a bowl combine tomatoes, pickles, olive oil, corn and set aside
2. Place the turkey slices over the tortillas and top with tomato mixture and mayonnaise
3. Roll and serve

Thyme cod

Servings: 2 | Preparation: 5 min | Cooking: 15 min

Ingredients
- 1 tablespoon olive oil

- ½ red onion
- 1 can tomatoes
- 2 3 springs thyme
- 2 3 cod fillets

Directions

1. In a frying pan heat olive oil and sauté onion, stir in tomatoes, spring thyme and cook for 5 6 min
2. Add cod fillets, cover and cook for 5 6 min per side
3. When ready remove from heat and serve

Veggie stir fry

Servings: 2 | Preparation: 10 min | Cooking: 20 min

Ingredients

- 1 tablespoon cornstarch
- 1 garlic clove
- ¼ cup olive oil
- ¼ head broccoli
- ¼ cup show peas
- ½ cup carrots
- ¼ cup green beans
- 1 tablespoon soy sauce
- ½ cup onion

Directions

1. In a bowl combine garlic, olive oil, cornstarch and mix well
2. Add the rest of the ingredients and toss to coat
3. In a skillet cook vegetables mixture until tender
4. When ready transfer to a plate garnish with ginger and serve

Chapter 4: Side Dishes

Minestrone soup

Servings: 6 | Preparation: 10 min | Cooking: 50 min

Ingredients

- 2 onions
- 1 cup peas
- 1 can tomatoes
- 2 cups tomato sauce
- 3 carrots
- 1 cup green beans
- 2 tbs basil
- 6 cups water
- 2 cloves garlic
- Salt
- 2 tbs cheese
- 1.5 cups kidney
- 2 cups celery
- 1 bell pepper

Directions

1. Put the onions, celery and carrots into a pot of water.
2. Add the green beans, peas, tomatoes and bell pepper when the water starts to boil, then allow to simmer for 30 min.
3. Add the tomato sauce and basil then season with salt.
4. Allow to simmer for 10 min, then add the garlic and simmer for 5 more min.
5. Serve topped with cheese.

Tuna salad

Servings: 4 | Preparation: 10 min | Cooking: 5 min

Ingredients

- ½ tsp lemon zest
- Salt
- Pepper
- 4 eggs
- 1/3 red onion
- ¾ lb green beans
- 1 can tuna
- 1 tsp oregano
- 6 tbs olive oil
- 3 tbs lemon juice
- 1 can beans
- 1 can black olives

Directions

1. Place the green beans, 1/3 cup water and salt to taste in a skillet.

2. Bring to a boil, covered.
3. Cook for 5 min.
4. Dump them onto a lined cookie sheet.
5. Mix the white beans, onion, olives and tuna.
6. Combine the oregano, lemon juice and zest, and oil in a separate bowl.
7. Pour the mixture over the tuna mixture.
8. Season and serve immediately with the boiled eggs.

Chicken skillet

Servings: 4 | Preparation: 10 min | Cooking: 30 min

Ingredients

- 1 tsp oil
- ½ cup carrots
- 1 zucchini
- 1 bell pepper
- ½ lb chicken
- 1 onion

Directions

1. Cut the chicken into strips, then cook in the oil until it gets brown.
2. Remove from the skillet and add the vegetables.
3. Cook until soft for 10 min, then add the chicken.
4. Season and serve immediately.

Spinach quesadillas

Servings: 4 | Preparation: 10 min | Cooking: 15 min

Ingredients

- 4 cups spinach
- 4 green onions
- 1 tomato
- ½ lemon juice
- 1 tsp cumin
- 1 tsp garlic powder
- Salt
- 1 cup cheese
- 4 tortillas

Directions

1. Cook all of the ingredients except for the cheese and tortillas in a skillet.
2. Cook until the spinach is wilted.
3. Remove to a bowl and add the cheese.
4. Place the mixture on half of the tortilla, fold the other half and cook for 2 min on each side on a griddle

Bean salad

Servings: 4 | Preparation: 10 min | Cooking: 0 min

Ingredients
- 1 can garbanzo beans
- 1 can red beans
- 1 tomato
- ½ red onion
- ½ lemon juice
- 1 tbs olive oil

Directions
1. Mix all of the ingredients together in a bowl.
2. Season with salt and serve immediately.

Garlic salmon

Servings: 4 | Preparation: 10 min | Cooking: 20 min

Ingredients
- 2 lb salmon
- 2 tbs water
- Salt
- 2 tbs parsley
- 4 cloves garlic

Directions
1. Preheat the oven to 400F.
2. Mix the garlic, parsley, salt and water in a bowl.
3. Brush the mixture over the salmon.
4. Place the fish on a baking tray and cover with aluminum foil.
5. Cook for 20 min.
6. Serve with vegetables.

Tuna wrap

Servings: 4 | Preparation: 10 min | Cooking: 0 min

Ingredients
- 6 ounces tuna
- 2 tsp yogurt
- ½ celery stalk
- Handful baby spinach
- ½ onion
- 2 tsp lemon juice
- 4 tortillas

Directions
1. Mix all of the ingredients except for the tortillas in a bowl.
2. Spread the mixture over the tortillas, then wrap them up.

3. Serve immediately.

Roasted chicken wrap

Servings: 4 | Preparation: 10 min | Cooking: 10 min

Ingredients
- 1 cup chicken breast
- 2 tsp yogurt
- 1/3 cup celery
- 8 tomato slices
- ½ onion
- 1 tbs mustard
- 2 tbs ketchup
- 4 tortillas

Directions
1. Cut the chicken as you desire and grill until done on each side.
2. Mix all of the ingredients except for the tortillas in a bowl.
3. Spread the mixture over the tortillas and add the chicken.
4. Serve immediately.

Lentil salad

Servings: 4 | Preparation: 10 min | Cooking: 0 min

Ingredients
- 1 cup cooked lentils
- 1 cup baby spinach
- 1 poached egg
- ¼ avocado
- ½ tomato
- 1 2 slices whole wheat bread

Directions
1. Mix all of the ingredients together except for the bread.
2. Toast the bread.
3. Serve immediately together.

Stuffed eggplant

Servings: 4 | Preparation: 10 min | Cooking: 50 min

Ingredients
- 1 eggplant
- 2 onions
- 1 red pepper
- ½ cup tomato juice
- ¼ cup cheese

Directions

1. Preheat the oven to 350F.
2. Cut the eggplant in half and cook for 30 min.
3. Cook the diced onion in 2 tbs of water until brown.
4. Add the pepper and add it to the onion, cooking for another 5 min.
5. Add the tomato juice and allow to cook for another 5 min.
6. Scoop out the eggplant.
7. Mix the eggplant with the onion mixture, then add it back into the eggplant shell.
8. Grate the cheese on top and bake for another 10 min.
9. Serve hot.

Broccoli & aurgula soup

Servings: 2 | Preparation: 5 min | Cooking: 20 min

Ingredients

- 1 tbs olive oil
- ¼ tsp thyme
- 1 cup arugula
- ½ lemon juice
- 1 head broccoli
- 1 clove garlic
- 2 cups water
- ¼ tsp salt
- ¼ tsp black pepper
- ½ yellow onion

Directions

1. Heat the oil in a saucepan.
2. Cook the onion until soft, then add the garlic and cook for another minute.
3. Add the broccoli and cook for 5 min.
4. Add the water, thyme, salt, and pepper.
5. Bring to boil, then lower the heat and cook for 10 min.
6. Transfer to a blender, blend, then add the arugula and blend until smooth.
7. Add the lemon juice and serve immediately.

Stuffed peppers

Servings: 4 | Preparation: 20 min | Cooking: 25 min

Ingredients

- ½ onion
- 1 cup mushrooms
- ½ yellow bell pepper
- 1 cup spinach
- 1 can tomatoes
- 1 tbs tomato paste
- 4 red bell peppers
- 1 lb ground turkey
- 2 tbs olive oil
- 1 zucchini
- ½ green bell pepper
- 1 tsp Italian seasoning
- ½ tsp garlic powder
- Salt
- Pepper

Directions

1. Bring a pot of water to a boil.
2. Cut the tops off the peppers, and remove the seeds.
3. Cook in water for 5 min.
4. Preheat the oven to 350F.
5. Cook the turkey until brown.
6. Heat the oil and cook the onion, mushrooms, zucchini, green and yellow pepper, and spinach until soft.
7. Add the turkey and the rest of the ingredients.
8. Stuff the peppers with the mixture.
9. Bake for 15 min.
10. Serve hot.

Potato salad

Servings: 6 | Preparation: 5 min | Cooking: 10 min

Ingredients

- 1 red onion
- 2 tsp cumin seeds
- 1 cloves garlic
- ½ cup olive oil
- 4 potatoes
- ½ cup lemon juice
- 2 tbs fresh parsley
- 1 ½ tsp salt
- 2 tsp turmeric powder

Directions

1. Steam the potatoes for 10 min, until tender.
2. Mix the lemon juice, turmeric, cumin seeds, and salt.
3. Place the potatoes in a bowl and pour the mixture over.
4. Add the onion and garlic and stir to coat.
5. Refrigerate until the potatoes are cold.
6. Add olive oil and herbs and stir.

Pork tacos

Servings: 4 | Preparation: 20 min | Cooking: 10 min

Ingredients

- 1 cucumber
- 1 cup red cabbage
- 1 ½ lbs ground pork
- 6 radishes
- 4 tsp sugar
- 2 tbs olive oil
- ¼ cup white wine vinegar
- 2 tbs soy sauce
- 2 tsp garlic powder
- 2 tbs sesame oil
- 4 scallions
- 2 tsp Sriracha
- 12 tortillas
- 2 tsp cilantro
- ½ cup sour cream
- Salt
- Pepper

Directions

1. Place the cucumbers, radishes, vinegar, 2 tsp sugar, salt, and pepper in a bowl.
2. Cook the scallions and cabbage in the oil until soft.
3. Add the pork, garlic powder, and 2 tsp sugar and cook for another 5 min.
4. Add the sesame oil, Sriracha, soy sauce and combine.
5. Season with salt and pepper.
6. Heat the tortillas in the microwave for a few seconds.
7. Spread sour cream on the tortilla, add the mixture, sprinkle cilantro over and add the cucumber and radishes.
8. Serve immediately.

Greek lamb meatballs

Servings: 4 | Preparation: 10 min | Cooking: 25 min

Ingredients

- 1 lb. ground lamb
- 1 egg
- 1 cloves garlic
- 1 handful parsley
- 1 tablespoon dried oregano
- 1 tsp dried rosemary
- ½ cup fetta cheese
- ¼ tsp salt

Directions

1. Preheat the oven to 325 F
2. In a bowl mix all ingredients
3. Form into meat balls
4. Bake for 20 25 min, remove and serve

Baked chilli chicken

Servings: 4 | Preparation: 10 min | Cooking: 30 min

Ingredients

- 2 lb. chicken drumsticks
- 3 tablespoons olive oil
- 2 cloves garlic
- 2 tablespoons lime juice
- 3 tsp lime zest
- 1 tsp chilli flakes
- salt

Directions

1. In a bowl place all ingredients except chicken drumsticks
2. Refrigerate and then add the drumsticks for 1 2 h
3. Preheat oven to 350 F
4. Arrange the chicken drumsticks on a greased oven tray and bake for 40 45 min
5. Remove and serve

Broccoli stir fry

Servings: 2 | Preparation: 10 min | Cooking: 15 min

Ingredients

- 1 head broccoli
- 1 handful cashews
- 1 tablespoons macadamia nut oil
- 2 tablespoons coconut aminos
- 1 tablespoon fish sauce
- 2 cloves garlic
- ¼ red pepper
- 1 tablespoon lime juice
- 6 oz. shrimp
- 1 tablespoon sesame seeds
- salt

Directions

1. In a frying pan heat oil over medium heat
2. Add garlic, sesame seeds, red pepper and cashews
3. Add shrimp and fry for 3 4 min
4. Remove and serve

Spinach Frittata

Servings: 2 | Preparation: 10 min | Cooking: 20 min

Ingredients
- ½ lb. spinach
- 1 tablespoon olive oil
- ½ red onion
- 2 eggs
- ¼ tsp salt
- 2 oz. cheddar cheese
- 1 garlic clove
- ¼ tsp dill

Directions
1. In a bowl whisk eggs with salt and cheese
2. In a frying pan heat olive oil and pour egg mixture
3. Add remaining ingredients and mix well
4. Serve when ready

Turnip Frittata

Servings: 2 | Preparation: 10 min | Cooking: 20 min

Ingredients
- ½ lb. spinach
- ¼ cup turnip
- ½ red onion
- 2 eggs
- ¼ tsp salt
- 2 oz. cheddar cheese
- 1 garlic clove
- ¼ tsp dill

Directions
1. In a bowl whisk eggs with salt and cheese
2. In a frying pan heat olive oil and pour egg mixture
3. Add remaining ingredients and mix well
4. Serve when ready

Squash Frittata

Servings: 2 | Preparation: 10 min | Cooking: 20 min

Ingredients
- 1 cup squash
- 1 tablespoon olive oil
- ½ red onion
- 2 eggs
- ¼ tsp salt
- 2 oz. cheddar cheese
- 1 garlic clove
- ¼ tsp dill

Directions
1. In a bowl whisk eggs with salt and cheese
2. In a frying pan heat olive oil and pour egg mixture
3. Add remaining ingredients and mix well
4. Serve when ready

Onion frittata

Servings: 2 | Preparation: 10 min | Cooking: 20 min

Ingredients
- 1 tablespoon olive oil
- ½ red onion
- 2 eggs
- ¼ tsp salt
- 2 oz. cheddar cheese
- 1 garlic clove
- ¼ tsp dill

Directions
1. In a bowl whisk eggs with salt and cheese
2. In a frying pan heat olive oil and pour egg mixture
3. Add remaining ingredients and mix well
4. Serve when ready

Fried chicken with almonds

Servings: 2 | Preparation: 10 min | Cooking: 25 min

Ingredients
- 1 cup bread crumbs
- ¼ cup parmesan cheese
- ¼ cup almonds
- 1 tsp salt
- 1 tablespoon parley leaves
- 1 clove garlic
- ½ cup olive oil
- 2 lb. chicken breast

Directions
1. In a bowl combine parsley, almonds, garlic, parmesan, bread crumbs, salt and mix well
2. In a bowl add olive oil and dip chicken breast into olive oil
3. Place chicken into the breadcrumb mixture and toss to coat
4. Bake chicken at 375 F for 20 25 min
5. When ready remove chicken from the oven and serve

Filet Mignon With Tomato Sauce

Servings: 4 | Preparation: 10 min | Cooking: 30 min

Ingredients

- 1 tsp soy sauce
- 1 tsp mustard
- 1 tsp parsley leaves
- 1 clove garlic
- 2 3 tomatoes
- 2 tsp olive oil
- 4 5 beef tenderloin steaks
- ½ tsp salt

Directions

1. In a bowl combine parsley, garlic, soy sauce, mustard and mix well
2. Stir in tomatoes slices and toss to coat
3. In a skillet heat olive oil and place the steak
4. Cook until golden brown for 3 4 min
5. Transfer skillet to the oven and bake at 375 F for 8 10 min
6. When ready remove and serve with tomato sauce

Zucchini noodles

Servings: 1 | Preparation: 5 min | Cooking: 15 min

Ingredients

- 2 zucchinis
- 1 tablespoon olive oil
- 1 garlic clove
- ½ cup parmesan cheese
- 1 tsp salt

Directions

1. Spiralize zucchini and set aside
2. In a skillet melt butter, add garlic and zucchini noodles
3. Toss to coat and cook for 5 6 min
4. When ready remove from the skillet and serve with parmesan cheese on top

Green beans with tomatoes

Servings: 4 | Preparation: 10 min | Cooking: 15 min

Ingredients

- 1 cup water
- 1 lb. green beans
- 2 tomatoes
- 1 tsp olive oil
- 1 tsp Italian dressing
- salt

Directions

1. In a pot bring water to a boil
2. Add green beans, tomatoes and boil for 10 12 min
3. Remove green beans and tomatoes to a bowl
4. Chop tomatoes, add Italian dressing, olive oil and serve

Roasted cauliflower rice

Servings: 2 | Preparation: 10 min | Cooking: 25 min

Ingredients

- 3 4 cups frozen cauliflower rice
- 1 tablespoon olive oil
- 2 garlic cloves
- ½ cup parmesan cheese

Directions

1. Place the cauliflower rice on a sheet pan
2. Sprinkle garlic and olive oil over the cauliflower rice and toss well
3. Spread cauliflower rice in a single layer in the pan
4. Roast cauliflower rice at 375 F for 20 25 min
5. When ready remove from the oven and serve with parmesan cheese on top

Roasted squash

Servings: 3 4 | Preparation: 10 min | Cooking: 20 min

Ingredients

- 2 delicata squashes
- 2 tablespoons olive oil
- 1 tsp curry powder
- 1 tsp salt

Directions

1. Preheat the oven to 400 F
2. Cut everything in half lengthwise
3. Toss everything with olive oil and place onto a prepared baking sheet
4. Roast for 18 20 min at 400 F or until golden brown
5. When ready remove from the oven and serve

Brussels sprout chips

Servings: 2 | Preparation: 10 min | Cooking: 20 min

Ingredients

- 1 lb. brussels sprouts
- 1 tablespoon olive oil

- 1 tablespoon parmesan cheese
- 1 tsp garlic powder
- 1 tsp seasoning

Directions
1. Preheat the oven to 425 F
2. In a bowl toss everything with olive oil and seasoning
3. Spread everything onto a prepared baking sheet
4. Bake for 8 10 min or until crisp
5. When ready remove from the oven and serve

Squash chips

Servings: 2 | Preparation: 10 min | Cooking: 20 min

Ingredients
- 1 lb. squash
- 1 tablespoon olive oil
- 1 tsp garlic powder
- 1 tsp seasoning

Directions
1. Preheat the oven to 425 F
2. In a bowl toss everything with olive oil and seasoning
3. Spread everything onto a prepared baking sheet
4. Bake for 8 10 min or until crisp
5. When ready remove from the oven and serve

Zucchini chips

Servings: 2 | Preparation: 10 min | Cooking: 20 min

Ingredients
- 1 lb. zucchini
- 1 tablespoon olive oil
- 1 tablespoon parmesan cheese
- 1 tsp garlic powder
- 1 tsp seasoning

Directions
1. Preheat the oven to 425 F
2. In a bowl toss everything with olive oil and seasoning
3. Spread everything onto a prepared baking sheet
4. Bake for 8 10 min or until crisp
5. When ready remove from the oven and serve

Carrot chips

Servings: 2 | Preparation: 10 min | Cooking: 20 min

Ingredients
- 1 lb. carrot
- 1 tablespoon olive oil
- 1 tablespoon parmesan cheese
- 1 tsp garlic powder
- 1 tsp seasoning

Directions
1. Preheat the oven to 425 F
2. In a bowl toss everything with olive oil and seasoning
3. Spread everything onto a prepared baking sheet
4. Bake for 8 10 min or until crisp
5. When ready remove from the oven and serve

Fried vegetables

Servings: 2 | Preparation: 10 min | Cooking: 15 min

Ingredients
- 1 cup red bell pepper
- ¼ cup cucumber
- ¼ cup zucchini
- ¼ cup asparagus
- ¼ cup carrots
- 1 onion
- 2 eggs
- 1 tsp salt
- 1 tsp pepper
- Seasoning
- 1 tablespoon olive oil

Directions
1. In a skillet heat olive oil and sauté onion until soft
2. Chop vegetables into thin slices and pour over onion
3. Whisk eggs with salt and pepper and pour over the vegetables
4. Cook until vegetables are brown
5. When ready remove from heat and serve

Onion sauce

Servings: 4 | Preparation: 10 min | Cooking: 55 min

Ingredients
- 1 onion
- 2 garlic cloves
- ¼ lb. carrots
- 1 potato
- 1 tablespoon balsamic vinegar
- ¼ tsp salt
- ¼ tsp black pepper

- 1 tablespoon olive oil
- 1 cup water

Directions

1. Chop all the vegetables and place them in a heated skillet
2. Add remaining ingredients and cook on low heat
3. Allow to simmer for 40 45 min or until vegetables are soft
4. Transfer mixture to a blender and blend until smooth
5. When ready remove from the blender and serve

Fish "cake"

Servings: 4 6 | Preparation: 10 min | Cooking: 50 min

Ingredients

- 2 tuna tins
- 2 potatoes
- 2 eggs
- 1 handful of gluten free flour
- 1 handful of parsley
- black pepper
- 1 cup breadcrumbs

Directions

1. Preheat the oven to 350 F
2. Boil the potatoes until they are soft
3. Mix the tuna with parsley, black pepper and salt
4. Roll fish into patties and dip into a bowl with flour, then eggs and then breadcrumbs
5. Place the patties on a baking tray
6. Bake at 350 F for 40 45 min
7. When ready remove from heat and serve

Sushi handrolls

Servings: 2 | Preparation: 10 min | Cooking: 25 min

Ingredients

- 1 sushi nori packet
- 4 tablespoons mayonnaise
- ½ lb. smoked salmon
- 1 tsp wasabi
- 1 cup cooked sushi rice
- 1 avocado

Directions

1. Cut avocado and into thin slices
2. Take a sheet of sushi and spread mayonnaise onto the sheet
3. Add rice, salmon and avocado
4. Roll and dip sushi into wasabi and serve

Steamed vegetables

Servings: 2 | Preparation: 10 min | Cooking: 10 min

Ingredients

- 1 carrot
- 2 sweet potato
- 2 parsnips
- 1 zucchini
- 2 broccoli stems

Directions

1. Chop vegetables into thin slices
2. Place all the vegetables into a steamer
3. Add enough water and cook on high until vegetables are steamed
4. When ready remove from the steamer and serve

Guacamole

Servings: 2 | Preparation: 5 min | Cooking: 5 min

Ingredients

- 1 avocado
- 1 lime juice
- 1 handful of coriander
- 1 tsp olive oil
- 1 tsp salt
- 1 tsp pepper

Directions

1. Place all the ingredients in a blender
2. Blend until smooth and transfer to a bowl

Chicken nachos

Servings: 4 6 | Preparation: 15 min | Cooking: 35 min

Ingredients

- 2 chicken breasts
- Tortilla chips
- Fajita seasoning
- ¼ cup cheddar cheese
- 4 5 mushrooms
- Guacamole
- ¼ cup peppers

Directions

1. In a pan heat olive oil and add chopped onion, sauté until soft
2. Add chicken, fajita seasoning and remaining vegetables
3. Cook on low heat for 10 12 min

4. Place tortilla chips into a baking dish, sprinkle cheese and bake in the oven until cheese has melted
5. Remove from the oven pour sautéed vegetables and chicken over and tortilla chips and serve

Scrambled eggs with salmon

Servings: 2 | Preparation: 10 min | Cooking: 20 min

Ingredients
- ½ lb. smoked salmon
- 2 eggs
- 1 avocado
- 1 tsp salt
- 1 tsp pepper
- 1 tps olive oil

Directions
1. In a bowl whisk the eggs with salt and pepper
2. In a skillet heat olive oil and pour the egg mixture
3. Add salmon pieces to the mixture and cook for 2 3 min per side
4. When ready remove from the skillet, add avocado and serve

Chicken with rice

Servings: 4 | Preparation: 10 min | Cooking: 25 min

Ingredients
- 2 chicken breasts
- 1 cup cooked white rice
- 2 tablespoons mayonnaise
- 1 tablespoon curry powder
- 1 zucchini
- 1 cup broccoli
- 1 tablespoon olive oil

Directions
1. Cut chicken breast into small pieces and set aside
2. In a pan heat olive oil and cook the chicken breast for 4 5 min
3. In another bowl combine mayonnaise, curry powder and add mixture to the chicken
4. Add remaining ingredients and cook for another 10 12 min or until the chicken is ready
5. When ready remove from the pot and serve with white rice

Roasted vegetables

Servings: 2 | Preparation: 10 min | Cooking: 50 min

Ingredients
- 1 carrot
- 2 sweet potatoes
- 1 butternut squash
- 2 parsnips
- 1 rosemary spring
- 2 bay leaves

Directions
1. Chop the vegetables into thin slices
2. Place everything in a prepare baking dish
3. Bake at 350 F for 40 45 min or until vegetables are golden brown
4. When ready remove from the oven and serve

Slaw

Servings: 1 | Preparation: 5 min | Cooking: 5 min

Ingredients
- 1 cabbage
- 1 bunch of baby carrots
- ½ cucumber
- 1 bun of cilantro
- 1 bunch of basil
- 1 onion

Directions
1. In a bowl mix all ingredients and mix well
2. Serve with dressing

Sriracha dressing

Servings: 1 | Preparation: 5 min | Cooking: 5 min

Ingredients
- 1 egg
- ¼ cup rice vinegar
- 1 tablespoon coconut aminos
- 1 tablespoon sriracha
- 1 tablespoon maple syrup

Directions
1. In a bowl mix all ingredients and mix well
2. Serve with dressing

Arugula salad

Servings: 1 | Preparation: 5 min | Cooking: 5 min

Ingredients
- 2 cups arugula leaves

- ¼ cup cranberries
- ¼ cup honey
- ¼ cup pecans
- 1 cup salad dressing

Directions

1. In a bowl mix all ingredients and mix well
2. Serve with dressing

Masoor salad

Servings: 1 | Preparation: 5 min | Cooking: 5 min

Ingredients

- ¼ cup masoor
- ¼ cup cucumber
- ½ cup carrot
- ¼ cup tomatoes
- ¼ cup onion

Salad dressing:

- ¼ tablespoon olive oil
- 1 tsp lemon juice
- ¼ tsp green chillies
- ½ tsp black pepper

Directions

1. In a bowl combine all ingredients together
2. Add salad dressing, toss well and serve

Muskmelon and pear salad

Servings: 1 | Preparation: 5 min | Cooking: 5 min

Ingredients

- 1 cup muskmelon
- ½ cup pear cubes
- ½ cup apple cubes
- Salad dressing

Directions

1. In a bowl combine all ingredients together
2. Add salad dressing, toss well and serve

Citrus watermelon salad

Servings: 1 | Preparation: 5 min | Cooking: 5 min

Ingredients

- 2 cups watermelon
- ¼ cup orange
- ¼ cup sweet lime
- ¼ cup pomegranate

Salad dressing:

- 1 tsp olive oil
- 1 tsp lemon juice
- 1 tablespoon parsley

Directions

1. In a bowl combine all ingredients together
2. Add salad dressing, toss well and serve

Carrot salad

Servings: 2 | Preparation: 5 min | Cooking: 5 min

Ingredients

- 1 ½ tbs lemon juice
- 1/3 tsp salt
- ¼ tsp black pepper
- 2 tbs olive oil
- 1/3 lb carrots
- 1 tsp mustard

Directions

1. Mix mustard, lemon juice and oil together
2. Peel and shred the carrots in a bowl
3. Stir in the dressing and season with salt and pepper
4. Mix well and allow to chill for at least 30 min

Moroccan salad

Servings: 2 | Preparation: 5 min | Cooking: 5 min

Ingredients

- 2 tbs lemon juice
- 1 tsp cumin
- 1 tsp paprika
- 3 tbs olive oil
- 2 cloves garlic
- 5 carrots
- Salt
- Pepper

Directions

1. Peel and slice the carrots
2. Add the carrots in boiled water and simmer for at least 5 min
3. Drain and rinse the carrots under cold water
4. Add in a bowl
5. Mix the lemon juice, garlic, cumin, paprika, and olive oil together
6. Pour the mixture over the carrots and toss then season with salt and pepper
7. Serve immediately

Avocado chicken salad

Servings: 2 | Preparation: 5 min | Cooking: 5 min

Ingredients

- 3 tsp lime juice
- 3 tbs cilantro
- 1 chicken breast
- 1 avocado
- 1/3 cup onion
- 1 apple
- 1 cup celery
- Salt
- Pepper
- Olive oil

Directions

1. Dice the chicken breast
2. Season with salt and pepper and cook into a greased skillet until golden
3. Dice the vegetables and place over the chicken in a bowl
4. Mash the avocado and sprinkle in the cilantro
5. Season with salt and pepper and add lime juice
6. Serve drizzled with olive oil

Asparagus frittata

Servings: 2 | Preparation: 10 min | Cooking: 20 min

Ingredients

- ½ lb. asparagus
- 1 tablespoon olive oil
- ½ red onion
- ¼ tsp salt
- 2 oz. cheddar cheese
- 1 garlic clove
- ¼ tsp dill

Directions

1. In a bowl whisk eggs with salt and cheese
2. In a frying pan heat olive oil and pour egg mixture
3. Add remaining ingredients and mix well
4. Serve when ready

Eggplant frittata

Servings: 2 | Preparation: 10 min | Cooking: 20 min

Ingredients

- ½ lb. eggplant
- 1 tablespoon olive oil
- ½ red onion
- ¼ tsp salt
- 2 oz. cheddar cheese
- 1 garlic clove
- ¼ tsp dill

Directions

1. In a bowl whisk eggs with salt and cheese
2. In a frying pan heat olive oil and pour egg mixture
3. Add remaining ingredients and mix well
4. Serve when ready

Stuffed sweet potatoes

Servings: 4 | Preparation: 10 min | Cooking: 20 min

Ingredients

- 2 lbs sweet potatoes
- 1 avocado
- 1/3 cup cilantro
- 1 jalapeno
- 2 tbs olive oil
- 1 cup black beans
- 1 red onion
- 2 garlic cloves
- 1 cup corn
- 1 cup tomatoes
- 2 tbs taco seasoning
- ½ tsp salt

Directions

1. Cook the sweet potatoes as you desire
2. Sauté the jalapeno and red onion in olive oil for 3 min
3. Add minced garlic and cook for 1 more minute
4. Add the black beans, corn, seasoning, salt, and pepper and cook 5 more min
5. Scoop out the potato insides and fill with the mixture
6. Serve with sour cream

Chicken and rice

Servings: 4 | Preparation: 10 min | Cooking: 20 min

Ingredients

- 1 cup rice
- 3 tsp seasoning
- 4 chicken breasts
- 2 ½ tbs butter
- 2 ½ cup chicken broth
- 1 lemon
- Salt

- Pepper

Directions

1. Season the chicken with salt, pepper and seasoning
2. Cook in melted butter until golden on both sides
3. Add in chicken broth, rice, lemon juice and remaining seasoning
4. Cook covered for at least 20 min

Liver and mashed vegetables

Servings: 4 | Preparation: 20 min | Cooking: 40 min

Ingredients

- 3 tsp rapeseed oil
- 350g sweet potato
- 150g parsnip
- 320g green beans
- 350g swede
- 3 cloves garlic
- 15 g flour
- 4 onions
- 1 pack liver
- 1 cube lamb stock
- Black pepper

Directions

1. Cook the onions in hot oil for about 20 min
2. Coat the liver with flour and pepper and cook in a pan until brown
3. Add the garlic to the onions and stir in 2 tsp of flour
4. Dissolve the stock cube in 450 ml water, then pour over the onions and bring to a boil
5. Add the liver and cook for 5 more min
6. Boil the vegetables covered for about 15 min
7. Mash the potato, parsnip and swede together
8. Serve the liver with the mashed vegetables

Broccoli casserole

Servings: 4 | Preparation: 10 min | Cooking: 15 min

Ingredients

- 1 onion
- 2 chicken breasts
- 2 tablespoons unsalted butter
- 2 eggs
- 2 cups cooked rice
- 2 cups cheese
- 1 cup parmesan cheese
- 2 cups cooked broccoli

Directions

1. Sauté the veggies and set aside
2. Preheat the oven to 425 F
3. Transfer the sautéed veggies to a baking dish, add remaining ingredients to the baking dish
4. Mix well, add seasoning and place the dish in the oven
5. Bake for 12 15 min or until slightly brown
6. When ready remove from the oven and serve

Potato chips

Servings: 2 | Preparation: 10 min | Cooking: 20 min

Ingredients

- 1 lb. zucchini
- 1 tablespoon salt
- 1 tsp smoked paprika

Directions

1. Preheat the oven to 425 F
2. In a bowl toss everything with olive oil and seasoning
3. Spread everything onto a prepared baking sheet
4. Bake for 8 10 min or until crisp
5. When ready remove from the oven and serve

Chicken stew with mushrooms

Servings: 4 | Preparation: 10 min | Cooking: 30 min

Ingredients

- ½ cup onion
- 1 cup cooked chicken
- 1 cup no salt chicken stock
- ¼ tablespoon seasoning
- ¼ tsp paprika
- ½ tsp garlic powder
- ¼ tsp black pepper
- 1 tablespoon cornstarch
- ¼ cup milk
- 1 clove garlic
- ¼ cup red pepper
- ¼ cup shitake mushrooms
- ¼ cup button mushrooms
- 1 cup kale
- 1 tablespoon olive oil

Directions

1. Sauté the onions and garlic together in a skillet
2. Add onions and the rest of vegetables
3. Sauté until they are soft

4. Add chicken stock, spices, cooked chicken and dry spices
5. In another container mix milk and cornstarch
6. Add to stew and simmer
7. When ready serve with rice or noodles

Chili thai sauce

Servings: 4 | Preparation: 10 min | Cooking: 10 min

Ingredients
- 1 cup water
- 1 tsp pepper flakes
- 1 tsp ketchup
- 3 tsp cornstarch
- ¾ cup vinegar
- ¼ cup sugar
- 1 tsp ginger
- 1 tsp garlic
- 1 tsp garlic

Directions
1. Boil water and vinegar
2. Add ginger, garlic, sugar, red pepper flakes and ketchup
3. Simmer for 5 10 min, add cornstarch and continue stirring, remove and serve

Grilled beak steak

Servings: 4 | Preparation: 10 min | Cooking: 20 min

Ingredients
- 2 tablespoons olive oil
- 1 onion
- 1 baguette
- ½ bunch arugula
- 1 tablespoon wine vinegar
- 3 cloves garlic
- ½ tsp hot pepper flakes
- 1 lb. beef

Directions
1. Mix vinegar, oil, garlic and pepper flakes in a bag and set aside
2. Add meat to marinade and refrigerate overnight
3. Remove steak from bag and grill steak for 4 5 min per side
4. Fry onion in a skillet and toss with marinade
5. Slice steak and top with onions and arugula

Panini

Servings: 2 | Preparation: 10 min | Cooking: 10 min

Ingredients
- 3 Panini buns
- 1 cup egg plant
- 1 cup cooked roast beef
- 2 tablespoons mayonnaise
- 1 tablespoon pesto sauce

Directions
1. Slice buns in half
2. In a bowl mix pesto sauce and mayonnaise and spread on each bun
3. Top with vegetables and roast beef

Tofu stir fry

Servings: 4 | Preparation: 10 min | Cooking: 10 min

Ingredients
- 1 cup white rice
- 1 tablespoon hoisin sauce
- 1 tablespoon rice vinegar
- 1 tsp cornstarch
- 1 cloves garlic
- 1 jalapeno pepper
- ½ cup basil leaves
- 3 tablespoons canola oil
- 1 package tofu
- 1 eggplant
- 3 scallions

Directions
1. Cook rice following the package instructions
2. In a skillet heat 1 tablespoon oil, add tofu and cook for 10 12 min
3. Transfer to a plate
4. Add vegetables and cook until tender, add sauce, toss and toss until thickened
5. Serve with basil and rice

Sesame asparagus

Servings: 2 | Preparation: 10 min | Cooking: 15 min

Ingredients
- 12 asparagus
- 1 lemon juice
- 1 tablespoon sesame oil
- 1 tsp sesame seeds

Directions

1. In a bowl mix lemon juice, sesame oil and sesame seeds
2. Wrap in tinfoil and bake at 350 for 15 min or until tender
3. Remove and serve

Basil pesto with pasta

Servings: 2 | Preparation: 10 min | Cooking: 20 min

Ingredients

- 1/3 lb. pasta
- ½ cup Parmesan cheese
- ½ cup olive oil
- 1 cup basil
- 2 cloves garlic
- ½ cup pine nuts

Directions

1. Cook pasta and set aside
2. In a bowl mix garlic, pine nuts and basil
3. Mix with Parmesan cheese and add oil
4. Serve over pasta

Tofu sticks

Servings: 4 | Preparation: 10 min | Cooking: 25 min

Ingredients

- 1 tsp tamari sauce
- 1 tsp seasoning
- 1 cup tofu
- 1 tablespoon water
- ¼ cup cornflake crumbs

Directions

1. In a bowl mix tamari with water
2. In another bowl mix cornflake and seasoning
3. Dip tofu into tamari sauce and then into seasoning
4. Place tofu slices on a baking sheet and bake at 325 for 15 18 min, remove and serve

Baked eggplant fries

Servings: 4 | Preparation: 10 min | Cooking: 25 min

Ingredients

- 1 eggplant
- 1 cup cornmeal
- ¼ tsp oregano
- ¼ tsp garlic powder

- ¼ tsp paprika
- 1 tsp olive oil
- 1 egg

Directions

1. Preheat oven to 375 F
2. In a bowl mix garlic powder, cornmeal, oregano and paprika
3. In a bowl beat the egg
4. Dip the eggplant fries in the beaten eggs and transfer to the cornmeal mixture
5. Place the eggplant fried on a baking sheet and bake for 20 min, remove and serve

Pita chips

Servings: 4 | Preparation: 10 min | Cooking: 10 min

Ingredients

- 2 pita rounds
- 2 tablespoons olive oil
- chili powder

Directions

1. Cut each pita into 8 wedges
2. Brush with olive oil and sprinkle with chili powder
3. Bake at 325 F for 12 min or until crisp
4. Remove and serve

Roasted red pepper dip

Servings: 2 | Preparation: 10 min | Cooking: 10 min

Ingredients

- 1 cup roasted red peppers
- 1 tablespoon olive oil
- 1 tsp lemon juice
- 1 clove garlic
- 1 tsp cumin

Directions

1. In a blender mix all ingredients and blend until smooth
2. Remove and serve with pita chips

Green pesto pasta

Servings: 2 | Preparation: 5 min | Cooking: 15 min

Ingredients

- 4 oz. spaghetti
- 2 cups basil leaves
- 2 garlic cloves

- ¼ cup olive oil
- 2 tablespoons parmesan cheese
- ½ tsp black pepper

Directions
1. Bring water to a boil and add pasta
2. In a blend add parmesan cheese, basil leaves, garlic and blend
3. Add olive oil, pepper and blend again
4. Pour pesto onto pasta and serve when ready

Roasted fennel

Servings: 4 | Preparation: 10 min | Cooking: 30 min

Ingredients
- 4 fennel bulbs
- 1 tablespoon olive oil
- 1 tsp salt

Directions
1. Slice the fennel bulb lengthwise into thick slices
2. Drizzle with olive oil and salt
3. Place the fennel bulb into a baking dish
4. Bake at 375 F for 25 30 min
5. When ready remove from the oven and serve

Spiced cauliflower

Servings: 4 | Preparation: 10 min | Cooking: 30 min

Ingredients
- 1 head cauliflower
- 2 tablespoons olive oil
- 1 tsp smoked paprika
- ¼ tsp cumin
- ¼ tsp coriander
- ¼ tsp salt
- ¼ tsp black pepper

Directions
1. In a bowl toss the cauliflower with olive oil, paprika, cumin, coriander, salt and pepper
2. Spread the cauliflower on a baking sheet
3. Bake for 20 min at 400 F
4. When ready remove from the oven and serve

Roasted butternut squash

Servings: 1 | Preparation: 10 min | Cooking: 35 min

Ingredients
- 1 butternut squash
- 2 shallots

- 2 tablespoons olive oil
- 1 tsp rosemary
- ½ tsp salt
- ¼ tsp black pepper

Directions
1. In a bowl combine all ingredients together
2. Add the butternut squash in the mixture and let it marinate for 10 15 min
3. Bake for 20 min at 425 F
4. When ready remove from the oven and serve

Fried chicken

Servings: 4 | Preparation: 10 min | Cooking: 20 min

Ingredients
- 2 chicken breasts
- ½ cup almond flour
- 1 tsp salt
- 1 tsp black pepper
- 2 eggs
- 1 cup bread crumbs
- ½ cup parmesan cheese

Directions
1. In a bowl combine flour, salt and pepper
2. In another bowl beat eggs and add to the flour mixture
3. Cut chicken breasts into thin slices and dip into the flour mixture
4. In another bowl combine bread crumbs and parmesan cheese
5. Take the chicken slices and dip into bread crumbs mixture
6. Place the chicken in frying pan and cook until golden brown
7. When ready remove from the pan and serve

Roasted chicken

Servings: 4 6 | Preparation: 10 min | Cooking: 40 min

Ingredients
- 1 whole chicken
- 1 celery
- 1 onion
- 4 cloves garlic
- 1 sprig of rosemary
- 1 bay leaf
- 1 tablespoon olive oil
- 1 tsp salt
- 1 tsp black pepper

Directions

1. In a pot heat olive oil and sauté onion, garlic and celery
2. Add chicken, rosemary, bay leaf, salt, black pepper and cook for 4 5 min
3. Remove from the pot and transfer to the oven
4. Bake for 30 35 min at 325 F
5. When ready remove from the oven and serve

Glazed salmon

Servings: 1 | Preparation: 10 min | Cooking: 30 min

Ingredients

- 1 salmon
- ¼ cup brown sugar
- 1 tablespoon lemon zest
- 1 tsp salt
- 1 tsp black pepper

Directions

1. In a bowl combine sugar, lemon zest, salt and pepper
2. Spread the mixture over the salmon and rub with the mixture
3. Bake at 350 F for 20 25 min
4. When ready remove from the oven and serve

Fish tacos

Servings: 8 12 | Preparation: 10 min | Cooking: 30 min

Ingredients

- 1 cup bread crumbs
- ¼ cup parmesan cheese
- 1 cup almond flour
- 2 eggs
- 2 tablespoons almond milk
- 1 lb. cod fish
- Tortillas
- 1 tsp Salt

Directions

1. In a bowl combine pepper, salt and flour
2. In another bowl whisk to eggs with milk
3. In another bowl combine bread crumbs with parmesan cheese
4. Cut the fish into thin strips and dip first into the flour mixture bowl, then egg mixture bowl and then into the bread crumbs mixture bowl
5. Fry for 5 6 min each fish strip or until golden brown
6. When ready transfer to a plate and serve

Simple steak

Servings: 4 6 | Preparation: 10 min | Cooking: 20 min

Ingredients

- 1 can celery soup
- 1 lb. cube steaks
- ¼ cup red onion
- 4 garlic cloves
- 1 stalk celery
- ¼ cup carrot
- 1 tsp cumin
- 1 tsp coriander
- salt

Directions

1. In a pan heat olive oil and sauté onion, cloves, celery and carrot
2. In a bowl combine celery soup with sautéed vegetables
3. Brown the cube steaks and set aside
4. Pour the sautéed vegetables and mixture into a pan, add cube steaks and cook until vegetables are soft
5. When ready remove from heat and serve

Cheese pesto

Servings: 2 | Preparation: 5 min | Cooking: 5 min

Ingredients

- 1 can spinach
- ¼ cup water
- ¼ cup cottage cheese
- ¼ cup basil
- 2 tablespoon parmesan cheese
- 1 tablespoon olive oil
- 3 cloves garlic
- 1 tsp black pepper

Directions

1. Place all ingredients in a blender and blend until smooth
2. When ready serve with cooked pasta

Rice salad

Servings: 4 | Preparation: 10 min | Cooking: 5 min

Ingredients

Salad:

- 3 tbs basil leaves
- 100g Kalamata olives

- 3 tbs pine nuts
- 2 green shallots
- ½ sun dried tomato
- 1 cup rice

Dressing:

- 3 tbs oil
- Pepper
- 2 tbs mustard
- 3 tbs lemon juice
- Salt
- 1 clove garlic

Directions

1. Cook the rice
2. Mix the dressing ingredients together
3. Mix the salad ingredients with the rice in a bowl
4. Add the dressing and serve

Salad with roasted strawberry dressing

Servings: 4 | Preparation: 10 min | Cooking: 50 min

Ingredients

- 1 pint fresh strawberries
- 1 red apple
- 1 sweet potato
- 1 large onion
- 1 tablespoon coconut oil
- 1 chopped cabbage
- ½ cup tomatoes
- 1 tablespoon almonds
- 1 tablespoon basil
- 2 tsp orange zest
- 1 banana

Directions

1. Preheat the oven to 375 F and place the strawberries on a baking sheet
2. On another baking sheet place, the potatoes and onions
3. Rub all the ingredients with with coconut oil and place them in the oven for 45 50 min
4. Remove from the oven and scoop out the sweet potato flesh
5. In a bowl mix tomato, almonds, cabbage, apple and basil
6. In a blender puree the roasted strawberries and banana pour over the salad mixture and toss to combine

Swiss chard salad

Servings: 2 | Preparation: 10 min | Cooking: 10 min

Ingredients

- 1 head cauliflower
- 1 tablespoon avocado oil
- 3 cups salad greens
- 1/3 cup red onion
- 1 pear
- harissa sauce
- 1 green bell
- 1 tablespoon parsley
- 1 tablespoon lemon zest
- 1 head Swiss chard
- 1 tomato

Directions

1. Preheat oven to 375 F and place the cauliflower on a baking sheet and drizzle with oil and salt
2. Roast for 35 40 min and remove when ready
3. In a bowl mix pepper, onion, parsley, Swiss chard, tomato and the roasted cauliflower
4. In another bowl whisk the lemon juice with harissa sauce and drizzle the dressing over salad

Green bean salad

Servings: 2 | Preparation: 10 min | Cooking: 10 min

Ingredients

- 2 lbs. green beans
- juice of 1 orange
- 1 tsp orange zest
- 2 carrots
- 1 apple
- 2 stalks celery

Directions

1. Stem the beans in pot over medium heat for 5 6 min and remove when ready
2. Add the carrots to the bowl and the steamed greens beans, celery and apple
3. In another bowl mix pepper, salt, orange juice and drizzle over the salad mixture

Zucchini soup

Servings: 4 | Preparation: 10 min | Cooking: 20 min

Ingredients

- 1 tablespoon olive oil
- 1 lb. zucchini

- ¼ red onion
- ½ cup all purpose flour
- ¼ tsp salt
- ¼ tsp pepper
- 1 can vegetable broth
- 1 cup heavy cream

Directions

1. In a saucepan heat olive oil and sauté zucchini until tender
2. Add remaining ingredients to the saucepan and bring to a boil
3. When all the vegetables are tender transfer to a blender and blend until smooth
4. Pour soup into bowls, garnish with parsley and serve

Brocoli soup

Servings: 4 | Preparation: 10 min | Cooking: 20 min

Ingredients

- 2 tablespoon olive oil
- 2 onons
- 2 garlic clvoes
- ¼ tsp red pepper flakes
- 2 lb. broccoli
- 1 potato

Directions

1. In a saucepan heat olive oil and sauté brocoli until tender
2. Add remaining ingredients to the saucepan and bring to a boil
3. When all the vegetables are tender transfer to a blender and blend until smooth
4. Pour soup into bowls, garnish with parsley and serve

Cauliflower soup

Servings: 4 | Preparation: 10 min | Cooking: 60 min

Ingredients

- 1 head cauliflower
- 1 clove garlic

- 1 tsp sage
- ½ tsp black pepper
- 5 cups chicken stock
- 1 head garlic
- 1 tsp olive oil
- 1 cup onion
- 1 cup apple
- 1 tsp thyme
- 1 tsp rosemary
- 8 baguette slices

Directions

1. Preheat oven to 325 F
2. Drizzle garlic head with olive oil and wrap in aluminum foil and roast for 25 30 min
3. Place baguette slices on a baking sheet and toast for 10 12 min
4. Squeeze the softened garlic cloves on the baguette slices
5. In a sauce pan add vegetables, spices, chicken stock and bring to boil
6. Reduce heat ad simmer for 20 30 min
7. With a blender, puree soup and garnish with garlic
8. Serve with baguette slices

Roasted cucumber

Servings: 3-4 | Preparation: 10 min | Cooking: 20 min

Ingredients

- 2 lb. cucumber
- 2 tablespoons olive oil
- 1 tsp curry powder
- 1 tsp salt

Directions

1. Preheat the oven to 400 F
2. Cut everything in half lengthwise
3. Toss everything with olive oil and place onto a prepared baking sheet
4. Roast for 18 20 min at 400 F or until golden brown
5. When ready remove from the oven and serve

Chapter 5: Smoothies and Drinks

Banana breakfast smoothie

Servings: 1 | Preparation: 5 min | Cooking: 5 min

Ingredients

- ½ cup vanilla yogurt
- 2 tsp honey
- Pinch of cinnamon
- 1 banana
- 1 cup ice

Directions

1. In a blender place all ingredients and blend until smooth
2. Pour the smoothie in a glass and serve

Cinnamon smoothie

Servings: 1 | Preparation: 5 min | Cooking: 5 min

Ingredients

- 1 cup soy milk
- 1 banana
- 1 tablespoon vanilla essence
- 1 cup strawberries
- ¼ tsp cinnamon

Directions

1. In a blender place all ingredients and blend until smooth
2. Pour smoothie in a glass and serve

Peanut butter smoothie

Servings: 1 | Preparation: 5 min | Cooking: 5 min

Ingredients

- 1 cup soy milk
- 1 banana
- 1 tablespoon peanut butter
- ¼ tsp cinnamon
- 1 cup ice

Directions

1. In a blender place all ingredients and blend until smooth
2. Pour smoothie in a glass and serve

Spinach smoothie

Servings: 1 | Preparation: 5 min | Cooking: 5 min

Ingredients

- 1 banana
- 1 cup ice
- ¼ cup blueberries
- 1 cup spinach

Directions

1. In a blender place all ingredients and blend until smooth
2. Pour smoothie in a glass and serve

Strawberry smoothie

Servings: 1 | Preparation: 5 min | Cooking: 5 min

Ingredients

- 1 cup strawberries
- 1 cup cranberry juice
- ½ cup orange juice
- 1 cup vanilla yogurt

Directions

1. In a blender place all ingredients and blend until smooth
2. Pour smoothie in a glass and serve

Vegan chocolate smoothie

Servings: 1 | Preparation: 5 min | Cooking: 5 min

Ingredients

- 2 bananas
- 2 tablespoons cocoa powder
- 1 tablespoon maple syrup
- ½ cup peanut butter
- 1 cup ice
- 2 cups almond milk

Directions

1. In a blender place all ingredients and blend until smooth
2. Pour smoothie in a glass and serve

Avocado smoothie

Servings: 1 | Preparation: 5 min | Cooking: 5 min

Ingredients

- 1 avocado
- 2 cups mango juice
- 1 cup orange juice
- 1 cup ice

Directions

1. In a blender place all ingredients and blend until smooth
2. Pour smoothie in a glass and serve

Low calorie smoothie

Servings: 1 | Preparation: 5 min | Cooking: 5 min

Ingredients

- 1 cup tomato juice
- ½ cup carrot juice
- 1 celery
- 1 cup spinach
- 1 cucumber
- 1 cup ice

Directions

1. In a blender place all ingredients and blend until smooth
2. Pour smoothie in a glass and serve

Berry smoothie

Servings: 1 | Preparation: 5 min | Cooking: 5 min

Ingredients

- 1 cup strawberries
- 1 cup blueberries
- 1 cup yogurt
- 1 cup beet juice
- 1 cup ice

Directions

1. In a blender place all ingredients and blend until smooth
2. Pour smoothie in a glass and serve

Cardamom smoothie

Servings: 1 | Preparation: 5 min | Cooking: 5 min

Ingredients

- 1 banana
- 2 dates
- 1 cup Greek yogurt
- 1 inch ginger
- ½ cup coconut milk
- ½ tsp cardamom

Directions

1. In a blender place all ingredients and blend until smooth

2. Pour smoothie in a glass and serve

Clementine smoothie

Servings: 1 | Preparation: 5 min | Cooking: 5 min

Ingredients

- 4 oz. clementine juice
- 2 oz. oats
- 2 oz. blueberries
- 2 pears
- 1 tablespoon honey
- 1 tsp mixed spice

Directions

1. In a blender place all ingredients and blend until smooth
2. Pour smoothie in a glass and serve

Pear smoothie

Servings: 1 | Preparation: 5 min | Cooking: 5 min

Ingredients

- 2 pears
- 1 banana
- 1 cup almond milk
- ½ cup vanilla yoghurt
- 1 tsp cinnamon

Directions

1. In a blender place all ingredients and blend until smooth
2. Pour smoothie in a glass and serve

Breakfast smoothie

Servings: 1 | Preparation: 5 min | Cooking: 5 min

Ingredients

- 1 banana
- 1 tsp coffee
- 1 tsp cinnamon
- 1 tsp honey
- 1 cup milk

Directions

1. In a blender place all ingredients and blend until smooth
2. Pour smoothie in a glass and serve

Banana smoothie

Servings: 1 | Preparation: 5 min | Cooking: 5 min

Ingredients
- 2 tablespoons cocoa powder
- 1 cup ice
- 1 banana
- 1 cup skimmed milk

Directions
1. In a blender place all ingredients and blend until smooth
2. Pour smoothie in a glass and serve

Green smoothie

Servings: 1 | Preparation: 5 min | Cooking: 5 min

Ingredients
- 1 banana
- 1 apple
- 1 kiwi
- 2 oz. spinach

Directions:
1. In a blender place all ingredients and blend until smooth
2. Pour smoothie in a glass and serve

Kale smoothie

Servings: 1 | Preparation: 5 min | Cooking: 5 min

Ingredients
- 2 oz. spinach leaves
- 1 cup soy milk
- 1 tablespoon peanut butter
- 1 tablespoon chia seeds
- 1 banana

Directions
1. In a blender place all ingredients and blend until smooth
2. Pour smoothie in a glass and serve

Green juice smoothie

Servings: 1 | Preparation: 5 min | Cooking: 5 min

Ingredients
- 2 apples
- 2 celery sticks
- 1 cucumber
- ½ cup kale leaves
- ¼ lemon

Directions
1. In a blender place all ingredients and blend until smooth
2. Pour smoothie in a glass and serve

Spicy smoothie

Servings: 1 | Preparation: 5 min | Cooking: 5 min

Ingredients
- 1 banana
- 2 oz. baby spinach
- 1 cup mango
- ¼ tsp jalapeno pepper
- 1 cup water

Directions
1. In a blender place all ingredients and blend until smooth
2. Pour smoothie in a glass and serve

Coconut smoothie

Servings: 1 | Preparation: 5 min | Cooking: 5 min

Ingredients
- 1 mango
- 1 banana
- 1 cup coconut milk
- 1 cup pineapple chunks
- 2 tablespoons coconut flakes

Directions
1. In a blender place all ingredients and blend until smooth
2. Pour smoothie in a glass and serve

Creamsicle smoothie

Servings: 1 | Preparation: 5 min | Cooking: 5 min

Ingredients
- 2 cups mango
- 1 carrot
- 1 tablespoon apple cider vinegar
- 1 tsp lemon juice
- 1 cup coconut milk
- 1 tsp honey

Directions

1. In a blender place all ingredients and blend until smooth
2. Pour smoothie in a glass and serve

Buttermilk smoothie

Servings: 1 | Preparation: 5 min | Cooking: 5 min

Ingredients

- 1 cup strawberries
- 1 cup buttermilk
- 1 cup ice
- 1 tsp honey
- 1 tsp agave syrup

Directions

1. In a blender place all ingredients and blend until smooth
2. Pour smoothie in a glass and serve

Parsley & pineapple smoothie

Servings: 1 | Preparation: 5 min | Cooking: 5 min

Ingredients

- 1 banana
- 1 cup pineapple
- ¼ cup parsley
- 1 tsp chia seeds
- 1 cup ice

Directions

1. In a blender place all ingredients and blend until smooth
2. Pour smoothie in a glass and serve

Pomegranate smoothie

Servings: 1 | Preparation: 5 min | Cooking: 5 min

Ingredients

- 1 cup pomegranate juice
- ¼ cup vanilla yogurt
- 3 cooked beets
- ¼ cup grapefruit juice
- 1 tablespoon honey
- 1 cup ice

Directions

1. In a blender place all ingredients and blend until smooth
2. Pour smoothie in a glass and serve

Cashew smoothie

Servings: 1 | Preparation: 5 min | Cooking: 5 min

Ingredients

- 1 cup cashew milk
- 1 cup vanilla yogurt
- 1 banana
- 1 cup pumpkin puree
- 1 cup ice

Directions

1. In a blender place all ingredients and blend until smooth
2. Pour smoothie in a glass and serve

Green Pineapple Smoothie

Preparation: 10 min| Cooking: 0 min| Servings: 2

Ingredients

- 1/2 cup chopped dandelion greens
- 1/2 cup arugula
- 2 cups chopped pineapple
- 1 medium banana, peeled
- 1 cup water
- 1 cup canned full-fat coconut milk, divided

Directions

1. Place dandelion greens, arugula, pineapple, banana, water and 1/2 cup coconut milk in a blender and blend until thoroughly combined.
2. Add remaining coconut milk while blending until desired texture is achieved.

Nutrition: Calories 315; Fat 17g ,Protein 3g; Sodium 51mg, Fiber 4g, Carbohydrates 38g, Sugar 26g

Chocolate Banana Smoothie

Preparation: 10 min| Cooking: 0 min| Servings: 2

Ingredients

- 1 cup chopped romaine lettuce
- 2 medium bananas, peeled
- 1 tablespoon cocoa powder
- 1/2 teaspoon vanilla bean pulp
- 2 cups oat milk, divided

Directions

1. Place romaine, bananas, cocoa powder, vanilla bean pulp, and 1 cup oat milk in a blender and blend until thoroughly combined.

2. Add remaining oat milk while blending until desired texture is achieved.

Nutrition: Calories 230; Fat 3g, Protein 7g; Sodium 113mg, Fiber 8g, Carbohydrates 49g, Sugar 13g

Peachy Orange Banana Smoothie

Preparation: 10 min| Cooking: 0 min| Servings: 2

Ingredients
- 1 cup chopped watercress
- 1 large orange, peeled
- 1 medium peach, pitted
- 1 medium banana, peeled
- 1 cup canned full-fat coconut milk, divided

Directions
1. Place watercress, orange, peach, banana, and 1/2 cup coconut milk in a blender and blend until thoroughly combined.
2. Add remaining coconut milk while blending until desired texture is achieved.

Nutrition: Calories 300; Fat 15gProtein 4g; Sodium 45mg, Fiber 5g, Carbohydrates 33g, Sugar 24g

Sweet Greens Smoothie

Preparation: 10 min| Cooking: 0 min| Servings: 2

Ingredients
- 2 cups spinach
- 1 medium banana, peeled
- 2 medium apples, cored and peeled
- 2 cups unsweetened vanilla almond milk, divided

Directions
1. Place spinach, banana, apples, and 1 cup almond milk in a blender and blend until thoroughly combined.
2. Add remaining almond milk while blending until desired texture is achieved.

Nutrition: Calories 183; Fat 3g, Protein 3g; Sodium 197mg, Fiber 6g, Carbohydrates 39g, Sugar 25g

Tart Pear Smoothie

Preparation: 15 min| Cooking: 0 min| Servings: 3

Ingredients
- 4 cups chopped romaine lettuce

- 4 medium pears, cored
- 1 medium banana, peeled
- 6 tablespoons lemon juice
- 2 cups water, divided

Directions
1. Place romaine, pears, banana, lemon juice, and 1 cup water in a blender and blend until thoroughly combined.
2. Add remaining water while blending until desired texture is achieved.

Nutrition: Calories 183; Fat 1g, Protein 2g; Sodium 8mg, Fiber 10g ,Carbohydrates 48g, Sugar 29g

Citrus Berry Smoothie

Preparation: 10 min| Cooking: 0 min| Servings: 2

Ingredients
- 1 cup chopped watercress
- 2 medium oranges, peeled
- 1 cup strawberries
- 1 cup blueberries
- 1 cup water
- 1 cup canned full-fat coconut milk, divided

Directions
1. Place watercress, oranges, strawberries, blueberries, water and 1/2 cup coconut milk in a blender and blend until thoroughly combined.
2. Add remaining coconut milk while blending until desired texture is achieved.

Nutrition: Calories 310; Fat 15g, Protein 4g; Sodium 46mg, Fiber 6g, Carbohydrates 35g, Sugar 26g

Mango Berry Smoothie

Preparation: 10 min| Cooking: 0 min| Servings: 2

Ingredients
- 1 cup chopped watercress
- 1 medium mango, pitted and peeled
- 1 cup raspberries
- 1.1/2 cups oat milk, divided

Directions
1. Place watercress, mango, raspberries, and 3/4 cup oat milk in a blender and blend until thoroughly combined.
2. Add remaining oat milk while blending until desired texture is achieved.

Nutrition: Calories 232; Fat 3g, Protein 6g; Sodium 91mg, Fiber 10g, Carbohydrates 50g, Sugar 26g

Cucumber Mint Smoothie

Preparation: 10 min| Cooking: 0 min| Servings: 1

Ingredients

- 1 cup chopped romaine lettuce
- 2 medium cucumbers, peeled and quartered
- 1/4 cup chopped mint
- 1 cup water, divided

Directions

1. Place romaine, cucumbers, mint, and 1/2 cup water in a blender and combine thoroughly.
2. Add remaining water while blending until desired texture is achieved.

Nutrition: Calories 40; Fat 0g, Protein 2g; Sodium 8mg, Fiber 4g, Carbohydrates 9g ,Sugar 4g

Banana Berry Smoothie

Preparation: 10 min| Cooking: 0 min| Servings: 2

Ingredients

- 1 cup chopped romaine lettuce
- 2 medium bananas, peeled
- 1 pint strawberries
- 1 pint blueberries
- 2 cups unsweetened vanilla almond milk, divided

Directions

1. Place romaine, bananas, berries, and 1 cup almond milk in a blender and blend until thoroughly combined.
2. Add remaining almond milk while blending until desired texture is achieved.

Nutrition: Calories 211; Fat 4g, Protein 4g; Sodium 175mg, Fiber 7g, Carbohydrates 46g, Sugar 26g

Green Citrus Smoothie

Preparation: 10 min| Cooking: 0 min| Servings: 2

Ingredients

- 1 cup chopped watercress
- 1 large grapefruit, peeled
- 2 medium oranges, peeled
- 1 medium banana, peeled
- 1 cup water, divided

Directions

1. Place watercress, grapefruit, oranges, banana, and 1/2 cup water in a blender and blend until thoroughly combined.
2. Add remaining water while blending until desired texture is achieved.

Nutrition: Calories 162; Fat 1g, Protein 3g; Sodium 7mg, Fiber 7g,Carbohydrates 41g, Sugar 27g

Cherry Pear Smoothie

Preparation: 10 min| Cooking: 0 min| Servings: 2

Ingredients

- 1 cup chopped iceberg lettuce
- 2 medium pears, cored
- 1 medium banana, peeled
- 1/2 cup pitted cherries
- 1/2 teaspoon vanilla bean pulp
- 2 cups unsweetened vanilla almond milk, divided

Directions

1. Place lettuce, pears, banana, cherries, vanilla bean pulp, and 1 cup almond milk in a blender and blend until thoroughly combined.
2. Add remaining almond milk while blending until desired texture is achieved.

Nutrition: Calories 216; Fat 3g, Protein 3g; Sodium 175mg, Fiber 8g, Carbohydrates 48g, Sugar 30g

Apple Peach Smoothie

Preparation: 10 min| Cooking: 0 min| Servings: 2

Ingredients

- 2 tablespoons rolled oats
- 1 cup chopped watercress
- 2 medium peaches, pitted
- 2 medium apples, cored and peeled
- 2 cups unsweetened vanilla almond milk, divided

Directions

1. Place oats, watercress, peaches, apples, and 1 cup almond milk in a blender and blend until thoroughly combined.
2. Add remaining almond milk while blending until desired texture is achieved.

Nutrition: Calories 198; Fat 4g, Protein 4g; Sodium 172mg, Fiber 7g, Carbohydrates 43g, Sugar 31g

Zucchini Apple Smoothie

Preparation: 10 min| Cooking: 0 min| Servings: 2

Ingredients
- 1 cup spinach
- 1 medium zucchini, chopped
- 3 medium carrots, peeled and chopped
- 2 medium apples, cored and peeled
- 2 cups water, divided

Directions
1. Place spinach, zucchini, carrots, apples, and 1 cup water in a blender and blend until thoroughly combined.
2. Add remaining water while blending until desired texture is achieved.

Nutrition: Calories 163; Fat 1g, Protein 4g; Sodium 90mg, Fiber 9g,Carbohydrates 40g, Sugar 28g

Farmers' Market Smoothie

Preparation: 10 min| Cooking: 0 min| Servings: 2

Ingredients
- 1 cup chopped romaine lettuce
- 2 medium tomatoes
- 1 medium zucchini, chopped
- 2 medium stalks celery, chopped
- 1 medium cucumber, chopped
- 1/2 cup chopped green onions
- 2 cloves garlic, peeled
- 2 cups water, divided

Directions
1. Place romaine, tomatoes, zucchini, celery, cucumber, green onions, garlic, and 1 cup water in a blender and blend until thoroughly combined.
2. Add remaining 1 cup water, if needed, while blending until desired texture is achieved.

Nutrition: Calories 86; Fat 1g, Protein 5g; Sodium 59mg, Fiber 6g, Carbohydrates 17g, Sugar 11g

Orange Broccoli Smoothie

Preparation: 10 min| Cooking: 0 min| Servings: 2

Ingredients
- 1 cup chopped romaine lettuce
- 1 cup chopped broccoli
- 1 medium zucchini, chopped
- 2 medium carrots, peeled and chopped
- 2 cups water, divided

Directions
1. Place romaine, broccoli, zucchini, carrots, and 1 cup water in a blender and blend until thoroughly combined.
2. Add remaining water while blending until desired texture is achieved.

Nutrition: Calories 71; Fat 1g, Protein 4g; Sodium 72mg, Fiber 5g, Carbohydrates 15g, Sugar 8g

Sweet Citrus Smoothie

Preparation: 10 min| Cooking: 0 min| Servings: 2

Ingredients
- 1 cup chopped watercress
- 1 large grapefruit, peeled
- 2 medium oranges, peeled
- 1 (1/2) piece gingerroot, peeled
- 1/2 medium lemon, peeled
- 1 cup water, divided

Directions
1. Place watercress, grapefruit, oranges, gingerroot, lemon, and 1/2 cup water in a blender and blend until thoroughly combined.
2. Add remaining water while blending until desired texture is achieved.

Nutrition: Calories 136; Fat 0g, Protein 3g; Sodium 7mg, Fiber 7g, Carbohydrates 35g, Sugar 24g

The Green Go-Getter Smoothie

Preparation: 10 min| Cooking: 0 min| Servings: 1

Ingredients
- 1 cup spinach
- 2 medium green apples, peeled and cored
- 1/2 medium banana, peeled
- 1 cup water, divided

Directions
1. Place spinach, apples, banana, and 1/2 cup water in a blender and blend until thoroughly combined.
2. Continue adding remaining water while blending until desired texture is achieved.

Nutrition: Calories 241; Fat 1g, Protein 2g; Sodium 29mg, Fiber 11g, Carbohydrates 63g, Sugar 44g

Homemade Tomato Juice

Preparation: 10 min| Cooking: 4 H| Servings: 4

Ingredients

- 10 large tomatoes, seeded and sliced
- 1 teaspoon lemon juice
- 1/4 teaspoon ground black pepper
- 1 tablespoon maple syrup

Directions

1. Place tomatoes in a 2-quart slow cooker. Cover; cook on low for 4–6 h.
2. Press cooked tomatoes through a sieve. Add remaining ingredients and chill.

Nutrition: Calories 95; Fat 1g, Protein 4g; Sodium 23mg, Fiber 6g, Carbohydrates 21g, Sugar 15g

Lemonade

Preparation: 10 min| Cooking: 3 H| Servings: 6

Ingredients

- 5 cups water
- 3/4 cup lemon juice
- 3/4 cup maple syrup
- 1 (2") piece gingerroot, peeled and sliced

Directions

1. Combine all ingredients in a 2-quart or smaller slow cooker. Cover and cook on high for 2–3 h (if mixture begins to boil, turn heat to low).
2. Turn to low to keep warm for serving, or chill and serve over ice. Remove gingerroot before serving.

Nutrition: Calories 109; Fat 0g, Protein 0g; Sodium 5mg, Fiber 0g, Carbohydrates 29g, Sugar 25g

Summer smoothie

Servings: 1 | Preparation: 5 min | Cooking: 5 min

Ingredients

- ½ cup Greek yogurt
- 2 cups raspberries
- 1 nectarine
- 1 cup ice

Directions

1. In a blender place all ingredients and blend until smooth
2. Pour smoothie in a glass and serve

Tropical smoothie

Servings: 1 | Preparation: 5 min | Cooking: 5 min

Ingredients

- 1 banana
- 1 pineapple
- 1 cup mango
- 1 cup almond milk

Directions

1. In a blender place all ingredients and blend until smooth
2. Pour smoothie in a glass and serve

Citrus smoothie

Servings: 1 | Preparation: 5 min | Cooking: 5 min

Ingredients

- 1 cup carrot juice
- 1 banana
- 1 cup pineapple juice
- 1 cup ice

Directions

1. In a blender place all ingredients and blend until smooth
2. Pour smoothie in a glass and serve

Mango smoothie

Servings: 1 | Preparation: 5 min | Cooking: 5 min

Ingredients

- 1 cup orange juice
- ¼ cup vanilla yogurt
- 1 cup mango
- 1 carrot
- 1 cup ice

Directions

1. In a blender place all ingredients and blend until smooth
2. Pour smoothie in a glass and serve

Tangerine smoothie

Servings: 1 | Preparation: 5 min | Cooking: 5 min

Ingredients

- 2 tangerines
- 1 cup pineapple

- 1 banana
- 1 cup ice

Directions
1. In a blender place all ingredients and blend until smooth
2. Pour smoothie in a glass and serve

Mocktail

Servings: 1 | Preparation: 10 min | Cooking: 0 min

Ingredients
- Ice
- 6 ounces soda water
- 3 lime slices
- 11 mint leaves
- 1 tbs honey

Directions
1. Add mint leaves and lime to a glass and muddle with a spoon.
2. Add honey, ice and soda.
3. Stir to combine.
4. Serve garnished with lime and mint.

Carrot smoothie

Servings: 1 | Preparation: 5 min | Cooking: 5 min

Ingredients
- 1 carrot
- 1 mango
- 2 tablespoons coconut flakes

Directions
1. In a blender place all ingredients and blend until smooth
2. Pour smoothie in a glass and serve

Ginger smoothie

Servings: 1 | Preparation: 5 min | Cooking: 5 min

Ingredients
- 2 cups pineapple
- 2 tablespoons lime juice
- 1 pice ginger

Directions
1. In a blender place all ingredients and blend until smooth
2. Pour smoothie in a glass and serve

Chatper 6: Dessert Recipes

Strawberry Ice Cream

Servings: 4 | Preparation: 15 min

Ingredients
- 1 cup fresh strawberries, hulled and sliced
- ½ small banana, peeled and sliced
- 2 tablespoon unsweetened coconut, shredded
- ½ cup coconut cream

Directions
1. In a powerful blender, add all ingredients and pulse until smooth.
2. Transfer into an ice cream maker and process according to manufacturer's directions.
3. Now, transfer into an airtight container and freeze for at least 3 to 4 h, stirring after every 30 min.

Nutrition: Calories: 101; Total Fat: 8.1g; Saturated Fat: 7.1g; Protein: 1.2g; Carbs: 7.7g; Fiber: 1.9g; Sugar: 4.5g

Mango Sorbet

Servings: 8 | Preparation: 10 min

Ingredients
- 3 cups frozen mango, peeled, pitted and chopped
- 10 fresh mint leaves
- 2 tablespoons fresh lime juice
- ½ cup chilled water

Directions
1. In a powerful blender, add all ingredients and pulse until smooth.
2. Transfer into serving bowls and serve immediately.

Nutrition: Calories: 38; Total Fat: 0.3g; Saturated Fat: 0.1g; Protein: 0.6g; Carbs: 9.4g; Fiber: 1.1g; Sugar: 8.5g

Chocolate Mousse

Servings: 4 | Preparation: 10 min

Ingredients
- ½ cup unsweetened almond milk
- 1 cup cooked black beans
- 4 Medjool dates, pitted and chopped
- ½ cup walnuts, chopped
- 2 tablespoons cacao powder

- 1 teaspoon organic vanilla extract
- 2 tablespoons fresh raspberries
- 4 fresh mint leaves

Directions
1. In a food processor, add all ingredients and pulse until smooth and creamy.
2. Transfer into serving bowls and refrigerate to chill before serving.
3. Garnish with raspberries and mint leaves and serve.

Nutrition: Calories: 342; Total Fat: 11g; Saturated Fat: 1.1g; Protein: 15.5g; Carbs: 50.8g; Fiber: 11.4g; Sugar: 15.8g

Berries Pudding

Servings: 3 | Preparation: 10 min

Ingredients
- 2 tablespoons raw hemp seeds, shelled
- 2 cups fresh mixed berries
- 2 ripe bananas, peeled
- 2 tablespoons unsweetened coconut milk
- 1-3 tablespoons maple syrup
- 2 tablespoons chia seeds
- 1|8 teaspoon ground cinnamon

Directions
1. In a food processor, add the berries, bananas and coconut milk and pulse until well combined.
2. Add the maple syrup and pulse until well combined.
3. Add the hemp seeds, chia seeds and cinnamon and pulse until well combined.
4. Transfer the pudding into a serving bowl.
5. Cover the bowl and refrigerate to chill for at least 2 h before serving.

Nutrition: Calories: 223; Total Fat: 7.8g; Saturated Fat: 2.7g; Protein: 5g; Carbs: 36.8g; Fiber: 7.8g; Sugar: 20.6g

Chocolaty Beans Brownies

Servings: 12 | Preparation: 15 min | Cooking time: 30 min

Ingredients
- 2 cups cooked black beans
- 12 Medjool dates, pitted and chopped
- 2 tablespoon organic vanilla extract
- ¼ cup cacao powder

- 1 tablespoon ground cinnamon

Directions

1. Preheat the oven to 350 degrees F. Line a large baking dish with parchment paper.
2. In a food processor, add all ingredients except cacao powder and cinnamon and pulse till well combined and smooth.
3. Transfer the mixture into a large bowl.
4. Add the cacao powder and cinnamon and stir to combine.
5. Now, transfer the mixture into prepared baking dish and with the back of a spatula, smooth the top surface.
6. Bake for about 30 min.
7. Remove from oven and let it cool.
8. With a sharp knife cut into 12 equal-sized brownies and serve.

Nutrition: Calories: 178; Total Fat: 0.9g; Saturated Fat: 0.3g; Protein: 7.8g; Carbs: 36.7g; Fiber: 7.3g; Sugar: 13.6g

Chocolate Mug Cake

Servings: 1 | Preparation: 5 min | Cooking time: 2 min

Ingredients

- ¼ cup almond flour
- ¼ teaspoon ground cinnamon
- Salt, as required 1 large organic egg
- ½ teaspoon organic vanilla extract
- ¼ cup banana, peeled and mashed
- 1-2 tablespoons 70% unsweetened mini chocolate chips

Directions

1. Grease a microwave-safe mug.
2. In a bowl, mix together flour, cinnamon and salt.
3. In another small bowl, add the egg and vanilla and beat well.
4. Add the banana and beat well.
5. Add the egg mixture into flour mixture and mix until just combined.
6. Gently, fold in the chocolate chips.
7. Transfer the mixture into prepared mug and microwave on High for about 2 min.
8. Remove from microwave and set aside to cool for about 5 min before serving.

Nutrition: Calories: 392; Total Fat: 28.1g; Saturated Fat: 7.6g; Protein: 8.7g; Carbs: 18.7g; Fiber: 6.3g; Sugar: 6.3g

Strawberry Cake

Servings: 10 | Preparation: 20 min | Cooking time: 35 min

Ingredients

For Cake:

- 2 cups almond flour
- ½ cup coconut flour
- ½ cup arrowroot powder
- 2 teaspoons baking soda
- Pinch of salt
- 1 cup unsweetened applesauce
- ½ cup raw honey
- 9 organic eggs
- 1 tablespoon organic vanilla extract
- 2 teaspoons apple cider vinegar

For Frosting:

- ¾ cup freeze-dried strawberries
- 1½ cups coconut oil, softened
- 1|3 cup raw honey
- ¼ cup arrowroot powder
- 2 tablespoons coconut flour
- Fresh strawberries, hulled and sliced (as required)

Directions

1. Preheat the oven to 325 degrees F. Grease 2 (9-inch) round cake pans.
2. For cake: in a large bowl, mix together flours, arrowroot, baking soda and salt.
3. In another bowl, add applesauce, honey, eggs, vanilla extract and vinegar and beat until well combined.
4. Add the egg mixture into flour mixture and mix until well combined.
5. Divide the mixture into prepared cake pans evenly.
6. Bake for about 25-35 min or until a toothpick inserted in the center comes out clean.
7. Remove from oven and place the pans onto wire rack to cool for about 10 min.
8. Carefully invert the cakes onto the wire rack to cool completely.
9. Meanwhile, for frosting: in a coffee grinder, add dried strawberries and pulse until powdered.
10. Through a fine strainer, strain the strawberry powder.
11. In a bowl, add remaining ingredients except fresh strawberries and beat until smooth.
12. Slowly, add strawberry powder, beating continuously until well combined.

13. Arrange one cake onto a platter and spread the strawberry mixture on top.
14. Place the second cake on top.
15. Now, spread the frosting over the cake.
16. Cut into desired sized slices and serve.

Nutrition: Calories: 638; Total Fat: 48.8g; Saturated Fat: 30.4g; Protein: 5.4g; Carbs: 43.1g; Fiber: 3.4g; Sugar: 29g

Apple Crisp

Servings: 4 | Preparation: 15 min | Cooking time: 20 min

Ingredients

For Filling:

- 2 large apples, peeled, cored and chopped
- 2 tablespoons fresh apple juice
- 2 tablespoons water
- ¼ teaspoon ground cinnamon

For Topping:

- ½ cup quick rolled oats
- ¼ cup unsweetened coconut flakes
- 2 tablespoons walnuts, chopped
- ½ teaspoon ground cinnamon
- ¼ cup water

Directions

1. Preheat the oven to 300 degrees F.
2. For filling: in a baking dish, place all the ingredients and gently mix.
3. For topping in a bowl, add all the ingredients and mix well.
4. Spread the topping over filling mixture evenly.
5. Bake for about 20 min or until top becomes golden brown.
6. Serve warm.

Nutrition: Calories: 201; Total Fat: 4.9g; Saturated Fat: 1.6g; Protein: 3.4g; Carbs: 38.2g; Fiber: 5g; Sugar: 23.9g

Banana Crumb

Servings: 2 | Preparation: 10 min | Cooking time: 25 min

Ingredients

- ¼ cup coconut, shredded
- 3 tablespoons coconut oil, melted

- 1 tablespoon fresh lemon juice
- ¼ teaspoon organic vanilla extract
- Pinch of ground cinnamon
- 2 medium bananas, peeled and sliced

Directions

1. Preheat the oven to 350 degrees F. Lightly, grease 2 ramekins.
2. In a bowl, add all ingredients except bananas and mix well.
3. In the bottom of the prepared ramekins, place the banana slices in and top with coconut mixture evenly.
4. Bake for about 25 min or until top becomes golden brown.
5. Serve warm.

Nutrition: Calories: 320; Total Fat: 24.2g; Saturated Fat: 20.8g; Protein: 1.7g; Carbs: 28.8g; Fiber: 4.1g; Sugar: 15.3g

Blueberry Crumble

Servings: 4 | Preparation: 15 min | Cooking time: 40 min

Ingredients

- ¼ cup coconut flour
- ¼ cup arrowroot flour
- ¾ teaspoon baking soda
- ¼ cup banana, peeled and mashed
- 2 tablespoons coconut oil, melted
- 3 tablespoons filtered water
- ½ tablespoon fresh lemon juice
- 1½ cups fresh blueberries

Directions

1. Preheat the oven to 300 degrees F. Lightly, grease an 8x8-inch baking dish.
2. In a large bowl, add all the ingredients except blueberries and mix well.
3. In the bottom of prepared baking dish, place blueberries evenly and top with flour mixture.
4. Bake for about 35-40 min or until top becomes golden brown.

Nutrition: Calories: 107; Total Fat: 7.2g; Saturated Fat: 6g; Protein: 1g; Carbs: 11.6g; Fiber: 2g; Sugar: 6.7g

Pear tart

Servings: 6 8 | Preparation: 25 min | Cooking: 25 min

Ingredients

- 1 lb. pears
- 2 oz. brown sugar
- ½ lb. flaked almonds
- ¼ lb. porridge oat
- 2 oz. flour
- ¼ lb. almonds
- pastry sheets
- 2 tablespoons syrup

Directions

1. Preheat oven to 400 F, unfold pastry sheets and place them on a baking sheet
2. Toss together all ingredients together and mix well
3. Spread mixture in a single layer on the pastry sheets
4. Before baking decorate with your desired fruits
5. Bake at 400 F for 22 25 min or until golden brown
6. When ready remove from the oven and serve

Cardamom tart

Servings: 6 8 | Preparation: 25 min | Cooking: 25 min

Ingredients

- 4 5 pears
- 2 tablespoons lemon juice
- pastry sheets

Cardamom filling:

- ½ lb. butter
- ½ lb. brown sugar
- ½ lb. almonds
- ¼ lb. flour
- 1 ¼ tsp cardamom
- 2 eggs

Directions

1. Preheat oven to 400 F, unfold pastry sheets and place them on a baking sheet
2. Toss together all ingredients together and mix well
3. Spread mixture in a single layer on the pastry sheets
4. Before baking decorate with your desired fruits
5. Bake at 400 F for 22 25 min or until golden brown
6. When ready remove from the oven and serve

Apple tart

Servings: 6 8 | Preparation: 25 min | Cooking: 25 min

Ingredients

- pastry sheets

Filling:

- 1 tsp lemon juice
- 3 oz. brown sugar
- 1 lb. apples
- 150 ml double cream
- 2 eggs

Directions

1. Preheat oven to 400 F, unfold pastry sheets and place them on a baking sheet
2. Toss together all ingredients together and mix well
3. Spread mixture in a single layer on the pastry sheets
4. Before baking decorate with your desired fruits
5. Bake at 400 F for 22 25 min or until golden brown
6. When ready remove from the oven and serve

Pistachios ice cream

Servings: 6-8 | Preparation: 15 min | Cooking: 15 min

Ingredients

- 4 egg yolks
- 1 cup heavy cream
- 1 cup milk
- 1 cup sugar
- 1 vanilla bean
- 1 tsp almond extract
- 1 cup cherries
- ½ cup pistachios

Directions

1. In a saucepan whisk together all ingredients
2. Mix until bubbly
3. Strain into a bowl and cool
4. Whisk in favorite fruits and mix well
5. Cover and refrigerate for 2 3 h
6. Pour mixture in the ice cream maker and follow manufacturer instructions
7. Serve when ready

Vanilla ice cream

Servings: 6-8 | Preparation: 15 min | Cooking: 15 min

Ingredients

- 1 cup milk
- 1 tablespoon cornstarch
- 1 oz. cream cheese
- 1 cup heavy cream
- 1 cup brown sugar
- 1 tablespoon corn syrup
- 1 vanilla bean

Directions

1. In a saucepan whisk together all ingredients
2. Mix until bubbly
3. Strain into a bowl and cool
4. Whisk in favorite fruits and mix well
5. Cover and refrigerate for 2 3 h
6. Pour mixture in the ice cream maker and follow manufacturer instructions
7. Serve when ready

Simple muffins

Servings: 8 12 | Preparation: 10 min | Cooking: 20 min

Ingredients

- 2 eggs
- 1 tablespoon olive oil
- 1 cup milk
- 2 cups whole wheat flour
- 1 tsp baking soda
- ¼ tsp baking soda
- 1 cup pumpkin puree
- 1 tsp cinnamon
- ¼ cup molasses

Directions

1. In a bowl combine all wet ingredients
2. In another bowl combine all dry ingredients
3. Combine wet and dry ingredients together
4. Pour mixture into 8 12 prepared muffin cups, fill 2/3 of the cups
5. Bake for 18 20 min at 375 F
6. When ready remove from the oven and serve

Cornbread muffins

Servings: 4 | Preparation: 10 min | Cooking: 20 min

Ingredients

- 1 cup whole wheat flour
- 1 can of Whole Kernel Corn 15 oz.
- ½ cup milk
- 1 egg

- ½ cup butter
- 1 tablespoon honey
- 1 tablespoon baking powder
- 1 tsp salt

Directions

1. Preheat oven to 375 F
2. Blend corn until smooth
3. In a bowl mix baking powder, salt and flour
4. In another bowl mix eggs, butter, corn, milk and honey
5. Pour over the flour mixture and mix well
6. Pour mixture into a cupcake pan and bake for 15 20 min

Morning muffins

Servings: 8 12 | Preparation: 10 min | Cooking: 25 min

Ingredients

- 1 cup oats
- ¼ cup unsweetened applesauce
- 2 egg whites
- 1 cup oat milk
- 1 cup whole wheat flour
- ¼ cup brown sugar
- ¼ tsp baking soda
- ¼ tsp salt
- 1 tsp cinnamon
- ½ cup blueberries

Directions

1. Preheat oven to 375 F
2. In a bowl combine all ingredients together and mix well
3. Fill 8 12 paper muffin cups with batter and fold in blueberries
4. Bake for 20 25 min, serve when ready

Fiber muffins

Servings: 8 12 | Preparation: 5 min | Cooking: 15 min

Ingredients

- 1 cup wheat bran
- 1 cup nonfat milk
- ¼ cup unsweetened applesauce
- 1 egg
- ¼ cup brown sugar
- ¼ cup all purpose flour
- ¼ cup whole wheat flour
- 1 tsp baking powder

- 1 tsp baking soda
- ¼ tsp salt
- 1 cup blueberries

Directions

1. Preheat oven to 400 F
2. In a bowl combine wheat bran and milk and set aside
3. In another bowl combine egg, brown sugar, apple sauce and stir in bran mixture, mix well
4. In another bowl combine baking soda, baking powder, wheat flour, all purpose flour and mix well
5. Stir flour mixture into bran and egg mixture and mix well
6. Fold in blueberries and fill muffin cups with batter
7. Bake for 12 15 min
8. When ready remove and serve

Strawberry muffins

Servings: 8 12 | Preparation: 10 min | Cooking: 20 min

Ingredients

- 2 eggs
- 1 tablespoon olive oil
- 1 cup milk
- 2 cups whole wheat flour
- 1 tsp baking soda
- ¼ tsp baking soda
- 1 tsp cinnamon
- 1 cup strawberries

Directions

1. In a bowl combine all wet ingredients
2. In another bowl combine all dry ingredients
3. Combine wet and dry ingredients together
4. Fold in strawberries and mix well
5. Pour mixture into 8 12 prepared muffin cups, fill 2/3 of the cups
6. Bake for 18 20 min at 375 F, remove when ready

Peach pecan pie

Servings: 8 12 | Preparation: 15 min | Cooking: 35 min

Ingredients

- 4 5 cups peaches
- 1 tablespoon preserves
- 1 cup sugar
- 4 small egg yolks

- ¼ cup flour
- 1 tsp vanilla extract

Directions

1. Line a pie plate or pie form with pastry and cover the edges of the dish depending on your preference
2. In a bowl combine all pie ingredients together and mix well
3. Pour the mixture over the pastry
4. Bake at 400 425 F for 25 30 min or until golden brown
5. When ready remove from the oven and let it rest for 15 min

Oreo pie

Servings: 8 12 | Preparation: 15 min | Cooking: 35 min

Ingredients

- pastry sheets
- 6 8 oz. chocolate crumb piecrust
- 1 cup half and half
- 1 package instant pudding mix
- 10 12 Oreo cookies
- 10 oz. whipped topping

Directions

1. Line a pie plate or pie form with pastry and cover the edges of the dish depending on your preference
2. In a bowl combine all pie ingredients together and mix well
3. Pour the mixture over the pastry
4. Bake at 400 425 F for 25 30 min or until golden brown
5. When ready remove from the oven and let it rest for 15 min

Grapefruit pie

Servings: 8-12 | Preparation: 15 min | Cooking: 35 min

Ingredients

- pastry sheets
- 2 cups grapefruit
- 1 cup brown sugar
- ¼ cup flour
- 5 6 egg yolks
- 5 oz. butter

Directions

1. Line a pie plate or pie form with pastry and cover the edges of the dish depending on your preference
2. In a bowl combine all pie ingredients together and mix well
3. Pour the mixture over the pastry
4. Bake at 400 425 F for 25 30 min or until golden brown
5. When ready remove from the oven and let it rest for 15 min

Directions

1. Preheat oven to 400 F, unfold pastry sheets and place them on a baking sheet
2. Toss together all ingredients together and mix well
3. Spread mixture in a single layer on the pastry sheets
4. Before baking decorate with your desired fruits
5. Bake at 400 F for 22 25 min or until golden brown
6. When ready remove from the oven and serve

Butterfinger pie

Servings: 8 12 | Preparation: 15 min | Cooking: 35 min

Ingredients

- pastry sheets
- 1 package cream cheese
- 1 tsp vanilla extract
- ¼ cup peanut butter
- 1 cup powdered sugar (to decorate)
- 2 cups Butterfinger candy bars
- 8 oz whipped topping

Directions

1. Line a pie plate or pie form with pastry and cover the edges of the dish depending on your preference
2. In a bowl combine all pie ingredients together and mix well
3. Pour the mixture over the pastry
4. Bake at 400 425 F for 25 30 min or until golden brown
5. When ready remove from the oven and let it rest for 15 min

Chocholate tart

Servings: 6 8 | Preparation: 25 min | Cooking: 25 min

Ingredients

- pastry sheets
- 1 tsp vanilla extract
- ½ lb. caramel
- ½ lb. black chocolate
- 4 5 tablespoons butter
- 3 eggs
- ¼ lb. brown sugar

Printed in Great Britain
by Amazon